Migration, Minorities and Citizenship

General Editors: **Zig Layton-Henry**, Professor of Politics, University of Warwick; and **Danièle Joly**, Professor, Director, Centre for Research in Ethnic Relations, University of Warwick

Titles include:

Muhammad Anwar, Patrick Roach and Ranjit Sondhi (*editors*)
FROM LEGISLATION TO INTEGRATION?
Race Relations in Britain

Sophie Body-Gendrot and Marco Martiniello (*editors*)
MINORITIES IN EUROPEAN CITIES
The Dynamics of Social Integration and Social Exclusion at the Neighbourhood Level

Naomi Cannon (*editor*)
IMMIGRATION AND INTEGRATION IN POST-INDUSTRIAL SOCIETIES
Theoretical Analysis and Policy-Related Research

Malcolm Cross and Robert Moore (*editors*)
GLOBALIZATION AND THE NEW CITY
Migrants, Minorities and Urban Transformations in Comparative Perspective

Adrian Favell
PHILOSOPHIES OF INTEGRATION
Immigration and the Idea of Citizenship in France and Britain

Simon Holdaway and Anne-Marie Barron
RESIGNERS? THE EXPERIENCE OF BLACK AND ASIAN POLICE OFFICERS

Danièle Joly
GLOBAL CHANGES IN ASYLUM REGIMES (*editor*)

HAVEN OR HELL?
Asylum Policies and Refugees in Europe

SCAPEGOATS AND SOCIAL ACTORS
The Exclusion and Integration of Minorities in Western and Eastern Europe

Atsushi Kondo (*editor*)
CITIZENSHIP IN A GLOBAL WORLD
Comparing Citizenship Rights for Aliens

Jørgen S. Nielsen
TOWARDS A EUROPEAN ISLAM

Jan Rath (*editor*)
IMMIGRANT BUSINESSES
The Economic, Political and Social Environment

Peter Ratcliffe (*editor*)
THE POLITICS OF SOCIAL SCIENCE RESEARCH
'Race', Ethnicity and Social Change

AF739446

John Rex
ETHNIC MINORITIES IN THE MODERN NATION STATE
Working Papers in the Theory of Multiculturalism and Political Integration

Carl-Ulrik Schierup (*editor*)
SCRAMBLE FOR THE BALKANS
Nationalism, Globalism and the Political Economy of Reconstruction

Steven Vertovec and Ceri Peach (*editors*)
ISLAM IN EUROPE
The Politics of Religion and Community

Östen Wahlbeck
KURDISH DIASPORAS
A Comparative Study of Kurdish Refugee Communities

John Wrench, Andrea Rea and Nouria Ouali (*editors*)
MIGRANTS, ETHNIC MINORITIES AND THE LABOUR MARKET
Integration and Exclusion in Europe

Migration, Minorities and Citizenship
Series Standing Order ISBN 0-333-71047-9
(outside North America only)

You can receive future titles in this series as they are published by placing a standing order. Please contact your bookseller or, in case of difficulty, write to us at the address below with your name and address, the title of the series and the ISBN quoted above.

Customer Services Department, Macmillan Distribution Ltd, Houndmills, Basingstoke, Hampshire RG21 6XS, England

Global Changes in Asylum Regimes

Edited by

Danièle Joly

City University
Library Information Services
Northampton Square

palgrave
macmillan

Editorial matter and selection © C Danièle Joly
Introduction & Chapters 1–10 © Palgrave Macmillan Ltd 2002

All rights reserved. No reproduction, copy or transmission of this publication may be made without written permission.

No paragraph of this publication may be reproduced, copied or transmitted save with written permission or in accordance with the provisions of the Copyright, Designs and Patents Act 1988, or under the terms of any licence permitting limited copying issued by the Copyright Licensing Agency, 90 Tottenham Court Road, London W1T 4LP.

Any person who does any unauthorised act in relation to this publication may be liable to criminal prosecution and civil claims for damages.

The author has asserted her right to be identified as the author of this work in accordance with the Copyright, Designs and Patents Act 1988.

First published 2002 by
PALGRAVE MACMILLAN
Houndmills, Basingstoke, Hampshire RG21 6XS and
175 Fifth Avenue, New York, N. Y. 10010
Companies and representatives throughout the world

PALGRAVE MACMILLAN is the global academic imprint of the Palgrave Macmillan division of St. Martin's Press, LLC and of Palgrave Macmillan Ltd. Macmillan® is a registered trademark in the United States, United Kingdom and other countries. Palgrave is a registered trademark in the European Union and other countries.

ISBN 0–333–91320–5

This book is printed on paper suitable for recycling and made from fully managed and sustained forest sources.

A catalogue record for this book is available from the British Library.

Library of Congress Cataloging-in-Publication Data

Global changes in asylum regimes/edited by Danièle Joly.
p. cm – (Migration, minorities, and citizenship)
Includes bibliographical references and index.
ISBN 0-333-91320-5
1. Asylum, Right of. 2. Refugees – Government policy. 3. Refugees – Legal status, laws, etc. I. Joly, Danièle. II. Series.

HV8652.G56 2002
341.4'88–dc21

2002072316

10 9 8 7 6 5 4 3 2 1
11 10 09 08 07 06 05 04 03 02

Printed and bound in Great Britain by
Antony Rowe Ltd, Chippenham and Eastbourne

For Nicolas and my parents

Contents

List of the Contributors

Michael Barutciski, Barreau du Québec, Canada

Agnès Callamard, Head of the Office of the Secretary-General, Amnesty International, UK

Cornelis D. de Jong, Co-ordinator, Global Forum on Fighting Corruption and Safeguarding Integrity II, Ministry of Justice, The Netherlands

Huberto Estrada-Soberanis, Human and Indigenous Rights Lawyer, Guatemala

Louis Gentile, Refugee Law Training Officer, UNHCR, UK

Mark Gibney, Belk Distinguished Professor, University of North Caroline-Ashville, USA

Danièle Joly, Director, Centre for Research in Ethnic Relations, University of Warwick

Morten Kjaerum, Director, Danish Centre for Human Rights, Denmark

John O. Oucho, Professor of Population and Sustainable Development, University of Botswana

Rosemary Preston, Director, International Centre for Education in Development, Department of Continuing Education, University of Warwick, Coventry, UK

Astri Suhrke, Senior Research Fellow, Chr. Michelsen Institute, Norway

Acknowledgement

This book includes a number of papers presented at a conference on New Asylum Regimes in the World (Warwick University 1998) which was sponsored by the ESRC.

Introduction

Danièle Joly

An analysis of asylum regimes as they are formulated today must necessarily be considered within the context of continuity and change in their historical development. In the post–World War II era an asylum regime was elaborated which mostly addressed European refugees and was governed by the 1951 Geneva Convention; it soon evolved into a liberal regime of entry coupled with generous conditions of long-term stay in most industrialised countries. Although the Geneva Convention became a universal instrument (with the removal of the geographical and historical limitations), other regions of the world developed their own sub-regimes. In Africa, the Organisation of African Unity prepared its own Convention in 1969, which met the conditions pertaining to the end of colonisation, the problems deriving from it and the establishment of newly independent states. This regime was one of reciprocity and sharing with much broader defining criteria than those of the Geneva Convention. This was characterised by the acceptance of mass influxes, short or long-term temporary protection and repatriation when possible (Suhrke, 1993). Asia demonstrated a kind of regional refugee regime with an internal practice of sharing (Suhrke and Hans, 1995), particularly in South Asia, while in South-East Asia a massive outflow from Indo-China in the wake of the US defeat resulted in some granting of temporary protection in neighbouring states combined with the global coordination of mass resettlement outside the region into industrialised states. In Latin America a strong tradition of asylum was somewhat frozen up by the successive military dictatorships which took over the Southern cone in the early 1970s and fanned refugees all over the world, whereas in Central America the 1984 Cartagena Declaration facilitated the reception of refugees across a variety of states. One central feature of that period appears to be the generally favourable ethos vis-à-vis refugees albeit through regionally determined differentiated formulae. Central and Eastern Europe remained outside the regime as those countries did not adhere to the Geneva Convention, but they nonetheless received a number of refugees from right-wing military dictatorships (such as Chile in 1973).

The UNHCR defined that period as 'reactive, exile-oriented and refugee specific' (quoted in Joly and Suhrke, 1997) and this is corroborated by a number of scholars who stress the exile bias of the regime (Chimmi, 1998). The underpinnings to this focus in the Western world were those of a world divided into two blocks poised against each other, wherein refugees acquired an inherent ideological value for the Western block in the discrediting of the communist model and where the emphasis on human rights and solidarity served to legitimate the liberal world. The guilt generated by the atrocities concomitant with Nazism and World War II also played a part. According to Chimmi (1998), this led to a positivist tradition and a depoliticised discourse in refugee studies (mostly occupied by lawyers) positing international law as an abstract system of rules which could be identified, objectively interpreted and enforced, that is a neutral language opposed to the politicised language of the Soviet Union. It was also a period of relative economic prosperity and expansion in the industrialised world and of hope for better prospects in the decolonised part of the world. Altogether this conjuncture made way for a relatively favourable approach to asylum on the part of governments.

The entire global context has changed and this provides a backdrop to the new asylum regimes. Regimes in distinct regions of the world are more interdependent and interconnected so that one can speak of a convergence towards a single regime. It is characterised by the search for solution rather than protection, by the diversified categories of persons of concern to refugee agencies such as UNHCR, by its humanitarian rather than human rights bias, by the trans-sovereign character of initiatives and many other features examined below. A new discourse carefully chisels an ethical and ideological foundation to the new regime. Finally, one aspect of the regime which is often neglected is the significant role of refugees as deliberate or unwitting movers of international policy and intervention; they have become one of the central political issues of the turn of the twenty-first century. The foundations of this regime are being forged by industrialised countries which influence the agenda worldwide through coordinated action. For some scholars the regime is the result of experimentation in refugee protection and humanitarian response, giving rise to unplanned, crisis-driven experiments (Newland, 1999) rather than a deliberate concerted plan. What is perceived as the failure of alternative methods leads to the assessment that the 1990s were characterised by a deterioration of the general observance of principles of international law (Newland, 1999). One lawyer speaks of 'threats' to refugee protection (Goodwin-Gill, 1996, pp. 3 and 5) while another fears 'an impending fundamental breakdown of the protection regime' (Hathaway et al., 1996, p. 4). It has also been argued that the multifaceted dimensions of the new regime concur to keep refugees away from industrialised countries (Joly, 1999). However, UNHCR describes it in a more positive light as 'proactive, homeland-oriented and refugee specific' (quoted in Joly and Surkhe, 1997). There is a fair consensus on the policy features which typify the new regime among scholars. Chimmi (1998) selects in-country protection, preventive protection, the right to remain, temporary protection (TP), closer cooperation with the Security Council and safe havens/safety zones. Mertus (1998) stresses states' refusal to grant asylum, containment, temporary protection, secondary holding states, repatriation; for Roberts (1998) the key aspects of the new regime comprise preventive action (also in countries at war), safety zones, UN Security Council authorised military intervention, temporary protection, voluntary/forced repatriation, monitored repatriation, Western states' reluctance to grant asylum. Some of the central features of this regime are examined below.

Worldwide regionalisation

Regionalisation is not so novel in the non-industrialised parts of the world as mentioned above, but it has become a universal and long-term approach in the 1990s with its adoption by European countries and the rest of the industrialised world. Its significance is made salient by the dominating role those countries play in the formulation of asylum regimes. This approach came to the fore with the conflict in former Yugoslavia whereby a kind of de facto burden-sharing among the countries of former Yugoslavia was promoted by the European Union: containment in the region became one key concept albeit with a narrow definition of the region (Joly et al., 1992). Moreover regionalisation was implemented by other industrialised states such as the US in the Caribbean, containing Haitians in Guantanamo. Nevertheless matters are not left up to 'the regions' as a concerted global coordination of these operations is taking place and bringing together industrialised states. In Europe it has taken the shape of a selective harmonisation led by the European Union through the formulation of a European asylum regime (Joly, 1999) including the response to refugee movements with a view to control borders (see the Resolutions on former Yugoslavia and the 46 Action Plan on the 'influx of migrants from Iraq and neighbouring countries' as analysed by Frelick, 1999). The EU even solicited advice from UNHCR to develop 'a regional approach to protection in appropriate cases involving cooperation with non-member states and the possibility of identifying safe areas within the region (internal flight options)' (quoted in Frelick, 1999, p. 25).

A reactive comprehensive approach

Furthermore, the regionalisation effort does not stand in isolation. It forms part of a fully fledged comprehensive policy with a great many components, which was formally endorsed by UNHCR in 1992 for the treatment of the refugee movements in former Yugoslavia. It is currently being applied throughout the world at the instigation of industrialised countries. Critics have argued that the primary purpose of such an approach was to ensure that the smallest possible number of refugees would reach the industrialised world. It includes preventive action, intervention in the country of origin, in-country protection, restrictive measures on asylum, regional containment, temporary protection and repatriation; it has been implemented through a variety of modes and instruments in varying combination according to the crisis involved and its geopolitical situation. Refugee issues have been repoliticised as the end of the Cold War was a crucial catalyst making it possible to intervene in countries of origin. The sacrosanct sovereignty principle does not hold sway in the same manner any longer, as noted by UNHCR:

> This is in keeping with a growing tendency for the international community to concern itself with conditions that until recently would have been treated as internal matters: violations of human rights, repression of minorities, indiscriminate violence and persecution. Such conditions can no longer be seen as falling within the realm of domestic concern, especially when they affect other countries by causing an outpouring of refugees (UNHCR, quoted by Newland, 1999, pp. 17–18).

Direct intervention in several countries of origin illustrates this new trend, as in Northern Iraq, Somalia, Haiti and Kosovo. A new conception of root causes has been formulated and implemented which does not, as in the 1980s, address structural conditions of inequality, oppression, racism, authoritarianism and totalitarianism located within states and the international system (Joly and Surkhe, 1997). The notion of early warning has faded. In the 1990s, a narrower definition has focused on more immediate causes of refugee movements particularly as it guides the implementation of policies. This is what has warranted our choice of the adjective *reactive* appended to comprehensivisation. Unwittingly refugees have become prime agents motivating major international policies and intervention through their sheer numbers and movements. The debate among social scientists demonstrates the complexities of the issues and the difficulties of unravelling implications for policies (Joly and Surhke, 1997). The comprehensive approach has been evaluated positively by some scholars in its aspects involving political reconciliation, the rehabilitation of institutions of government and civil society, the international supervision of elections, and economic reconstruction. Newland (1999) identifies a number of 'innovative' measures such as temporary protection, safe havens, cross-border delivery of assistance and the use of peace-keeping troops for the delivery of humanitarian assistance. But the comprehensive approach is more often criticised for its deleterious impact on protection through *inter alia* prioritising the keeping of refugees as closely as possible to the country of origin and returning them as soon as is practicable.

Within this comprehensive approach, safe havens have been singled out as the target of much controversy. Operation Provide Comfort in Northern Iraq has been both celebrated as a success and deplored as a failure. According to Frelick (1999) it follows a host country logic which introduces preventive protection on the grounds that refugees from Iraq pose a threat to international peace and security (thus motivating the Security Council Resolution 688). The author unpacks subsequent developments in Iraq to demonstrate that the safety of the area could not be guaranteed any more in 1996. In Bosnia, the safety of Srebrenica and other 'safe areas' was to be guaranteed under two resolutions of the Security Council, eventually resulting in human tragedy on a massive scale. A plethora of terms indicates the uncertainty surrounding those notions: safe havens, safety zones, safety corridors, open relief centres and humanitarian zones (Landgren, 1995).

Restricted asylum

The rationale sustaining this approach has been the growing reluctance of states to offer asylum-based protection (Newland, 1999; Roberts,

1998) often attributed to their concern with the economic burden and the exacerbation of existing racial, ethnic and national tensions; this trend was initiated by industrialised countries which multiplied measures designed to pursue it but then created a model influencing reception countries in other parts of the world as testified by the UNHCR, 'non-compliance with international treaty obligations for refugees is becoming something of a global norm' (MacNamara, 1997, p. 57, quoted by Suhrke, 1998). For Suhrke (1998) the most dramatic feature of the refugee scene in the 1990s was thus the globalised restriction on asylum. It has sometimes led to the coining of the phrase 'the non-entrée' regime (Chimmi, 1998). The European Union in particular prepared conventions and a great number of soft instruments to that effect (Joly, 1996). The theme of 'bogus' asylum-seekers abusing the asylum system is being peddled repeatedly to justify restrictions. Non-industrialised countries have also been shown to refuse entry in an increasing manner: it has been argued that this is grounded in the problems of declining economies, population pressures and a growing awareness of the ecological cost of hosting large refugee populations exacerbated by the example originating from the richer states (Joly and Surkhe, 1997). Paradoxically it is when an increased number of states adhere to the Geneva Convention that it becomes more and more residual in the percentage of refugees being awarded Convention status (only 10 per cent in Europe). The wings of the Convention are being clipped through an array of measures, including a joint action by the European Union on its definition of a refugee which excludes those for whom agents of persecution are not the state (Joly, 1999). In the meantime, the dismantling of communist regimes and the end of the Cold War have entailed that Central and Eastern European countries are gradually signing the Convention but are at the same time queuing up to adopt the European Union *acquis communautaire* and its asylum regime.

The new reality of protection

Protection itself is assuming new meanings. Roberts (1998) identifies a dichotomy which spans on the one hand legal protection, that is, state protection and refugee status and on the other hand physical protection. Under the previous asylum regime no noticeable discrepancy separated the two. Protection then also used to imply the quest for three possible solutions: permanent settlement in the country of exile (that was generally the case in industrialised countries), resettlement after a temporary stay in a transit country, or repatriation from the latter. While it generally used to involve a durable solution after the crossing of an international border its meaning has now shifted to in-country protection and repatriation from temporary solutions if a border was crossed. In the industrialised world some scholars have referred to a non-integration programme (Joly, 1996). What has undoubtedly happened is that more restrictive asylum policies have been paired with less favourable reception/settlement policies. On the whole, quotas for resettlement as a durable solution are very limited: ten states receive between 30,000 and 50,000 annually (Suhrke, 1998) while the global burden-sharing and permanent settlement offers witnessed on the occasion of the Vietnamese refugee movement were replaced for Bosnians and Kosovans by temporary protection for limited numbers. A good number of formulae stressing the search for solutions have been elaborated 'protecting' people *in situ* (hence the importance accorded to internally displaced persons): in the region of origin, under other statuses than the Geneva Convention status in reception countries, including, for the first time in Europe, temporary protection. One theme, which is slow to emerge in agencies' concerns and scholarly writings is the question of women refugees, despite their overwhelming numbers and specific situations.

However, the main emphasis has been laid on repatriation, which has gained great credence among policy-makers and NGOs and is customarily acclaimed as the optimal solution for refugees with a view to sparing them the trauma of exile. This is why the terminology used by governments and agencies concerned focuses on solutions rather than protection. Repatriation has become a central concept: ten million returned to their countries of origin between January 1991 and early 1997 (Roberts, 1998). In Central America a regional process of peace with international representation incorporated a plan for the return of refugees; in the region the refugees continue to play an active role in the peace process as they had in their paths to exile and countries of reception. In parallel to this development the US introduced stricter border enforcements through multilateral and bilateral agreements (two Acts in 1996) to return aliens to so-called third countries while Guatemala introduced severe sanctions for assistance to undocumented aliens (between five and eight years in prison) (Nezer, 1999). Forcible returns have been numerous in different areas of the world: from Iran to Afghanistan and Azerbaijan, from Bangladesh to Burma, from Thailand to Burma and Cambodia, from Tanzania and the Congo to Rwanda, from Germany to Bosnia, from the US to Haiti and Cuba. Repatriation has sometimes been monitored by international agencies including UNHCR and may become one component of a development aid package to reconstruct a region formerly in conflict (as in Bosnia). Some industrialised countries have also offered return programmes to refugees settled on their territory (such as Norway).

Institutional actors

The leading actors in this process are the governments of the industrialised world through intergovernmental bodies and supra-national agreements. The European Union is a major player together with the Inter-governmental Consultations on Asylum, Refugee and Migration Policies in Europe, North America and Australia which comprise the main industrialised countries and the UNHCR. In addition, international non-governmental organisations (INGOs) and NGOs attempt to influence the agenda and play an important role in the field; it is pointed out that NGOs now collectively transfer more resources to Southern countries than the world bank (Mertus, 1998). The United Nations Security Council is called upon; NATO takes it upon itself to intervene militarily but also provides humanitarian assistance.

UNHCR has become embroiled in controversies and its relationship to governments and donor countries has been the target of sharp criticism. In some cases, the agency has been supported for extending its concern to new categories of persons and mutating from a refugee organisation to a broad-based humanitarian refugee agency. For instance, UNHCR monitoring of internally displaced persons and returnees has sometimes been perceived as a positive extension of its mandate and an innovative change in the regime through providing some degree of assurance and safety (Roberts, 1998). An opposing view is that the protection mandate of UNHCR is undermined by the pressures of its expanded humanitarian assistance role (Rudge, 1998) or even that its humanitarian responsibilities and its protection mandate are potentially incompatible (Goodwin-Gill, 1999). UNHCR has also been accused of legitimating and furthering the agenda of industrialised states in the pursuance of their interests through prioritising concepts such as in-country protection, the right to remain and repatriation (Chimmi, 1998). New UNHCR concerns embrace substantial numbers (13 million), who are not refugees but Internally Displaced Persons (IDPs), returnees, war-affected populations in former Yugoslavia, relocated populations in the Russian Federation, and stateless peoples (Roberts, 1998). 'Uprooted populations', 'displaced people' and 'involuntary migrants' are the new terms used which tend to replace the concept of refugee (Joly and Suhrke, 1997).

The paradigm shift

This major shift of paradigm can be attributed to several possible underlying factors. It has been argued that the end of the Cold War has reduced the importance of international relations which gave some refugees an intrinsic ideological value and thus facilitated the institution of asylum for all (Joly, 1996). The new regime, defined by some as a 'post-cold war paradigm (Mertus, 1998) appears to be driven by narrow domestic considerations at a time when there is a retreat in values of universalism and solidarity (Rudge, 1998), partly as a consequence of an overbearing neoliberal economic model which let loose the forces of the market. An introverted conception of the national interest is prevailing in industrialised states and it is perceived that refugees are representing a threat to society's political regime, cultural identity, socio-economic order and environment and national security (Weiner, 1996)). This is questioned by Frelick (1999) who considers as untested the proposition that societies in Western Europe and North America are hostile to immigration. Furthermore, these notions are being fundamentally challenged with a criticism of the unquestioned acceptance of states that they should award more privileges to their citizens than to others (Gibney, 1991).

According to another interpretation, the institution of asylum is undermined by the internal weakening of states vis-à-vis supra-national institutions in some regions of the world, compounded by the failure of other states (Rudge, 1998). The trend is that of massive cutbacks in social budgets for the vulnerable sectors of home societies breaking up the ethos of social cohesion, and affecting even more severely solidarity with outsiders such as refugees. Moreover, there appears to be a shift away from the state in the area of protection as receiving states are less concerned about the human rights of the uprooted and more about their own rights 'to protect their own culture and standard of living from foreign intruders' (Mertus, 1998) combined with stronger states' control over their borders. Mertus (1998) attributes this trend to an enhanced globalisation manifested through several factors: the increased connectedness of states, the interconnectedness of states and individuals globally, the wider participation in international and national problems through NGOs and new social movements, the greater involvement of forces above the states such as transnational cooperation and collective transnational solutions. While a broader interpretation of protection can be facilitated by international bodies, fewer rights appear to derive from it as only states can award status and concomitant rights; this appears to be confirmed by the limited rights which refugees enjoy in refugee camps under international humanitarian protection (Callamard, 1995).

The ongoing debate about the causes of displacement directly relates to policies vis-à-vis refugees: one view attributes them to internal rather than inter-state conflict, and competing power struggles divided by ethnic and national loyalties which states are unable to control (Mertus, 1998). Other scholars such as Chimmi (1998) argue that internalist explanations for refugee movements are advanced by industrialised countries with the aim of laying the blame for displacement on countries of origin. As a consequence, other countries would then have no responsibilities towards the forced migrants concerned and would thus be able to justify containing them close to their area of origin, repatriating them and intervening in their homeland to prevent or stop their movement. Chimmi (1998) also shows how a 'myth of difference' has been created contrasting the refugees of the Cold War era to contemporary non-European refugees, at the service of a policy of containment. In his opinion, this interpretation serves to exonerate imperialism which he deems at the root of most serious crises producing refugees through its history and currently as a result of the 'destructive impact' of the neoliberal economic model.

This book explores in greater detail the themes mentioned above, bringing together writings by practitioners and academics (some of whom are both). It addresses the question of new asylum regimes in the world through the examination of key issues thematically and through regional case studies.

Gibney in chapter 1 shows conclusively the exceptionally strong relationship between levels of human rights abuses and the phenomenon of refugee flight. He establishes that the most violent countries in the world produce nearly all the world's refugees, thus refuting the myth that the majority of asylum-seekers are abusing the system. Moreover, he argues that most of this violence is quite predictable and the details of it known with certainty. This leads him to turn the whole question on its head, arguing that one could consider every serious human rights abuse in the world as a failure of refugee protection and in addition that it is pretty clear to everyone who needs protection.

Gentile in chapter 2 sets out to dispel four 'smug' myths of international protection. He first refutes the argument that the international community has made significant progress in protecting human rights since World War II. He then challenges the notion that universal human rights principles (including asylum and refugee law) are respected in the developed world but for various reasons are nearly impossible to enforce in the developing world. He denies that the international community ensures the protection of and assistance to most refugees within acceptable minimum standards. Finally, he invalidates the view that the developed world is being overwhelmed by bogus asylum-seekers.

Joly in chapter 3 makes a detailed analysis of the temporary protection mechanism developed during the conflict in former Yugoslavia at the initiative of UNHCR and with European Union leadership. She examines the circumstances bringing it about, the instruments and statuses implemented, the criteria advanced to warrant TP, the standards of treatment of temporary protected persons, the concomitant comprehensive action and the actors involved. She concludes that temporary protection *à l'européenne* constitutes the cornerstone of a new European asylum regime which maximises asylum restrictions and undermines social rights in the reception country.

Barutciski and Suhrke in chapter 4 examine the nature of the challenge and the adequacy of the solutions that were developed for the Kosovo refugee crisis The challenge was to persuade a host country, Macedonia, to admit a massive influx of refugees that the government initially rejected. The eventual solution was based on a 'burden-sharing' scheme involving transfer of refugees to other countries, both in the region and outside. The authors find that while the two innovative programmes (called 'humanitarian transfer' and 'humanitarian evacuation') solved the immediate protection problem, both the programmes and the way they were handled remained controversial.

De Jong in chapter 5 examines how European cooperation in the field of asylum and immigration works in practice through a detailed study of the European Union Action Plan on the influx of migrants from Iraq and the neighbouring region. He notes that the plan became diverted from its initial purpose as its implementation lessened the asylum dimension and over-emphasised elements related to illegal immigration. In his view the plan and its practice failed to demonstrate Europe's ability to show solidarity to member states confronted with a significant increase in asylum applications. De Jong then advocates an innovative approach and proposes a model of shared responsibility in keeping with international instruments.

Estrada-Soberanis in chapter 6 examines the return of refugees to Guatemala within the framework of the peace process in Central America. He situates the human rights issue within the history of conflict in Guatemala and thereafter demonstrates how the displaced populations together with popular organisations achieved the recognition of their fundamental claims in the Agreement of the Resettling of Populations Displaced by the Armed Conflict. As put forward by the Guatemalan Civil Society Assembly, this includes those who were to be covered under the category of uprooted people: it establishes their participation in the design, decision, execution and monitoring of the resettlement strategy, and recognises that extreme poverty and the agrarian structure are two key components of the cause of conflict. However, Estrada-Soberanis also shows how the positive role of the UN was undermined by the policies of financial institutions such as the International Monetary Fund (IMF) and the World Bank under US influence.

Callamard in chapter 7 seeks to highlight issues of gender in the refugee experience through a review of existing evidence on the discrimination faced by refugee women in terms of access to international assistance, income and physical protection. She argues that discrimination and violence against refugee women are politically determined and politically sanctioned, under the action or influence of international, national and local actors, and therefore that the situation of refugee women in camps amounts to persecution under the accepted definition. Moreover, according to Callamard, if the militarisation and criminalisation of refugee camps constitute major obstacles with regard to the protection of refugee women, answers to this militarisation, including forced repatriation to unsafe areas, are no less threatening and constitute major setbacks.

Oucho in chapter 8 seeks to demonstrate that forced migration, which generates refugees and internally displaced persons (IDPs), will be Africa's liability well into this millennium, unless durable solutions are found to contain the menace. The tide of both types of displaced persons (DPs) has increased and expanded spatially over the years in Africa, in the case of refugees rendering individual states the status of either senders or recipients or both. Some sub-regional perspectives are provided as are national situations which help to illustrate the nature and magnitude of the problem. Determinants and consequences of population displacement are considered in generic categories such as political, economic, social and environmental factors which vary from one period to another and from country to country. Thereafter, attention is drawn on how to convert Africa's current liability to an asset through national reconstruction and reconciliation, carefully designed research and policy based on research findings and the search for durable peace.

Preston in chapter 9 locates trends in contemporary practice of refugee law in relation to change in the management of the global economy. She reviews the social implications of proposals to reformulate international refugee law so as to take account of these changes and examines the implications of the language of temporary protection and return in safety and dignity for the status and treatment of people seeking refuge from persecution and violence across international borders. With increasingly restrictive asylum practices undermining refugee law, this chapter suggests that the question is not so much one of reducing the scope of the law to accommodate them, but of examining the implications of threats to the very principles of international law posed by global mechanisms of liberal governance.

Finally in chapter 10 Kjaerum deals with developments in the NGO community in the 1990s and their impact on the protection of refugees, focusing primarily on human rights organisations which have seen much development in recent years. They are beginning to address problems which were exclusively perceived as humanitarian and social issues in the past. Consequently Kjaerum notes that a stronger human rights oriented NGO community is emerging at the domestic level in several parts of the world, which is concerned with the protection of refugees. He concludes that increased collaboration between humanitarian organisations, intergovernmental institutions and national human rights organisations could bring new perspectives into the protection regimes and in particular create a bottom-up approach at the global level.

Bibliography

Callamard, Agnès (1995) 'Populations under Fire, Populations under Stress', Ph.D. dissertation, New York: New School for Social Research.

Chimmi, B. S. (1998) 'The Geopolitics of Refugee Studies: a View from the South', *Journal of Refugee Studies*, II, 4, December 1998, pp. 350–75.

Edminster, Steven (1999) 'Recklessly Risking Lives: Restrictive Interpretation of "Agents of Persecution" in Germany and France', in *World Refugee Survey 1999*, US Committee for Refugees, pp. 30–9.

Frelick, Bill (1999) 'Down the Rabbit Hole: the Strange Logic of Internal Flight Alternatives', in *World Refugee Survey 1999*, US Committee for Refugees, pp. 27–9.

Gibney, Mark (1991) 'US Foreign Policy and the Creation of Refugee Flows', in H. Adelman (ed.) *Refugee Policy: Canada and the United States*, Toronto: York Lanes Press, pp. 81–114.

Goodwin-Gill, Guy (1996) 'Refugee Identity and the Fading Prospect of International Protection', Conference on *Refugee Rights and Realities*, Nottingham, 30 November.

Goodwin-Gill, Guy (1999) 'Refugee Identity and Protection's Fading Prospect', in Frances Nicholson and Patrick Twomey (eds) *Refugee Rights and Realities: Evolving International Concepts and Regimes*, Cambridge: CUP, pp. 220–52.

Hathaway, James et al. (1996) 'Towards the Reformulation of International Refugee Law: a Model for Collectivised and Solution-oriented Protection'. consultative workshops in London and Washington, 4 and 11 October.

Joly, Danièle (1996) *Haven or Hell: Asylum Policies and Refugees in Europe*, Oxford, Macmillan.

Joly, Danièle (1999) 'A New Asylum Regime in Europe', in Frances Nicholson and Patrick Twomey (eds), *Refugee Rights and Realities*, Cambridge: CUP, pp. 336–57.

Joly, Danièle and Astri Suhrke (1997) 'Asylum: Changing Concepts and Practices', paper prepared for IUSSP Committee on South–North Migration, Barcelona, 7–10 May.

Joly, Danièle et al. (1992) *Refugees: Asylum in Europe?*, London: MRG, 1992; also published by Westview, USA, 1992.

Landgren, Karin (1995) 'Safety Zones and International Protection: a Dark Grey Area', *IJRL* 8, 3, pp. 416–32.

Mertus, Julie (1998) 'The State and the Post-Cold War Refugee Regime: New Models, New Questions', *IJRL*, 10, 3, pp. 321–49.

Newland, Kathleen (1999) 'The Decade in Review', in *World Refugee Survey 1999*, US Committee for Refugees, pp. 14–21.

Nezer, Melanie (1999) 'The Pueblor Process: U.S. Migration Controls Move South of the Border', in *World Refugee Survey*, US Committee for Refugees, pp. 40–5.

Roberts, Adam (1998) 'More Refugees, Less Asylum: a Regime in Transformation', *Journal of Refugee Studies*, 11, 4, December 1998, pp. 375–96.

Rudge, Philip (1998) 'Reconciling State Interests with International Responsibilities: Asylum in North America and Western Europe', *IJRL*, 10, 1/2, January–April pp. 7–21.

Suhrke, Astri (1993) Safeguarding the Right to Asylum. Expert Group Meetings on Population Distribution and Migraton, Santa Cruz, Bolivia, 18–22 January.

Suhrke, Astri (1998) 'Burden-sharing during Refugee Emergencies: the Logic of Collective versus National Action', *Journal of Refugee Studies*, 11, 4, December pp. 375–415.

Suhrke, Astri and Asha Hans (1995) 'Responsibility Sharing', Study in Action No. 4, Toronto 1, 18–21 May, discussion paper.

Weiner, Myron (1996) *The Global Migration crisis*, New York: Harper Collins.

1
Certain Violence, Uncertain Protection

Mark Gibney

Introduction

Each February the US State Department publishes its Country Reports on Human Rights Practices. This 1,300-plus page tome is a compendium of the human rights practices of the previous year for every country in the world – except, conveniently enough, the United States. Several months after this, Amnesty International publishes its own world human rights report for the previous year, covering much the same territory as the State Department does (but including the US). Both texts provide a full litany of much of what is wrong with the world. Even a quick glance at either volume provides stunning evidence that: torture is a common practice in a whole host of countries in the world; 'summary executions' and 'disappearances' are frequently employed to kill enemies of ruling governments; prison conditions in one country after the other are nothing short of barbaric as thousands of prisoners are left to literally rot to death; female genital mutilation continues unabated in a host of African countries; and tens of thousands of civilians are killed and brutalised in civil wars each year. This sickening evidence of our inhumanity to one another goes on and on, and, rather than seeing any kind of improvement, there are indications that human rights conditions throughout the Third World are only getting worse.

What does all this have to do with refugees? In some ways human rights has everything to do with refugee protection, but apparently in other ways the relationship between the two is fairly weak, and at times even non-existent. This chapter focuses on two aspects of this relationship, but particularly on the failure of the refugee regime to be informed by human rights practices.

The first part reports on empirical studies that show, rather conclusively, that there is an exceptionally strong relationship between levels of human rights abuses and the phenomenon of refugee flight. That is, the most violent countries in the world produce nearly all of the world's refugees. Another noteworthy phenomenon is that refugees almost always flee to countries where human rights practices are better than they are in their respective countries of origin (and this analysis is merely looking at refugee populations in the Third World, and it does not include Western countries where human rights conditions would invariably be considerably better). This finding is further evidence of the bona fides of the claims being presented. One problem, however, is that as violence has spread in the world there are fewer and fewer countries that can serve as a 'safe haven', and the safety valve that once might have been provided by the West has been reduced considerably. This leads to the final point in this section, which is that there is no empirical basis for the widespread charge made throughout Europe and the United States that asylum seekers are abusing the refugee system. The data, in fact, shows just the opposite: asylum seekers in both Europe and the United States are, in overwhelming numbers, from the most violence-plagued countries in the world.

The second part also focuses on the relationship between human rights and refugee protection, but it ventures into completely new territory. What I am attempting to do in this section is to begin to establish standards by which we can judge how well we have been providing refugee protection. We all know the number of refugees in the world and the number of displaced persons, but this data tells us much less than we think it does. What this tells us is how many people are being protected (in some form), but it tells us absolutely nothing about how many are in need of protection, or how many could be protected – through refugee relief or otherwise.

There is a terrible misperception that political violence is random. The truth is that violence is quite predictable. We know with some degree of accuracy what countries will experience it, what forms this violence will take, who will be its victims and so forth. But we have not used this information well. It is one thing to rationalise that the world community often finds it difficult if not impossible to provide protection to people when violence breaks out somewhere in the world in a sudden and unexpected manner. It is quite another thing, however, when the international community knows full well where political violence will occur – but still does not offer protection as refuge or otherwise.

Human rights and refugees

The first thing that must be established is just how violent the world we live in is. For more than a decade I have directed a project that measures political violence in nearly every country in the world on a scale of 1–5 depending on levels of human rights abuses.[1] The data comes from both the Amnesty and the State Department Country Reports. The results – the Political Terror Scale (PTS) – are listed in Appendix A (p. 32). In 1980, the average PTS score for countries in the Third World was 2.71. Since that time there has been a steady increase in violence.[2] By 1993, the average PTS score in the Third World was more than 3.0. This increase might not seem so much but consider this: in 1980 only 20 per cent of the countries in the Third World had a PTS score of more than 3, but by 1993 this number had increased so that more than half of the countries had this score or higher.

One of the consequences of this violence has been the creation of refugee flows. As I reported recently with two of my colleagues, the

Table 1.1: Human rights rankings of refugee producing nations

Year	*PTS<2.5 (%)*	*PTS 3–3.5 (%)*	*PTS 4–5 (%)*	*Unknown PTS*	*Total refugees*	*# of nations*
1980	3(2)	8(5)	47(5)	43(3)	4,934,900	15
1981	10(4)	14(7)	68(4)	8(2)	5,362,590	17
1982	4(4)	4(5)	90(3)	2(1)	4,985,600	13
1983	5(3)	8(8)	86(8)	1(1)	5,778,860	20
1984	5(2)	30(12)	63(8)	2(1)	6,954,000	23
1985	5(2)	9(8)	84(15)	2(1)	7,814,700	26
1986	4(3)	5(5)	89(16)	2(1)	9,308,300	25
1987	3(2)	4(8)	91(16)	2(1)	10,802,270	27
1988	2(1)	17(9)	80(16)	1(1)	12,031,020	27
1989	4(4)	21(11)	73(13)	2(1)	12,253,580	29
1990	1(4)	15(7)	82(20)	1(1)	13,706,100	32
1991	<1(1)	22(14)	76(17)	2(1)	13,715,550	33
1992	1(3)	5(9)	92(21)	2(1)	11,390,300	34
1993	9(6)	19(11)	72(19)	<1(1)	10,627,200	37

Notes: We have included in our study those refugees who have originated in developing countries seeking protection in developing countries. Refugees who seek asylum in developed countries have been excluded. Regrettably refugees whose numbers and origins could not be accurately determined had to be omitted from our study.
The figures in parentheses are the number of nations involved. Source: Mark Gibney, Clair Apodaca and James McCann (1996) 'Refugee Flows, the Internally Displaced and Political Violence (1980–1993): an Exploratory Analysis', in Alex P. Schmid (ed.), *Whither Refugee? The Refugee Crisis: Problems and Solutions*, Leiden, the Netherlands: PIOOM, pp. 45–66 (53).

overwhelming majority of refugees in the world has been from countries experiencing gross levels of human rights abuses, which we defined as either a Level 4 or Level 5 country.[3] I have reprinted Table 3 from that study and labelled it Table 1.1. These results are very consistent with other empirical studies that have also found that violence is what creates and perpetuates refugee flows.[4]

We also examined where it was that refugees went to. If they 'fled' to countries where human rights practices were generally as bad as their country of origin or worse, one might question whether other factors – such as economic factors – might be prompting migratory flows, rather than the desire for protection. What we found instead was that a significant majority of refugees migrated to countries where human rights practices were better than in their respective countries of origin, although, admittedly, there were more instances than we anticipated where refugees migrated to countries where human rights conditions were actually worse. I have reprinted Table 5 from that study and labelled it Table 1.2.

Table 1.2: Receiving country's human rights rankings in relation to refugee producing nation for select countries

	Refugees going to places with					
Year	*Better human rights records(%)*	*Worse human rights records(%)*	*Same human rights records(%)*	*Unknown human rights records(%)*	*Total refugees*	*# of nations*
1980	69	7	15	9	4,934,900	15
1981	64	9	9	18	5,362,590	17
1982	80	5	8	7	4,985,600	13
1983	80	9	10	1	5,778,860	20
1984	74	17	6	3	6,954,000	23
1985	77	13	7	3	7,814,700	26
1986	85	12	<1	3	9,308,300	25
1987	60	31	3	6	10,802,270	27
1988	56	27	14	3	12,031,020	27
1989	61	7	26	6	12,253,580	29
1990	81	6	10	3	13,706,100	32
1991	82	12	1	5	13,715,550	33
1992	79	11	6	4	11,390,300	34
1993	68	14	6	12	10,627,200	37

Source: Mark Gibney, Clair Apodaca and James McCann (1996) 'Refugee Flows, the Internally Displaced and Political Violence (1980–1993): an Exploratory Analysis', in Alex P. Schmid (ed.), *Whither Refugee? The Refugee Crisis: Problems and Solutions,* Leiden, the Netherlands: PLOOM, pp. 45–66 (55).

These findings purposely excluded the Western countries, and obviously it is vital to examine this phenomenon as well, particularly in the light of the fact that as violence continues to escalate in the Third World the possibility of finding countries of 'safe haven' becomes less and less likely. Let me begin with the refugee practices of the United States. One issue that I have pursued for some time is to uncover the relationship between human rights and US refugee policy.[5] The data indicate that there is very little connection between the two. Or to phrase this in a less delicate way: the United States has not really had a refugee policy as such, but a well-disguised immigration system masquerading as a refugee admission policy. The fact is that the vast majority of the 'quota refugees' who have been admitted to the United States since the passage of the 1980 Refugee Act have been from countries experiencing only 'fair' or 'moderate' levels of human rights abuses. Refugees from countries experiencing the very highest levels of human rights abuses – and, remember, this constitutes most of the world's refugee population – have not been given safety in the United States,[6] although there are at least some indications that this is beginning to change.[7]

Where there is at least some connection between human rights practices and refugee protection is United States' asylum policy. For example, during the 1980s fully 4/5 of those who *applied* for asylum during the decade (using the State Department as a data source) were from countries experiencing gross levels of human rights abuses (Levels 4 and 5), as were a comparable number of those who were *granted* refugee status. While this relationship was not as strong as this for the present decade, still, there is solid evidence that any 'abuse' of the asylum system is merely in the minds of American politicians and now the American public. The reason for this conclusion is simply this: the vast majority of asylum seekers in the United States come from exactly the kinds of countries one would expect those needing protection to come from, namely, countries experiencing extraordinarily high levels of political violence. We might not like to believe this, and we might not like the moral and legal position that this places us in, but it is true nonetheless.

What about Europe? Less empirical work has been done here, but what there is in many ways mirrors the American experience. In a study that focused on Dutch asylum policy, Daan Bronkhorst uncovered a number of apparent inconsistencies in asylum practice. For starters, Bronkhorst found that there were enormous inconsistencies between the European countries in terms of their treatment of the claims of individuals from the same country.

> [T]here are no grounds to assume that ... Turkish asylum seekers in Germany are generally of a different type than Turkish asylum seekers in the Netherlands or Denmark. Yet the Netherlands have admitted a percentage six times higher than that in the FRG. Tamils have stood hardly a chance of being admitted in the Netherlands or Germany, while a broad majority has been recognised as refugees in France. Similar disparities are to be noted regarding other groups.

Bronkhorst continues:

> *Within* West European countries, the variance is remarkable as well. In Denmark, Somalians had a much better rate of acceptance than Turks, while in the Netherlands it was the other way round. In the UK, Ethiopians fare somewhat better than Iraqis, while in the FRG Ethiopians had only half the chance of Iraqis.

Perhaps belabouring the obvious, Bronkhorst writes:

> What comes out from this ... is that various European governmental bodies responsible for refugee determinations do not seem to agree at all about which groups of asylum seekers contain a high percentage of 'genuine' refugees, and which groups do not.[8]

Bronkhorst also constructed a human rights scale that is in many ways similar to the Political Terror Scale.[9] He then examined whether there was any relationship between human rights violations in another country and the Dutch refugee response. His data showed very little connection in that refugee admissions seemed almost random. Table 3 of that study is reproduced here as Table 1.3.

Can these findings be extended to Europe quite generally? Using data provided by the UNHCR Food and Statistical Unit, what I have done for one year (1993) is to break down the asylum seeker population in Europe by nationality as well as by levels of political terror in their country of origin (and here I have taken the average for Amnesty and the State Department). The results are produced in Table 1.4. At first glance there appears to be little connection between levels of human rights abuses and asylum applications. For example, the largest number of applicants are individuals from countries with a human rights score of 2.0, which represents only moderate levels of political terror. Could this indicate that the accusation of frauding which the extreme right levels at asylum seekers might be corroborated by statistics?

Table 1.3: Scale of human rights violations in some refugee countries (index 1981–89) and admission in the Netherlands (percentage of applications for 1983–89)

Country	*Violations 'index'*	*Admissions*
Iraq	24	25
Iran	21	45
Afghanistan	18	20
Lebanon	18	<2
Ethiopia	17	20
Sri Lanka	17	<2
Somalia	16	5
Pakistan	15	<2
Bangladesh	15	<2
Zaire	15	<2
Turkey	14	35
Rumania	10	10
Ghana	9	<2
Poland	8	5
Suriname	7	10

Source: Daan Bronkhorst (1991) 'The "Realism" of a European Asylum Policy: a Quantitative Approach', *Netherlands Quarterly of Human Rights*, 2, pp. 142–58 (149).

A closer scrutiny of the data points to the opposite conclusion and a negative answer to the above question. What Europe is panicking over are the asylum seekers from the Third World much more than those from other European countries (although it is interesting to note that in 1993 there were 318,300 asylum seekers from other European countries compared with only 182,400 from non-European countries). To see what the data would look like for Third World asylum applicants, I simply removed European applicants from my calculations. These results are considerably different, and summarised in Table 1.5 (p. 24). No doubt the most impressive finding is that nearly 70 per cent (69.6) of the non-European asylum applicants in 1993 were from countries experiencing gross levels of human rights abuses (Level 4 and higher), and, concomitant with that, only 10.6 per cent were from Level 2 countries and below.

Like some of their American counterparts, a number of public officials in Europe have been stirring up nativist sentiments against asylum seekers, particularly against those from the Third World. The empirical evidence shows, however, that the frequent charge of widespread abuse of the asylum system seems to be completely unfounded – or at least with respect to Third World applicants. Similar to the situation in the

Table 1.4: Asylum seeker populations in western Europe, 1993

PTS level	*Country*	*# of asylum seekers*	*PTS level*	*Country*	*# of asylum seekers*	*PTS level*	*Country*	*# of asylum seekers*
5.0	Bosnia*	75,700	3.5	Pakistan	6,500	1.5	Macedonia*	1,800
	India	9,300		Iran	7,000		Ukraine*	4,900
	Zaire	11,500		Lebanon	3,900		Ghana	5,400
	Iraq	9,000		Ethiopia	1,900			12,100
	Liberia	4,200		Syria	1,600			
	Angola	3,800			20,900			
	Columbia	800				1.0	Poland*	3,300
	Sudan	1,400						
		115,700						
4.5	Turkey	25,000	3.0	Cuba	500			
	Somalia	13,000		Morocco	100			
	Sri Lanka	12,100		Senegal	2,200			
	Algeria	13,700		Guinea	1,800			
	Afghanistan	7,700		China	6,600			
	Togo	4,400		Bangladesh	2,500			
	Georgia*	1,800			13,700			
		77,700						
			2.5	Russian Republic*	7,800			

Table 1.4: Asylum seeker populations in western Europe, 1993 *con't*

PTS level	*Country*	*# of asylum seekers*	*PTS level*	*Country*	*# of asylum seekers*	*PTS level*	*Country*	*# of asylum seekers*
4.0	Serbia*	96,800	2.0	Mali	1,600			
	Haiti	300		Romania*	85,000			
	Nigeria	4,200		Bulgaria*	25,000			
	Peru	1,700		Vietnam	12,400			
	Philippines	100		Armenia*	7,300			
	Sierra Leone	2,300		Albania*	6,300			
	Egypt	2,300			137,600			
	Croatia*	2,600						
		110,300						

* = European (318,300)   Non-European (182,400)

Table 1.5: Non-European asylum seekers (1993)

Level	*# Applied*	*Percentage*
5.0	40,000	22.0
4.5	75,900	41.6
4.0	10,900	6.0
3.5	20,900	11.4
3.5	15,300	8.3
2.5	–	–
2.0	14,000	7.6
1.5	5,400	3.0
1.0	–	–

United States, the vast majority of non-Europeans who applied for asylum (at least in 1993) were from countries experiencing the very highest levels of political terror in the world. Even if one thought that Third World asylum seekers do not 'belong' in Europe in the sense that protection could be sought elsewhere, there should be no gainsaying the fact that these individuals are migrating from extraordinarily violent societies. And as violence spreads in the world, these countries are now being surrounded by other violent countries as well.

Refugee scholars do know how, where, or how, to place human rights within the context of refugee protection. Nobody, of course, has ever suggested that human rights conditions or practices in other countries are not important to the refugee enterprise. In fact, refugee scholars have been prompt (in theory at least) to affirm the importance of human rights practices in refugee affairs.[10] Still, in practice, there is an enormous hesitancy to erect a human-rights-centred refugee policy. Much of this ambivalence can be found in the writings of David Martin. Martin has written:

> One common mistake, made by both the left and the right, is to assume that the existence of serious human rights problems in a country should translate into a finding that virtually all emigrés from that country are refugees.[11]

Instead, Martin agues, 'something more' than human rights violations is needed in order to provide refugee protection, and that 'something more' is the fact that the individual is likely to be targeted by the persecutors upon his return. And in a statement that summarises well the manner in which international law is presently interpreted, Martin writes:

> Every effort should be made to avoid the use of dichotomous images and to break the ready links people rush to forge between human rights policy and asylum determinations. Obviously, an important relationship exists between human rights abuses in the home country and the merits of asylum claims by that country's nationals. But it is hardly a one-to-one correlation.[12]

Martin is indeed correct about the one-to-one correlation. But where does this leave one? I would suggest it leads to a very dangerous slippery slope. We begin by rationalising that human rights violations do not necessarily translate into bona fide claims for refugee status. From there we have set things up – mainly for our own benefit – so that individuals have to show 'something more'. But very few are able to show 'something more'. All (!) that they can show is that they live in societies that for most of us would be unimagined levels of violence and death. But that is not good enough, or at least not good enough to receive refugee protection from Western industrialised countries. And this is why someone like Martin could (as he has) describe asylum applications from Central America during the 1980s as 'manifestly unfounded', yet still maintain that human rights practices are (and should be) important in refugee determinations. There is an inconsistency in these two views that I find unnerving.

Measuring refugee protection

As one who reads both the Amnesty International and State Department Reports each year, let me tell you that this is truly a mind-numbing experience. It is not simply the incredible levels of human rights abuses that take place in country after country. This, by itself, would be bad enough. More than this, however, it is the fact that in reading these reports one is struck with the sense that year after year, decade after decade, absolutely nothing has changed – and, worst of all, that nothing *will* change either. And what I am speaking about here is not only to be found in the never-ending civil wars in places like Afghanistan and the Sudan. But I am also speaking about the killing of street children in Brazil, the systematic butchering of women's genitals in countries like Egypt, the atrocious prison conditions in a country like Peru, and so on. These same, exact phenomena occur in these same, exact countries year after year after year. Yet nothing happens.

Perhaps it is for this reason that I have always found the term 'early warning' rich with irony. To my way of thinking, there is a world full of early warning. Not necessarily a warning to those of us in the West about oncoming refugee flows, but a warning to all about areas where violence seems to be perpetual. In fact, there is much more than warning; there is something approaching near certainty. It is already known, for example, that approximately 70,000 people will be killed in wars every year,[13] and we already have a pretty fair idea of where this will take place. It is known that this year, like those preceding it, another 2 million women will be forced to undergo female genital mutilation. And if one chooses to do so, one could easily catalogue which countries these women live in, but more than this, who many of these young girls are – and perhaps even who will perform these rituals! In terms of torture, there is not only a very good estimation of where it will occur and who will be its victims, but we even know the particular methods by which it will be practised in various countries. In short, an enormous amount is known about violence. There are very few surprises here. What is much less known is how this violence can be stopped. And I would also suggest that much less is known about protecting the victims of this violence than is assumed.

In the absence of any other form of effective international mechanisms,[14] refugee relief has been almost the sole means of protecting those suffering from human rights abuses. But this reaches only a fraction of those who suffer. As Andrew Shacknove has pointed out, what differentiates refugee populations is their relationship to the international community. He writes: 'Refugees, unlike all others deprived of their basic needs, have a well-founded fear that recourse to their own governments is futile and are, in addition, within the reach of the international community.'[15]

But it is this notion of being within the reach of the international community that is problematic. The notion of 'reach' would seem to suggest that the international community is pretty much doing everything in its power to offer protection to as many as it possibly can – albeit, within the confines of the nation-state system. The reality, of course, is anything but this. The days of 'reaching' to bring refugees to our countries are long gone, and it is not likely that we will ever see these days again. In fact, it is no great secret that things are working in reverse. The real tragedy, however, is that the West has put nothing in its place.

One of the problems is that we have never tried to establish standards against which we could measure how successful our efforts at refugee protection have been. Are we doing a good job of refugee protection? A bad job? How does anyone know? What, exactly, are we trying to measure? What, exactly, are we trying to achieve? If several hundred thousand civilians are killed in the crossfire of a civil war in a country, is this an indictment of the refugee regime?

To begin to fill this vacuum, allow me to first propose the standard that every serious human rights abuse in the world constitutes a failure of refugee protection. The purpose of refugee relief, after all, is to offer protection. And if individuals are not being protected then refugee relief is not doing what it was intended to do. This position, of course, is too extreme. But it is essential that we do not retreat to a position (the one that we are at now) where the existence of gross and systematic levels of human rights abuses is treated as having little bearing in terms of considering the effectiveness of refugee protection. The point here – and it is a point that comes screaming out of the pages of both the State Department and the Amnesty International Country reports – is that most of the violence in the world is quite predictable. It is one thing to say that victims of human rights abuses are beyond our 'reach' when violence suddenly and unexpectedly breaks out in another country. In those instances, perhaps, there is little that the international community can do.

It is, however, something else altogether different when we know *where* violence will strike, *how* it will occur and *who* it will be aimed at. To suggest that the victims of *this* kind of violence – the kind of violence that most of the world suffers from – are somehow beyond our reach does not say much about us. Certainly offering relief of any kind would be a political problem of the highest magnitude. But it is vital that we recognise that most of the limitations are those that we have placed there ourselves – either by our own actions or in most cases by our inactions.

Let me present a 'modest proposal' along these lines: refugee protection can be said to have failed when individuals suffer human rights violations that are in some way avoidable. Let me be clear: I am not promoting refugee relief as the best means of dealing with human rights violations in the world. In a myriad of ways refugee relief is the least-preferred option. It is expensive; it assists only a tiny fraction of those who suffer the same kind of treatment; finally, it allows one to pretend that much more is accomplished than is really accomplished.[16] It also has allowed those of us in the West to live in a surreal world where violence is escalating but refugee flows are declining – and it somehow makes it possible to conclude from this that our efforts at refugee protection have been successful.

Conclusion

The Western countries are no longer desirous of receiving refugee populations, and they have taken a number of measures to achieve this result, including carrier sanctions, very stringent visa restrictions and expedited procedures. To assist these measures, a myth has been perpetuated that most asylum seekers are abusing the system. But it is important to note that these wild charges and stereotypes of asylum seekers are not based on any kind of empirical evidence. If, instead, one was to examine human rights data one would see quite convincingly that asylum seekers in Europe and the United States are fleeing from some of the most violent countries in the world. This we can establish as a matter of fact. But these facts run directly contrary to the policy that the Western countries wish to pursue, and because of this asylum seekers stand little chance.

Another popular idea is that political violence is random. And the reason why no attempt is made to measure efforts at refugee protection is that it is simply assumed that Western industrialised countries are doing their best in a world gone crazy. But most political violence in the world is not random. Instead, we have a very good idea of where violence will occur and who its victims will be. Thus, we have a good idea – before the fact – of who needs protection. And continual failure to provide this speaks volumes about refugee protection, and it also says a great deal about our societies.

Bibliography

Aleinikoff, T. Alexander (1991) 'The Meaning of "Persecution" in United States Asylum Law', *International Journal of Refugee Law*, 3, pp. 5–29.

Bronkhorst, Daan (1991) 'The "Realism" of a European Asylum Policy: a Quantitative Approach', *Netherlands Quarterly of Human Rights*, 2, pp. 142–58.

Eckhardt, William (1989) 'Civilian Deaths in Wartime', *Bulletin of Peace Proposals*, 20, pp. 89–98

Gibney, Mark (1987) 'A "Well-Founded Fear" of Persecution', *Human Rights Quarterly*, 10, pp. 109–21.

Gibney, Mark (forthcoming) 'The Divorce between Refugee Determinations and the Pursuit of Human Rights Objectives through the Conduct of U.S. Foreign Policy', in Lydio Tomasi (ed.), *In Defense of the Alien*, vol. 19, New York: Center for Migration Studies.

Gibney, Mark (forthcoming) 'In Search of a United States Refugee Policy', in David Forsythe (ed.), *The United States and Human Rights: Looking Outward and Inward*, Lincoln, NE: University of Nebraska Press.

Gibney, Mark, Clair Apodaca and James McCann (1996) 'Refugee Flows, the Internally Displaced and Political Violence (1980–1993): an Exploratory

Analysis', in Alex P. Schmid (ed.), *Whither Refugee? The Refugee Crisis: Problems and Solutions*, Leiden, the Netherlands: PIOOM, pp. 45–66.
Gibney, Mark, Vanessa Dalton and Marc Vockell (1992) 'USA Refugee Policy: a Human Rights Analysis Update', *Journal of Refugee Studies*, 5, pp. 33–46.
Hathaway, James (1990) 'A Reconsideration of the Underlying Premise of Refugee Law', *Harvard International Law Journal*, 31, pp. 129–83.
McCann, James and Mark Gibney (1996) 'An Overview of Political Terror in the Developing World, 1980–91', in David Louis Cingranelli (ed.), *Human Rights and Developing Countries*, Greenwich, CT: JAI Press, pp. 15–27.
Martin, David (1990) 'Reforming Asylum Adjudication: On Navigating the Coast of Bohemia', *University of Pennsylvania Law Review*, 138, pp. 1,247–1,381.
Schmeidl, Susanne (1996) 'Causes of Forced Exodus: Five Principal Explanations in the Scholarly Literature and Six Findings from Empirical Research', in Alex P. Schmid (ed.), *Whither Refugee? The Refugee Crisis: Problems and Solutions*, Leiden, the Netherlands: PIOOM, pp. 15–43.
Shacknove, Andrew (1985) 'Who Is a Refugee?', *Ethics*, 95, pp. 274–84.
Tomasevski, Katarina (1997) *Between Sanctions and Elections: Aid Donors and Their Human Rights Performance*, London: Pinter.
Wallensten, Peter and Karin Axell (1993) 'Armed Conflict at the End of the Cold War, 1989–92', *Journal of Peace Research*, 30, pp. 331–46.

Notes

1. The five categories are as follows:
   Level 1: Countries ... under a secure rule of law, people are not imprisoned for their views, and torture is rare or exceptional ... Political murders are extraordinarily rare.
   Level 2: There is a limited amount of imprisonment for non-violent political activity. However, few are affected, torture and beatings are exceptional ... Political murder is rare.
   Level 3: There is extensive political imprisonment, or a recent history of such imprisonment. Execution or other political murders and brutality may be common. Unlimited detention, with or without trial, for political views is accepted ...
   Level 4: The practices of Level 3 are expanded to larger numbers. Murders, disappearances, and torture are a common part of life ... In spite of its generality, on this level violence affects primarily those who interest themselves in politics or ideas.
   Level 5: The violence of Level 4 has been extended to the whole population ... The leaders of these societies place no limits on the means or thoroughness with which they pursue personal or ideological goals.
2. See generally, James McCann and Mark Gibney, 'An Overview of Political Terror in the Developing World, 1980–1991', in David Louis Cingranelli (ed.), *Human Rights and Developing Countries*, Greenwich, CT: JAI Press, 1996.
3. Mark Gibney, Clair Apodaca and James McCann, 'Refugee Flows, the Internally Displaced and Political Violence (1980–1993): an Exploratory Analysis', in Alex P. Schmid (ed.), *Whither Refugee? The Refugee Crisis: Problems and Solutions*, Leiden, the Netherlands: PIOOM, 1996.

4. See generally, Susanne Schmeidl, 'Causes of Forced Exodus: Five Principal Explanations in the Scholarly Literature and Six Findings from Empirical Research', in Schmid, *supra* note 3; William Deane Stanley, 'Economic Migrants or Refugees from Violence? A Time-Series Analysis of Salvadoran Migration to the United States', *Latin American Research Review*, 22, 1987, pp. 132–55.
5. Mark Gibney, 'A "Well-Founded Fear" of Persecution', *Human Rights Quarterly*, 10, 1987, pp. 109–21; Mark Gibney, Vanessa Dalton and Marc Vockell, 'USA Refugee Policy: a Human Rights Analysis Update', *Journal of Refugee Studies*, 5, 1992, pp. 33–46; Mark Gibney, 'In Search of a United States Refugee Policy', in David Forsythe (ed.), *The United States and Human Rights: Looking Outward and Inward* (Lincoln, NE: University of Nebraska Press, forthcoming).
6. To choose an example that is not atypical, in 1989 the United States admitted 98,076 refugees through its overseas refugee processing programme. More than 80 per cent of those admitted (85.7 using Amnesty as a data source and 83.1 using the State Department) were from Level 2 and Level 3 countries (which is essentially a reflection of the limited amount of human rights violations – at least violations of the integrity of the person – in the then-newly created Russian Republic and in Vietnam). By way of stark contrast, only 47 refugees (out of the 98,076 who were admitted) were from a Level 5 country.
7. See Gibney, 'In Search of a United States Refugee Policy'. Since 1992 there has been a much stronger relationship between levels of human rights abuses and US refugee admissions. This appears to be influenced by several factors, including US military involvement in those countries (which helps to explain the greatly increased number of refugees from Iraq, Somalia and Bosnia), but also, perhaps, a genuine commitment to the protection of human rights through refugee protection. For example, although the percentage of refugees from Level 5 countries had never been above 10 per cent prior to 1994 (and was often considerably less), there has been a substantial increase in this number since that time. In fact, if one includes refugees from Level 4 countries, more than half of the refugees admitted to the US since 1994 have been from countries experiencing gross levels of human rights abuses – which is a far cry from previous practice.
8. Daan Bronkhorst, 'The "Realism" of a European Asylum Policy: a Quantitative Approach', *Netherlands Quarterly of Human Rights*, 2, 1991, pp. 142–58 (148).
9. On the basis of the Amnesty International Report, Bronkhorst created a scale of human rights violations in each of five categories: political prisoners, cases of torture, executions, 'disappearances', and extra-judicial executions. The index number for each category is 1 for upto 10 cases, 3 for 10 to 100 cases, and 5 for more than 100 cases in that category. So the highest (i.e., worst) score a country could receive would be a 25.
10. See generally, James Hathaway, 'A Reconsideration of the Underlying Premise of Refugee Law', *Harvard International Law Journal*, 31, 1990, pp. 129–83; T. Alexander Aleinikoff, 'The Meaning of "Persecution" in United States Asylum Law', *International Journal of Refugee Law*, 3, 1991, pp. 5–29.

11. David Martin, 'Reforming Asylum Adjudication: On Navigating the Coast of Bohemia', *University of Pennsylvania Law Review*, 138, 1990, pp. 1,247, 1,270.
12. Ibid. at p. 1,279.
13. William Eckhardt, 'Civilian Deaths in Wartime', *Bulletin of Peace Proposals* 20, 1989, pp. 89–98; Peter Wallensteen and Karin Axell, 'Armed Conflict at the End of the Cold War, 1989–92', *Journal of Peace Research*, 30, 1993, pp. 331–46.
14. See generally, Katarina Tomasevski, *Between Sanctions and Elections: Aid Donors and Their Human Rights Performance*, London: Pinter, 1997.
15. Andrew Shacknove, 'Who Is a Refugee?', *Ethics*, 95, 1985, pp. 274, 282.
16. I made this argument in a recent piece that focused on the granting of asylum to a woman who feared facing female genital mutilation back in her home country of Togo. My point is that as novel and as commendable as this victory happened to be, the granting of asylum to this particular woman (and a handful like her each year) would offer absolutely no protection whatsoever to the other two million who will face this barbarous practice this year. What I call for is a much closer connection between US asylum/refugee policy and the conduct of American foreign policy. If the US believes that female genital mutilation constitutes an egregious human rights violation – and the granting of refugee status is proof positive of this proposition – then it is (or should be) incumbent on all of us to take serious measures to halt these practices. What has happened instead is that the US and several other Western countries have outlawed the practice domestically. This, however, does nothing for women who will face this practice but who will not be able to get to the West – which will be nearly all of the women in the world who face this butchery. Mark Gibney, 'The Divorce between Refugee Determinations and the Pursuit of Human Rights Objectives through the Conduct of U.S. Foreign Policy', in Lydio Tomasi (ed.), *In Defense of the Alien*, vol. 19, New York: Center for Migration Studies (forthcoming).

Appendix A: Political terror scale 1980–96

	80		81		82		83		84		85		86		87		88		89		90		91		92		93		94		95		96	
	a	s	a	s	a	s	a	s	a	s	a	s	a	s	a	s	a	s	a	s	a	s	a	s	a	s	a	s	a	s	a	s	a	s
AFGH	5	5	5	5	5	5	5	5	4	5	5	5	5	5	4	5	4	5	4	5	4	4	4	5	4	5	4	5	5	5	5	5	4	5
ALBA	3	3	3	3	3	3	3	3	3	3	3	3	3	3	3	3	3	3	3	3	3	3	3	2	2	2	2	2	3	2	3	2	3	2
ALGE	2	1	2	1	2	1	2	1	2	2	2	2	2	2	2	2	4	3	2	2	2	2	3	3	4	4	4	5	5	5	5	5	5	5
ANGO	3	3	3	3	3	3	3	5	3	3	3	5	4	5	4	5	4	4	4	4	4	4	3	3	4	5	5	5	5	5	4	5	4	5
ARG	5	4	5	3	3	3	3	3	2	2	2	1	2	2	2	2	2	2	3	2	3	2	3	2	2	2	2	2	2	2	2	2	3	2
BAHR	3	2	3	2	3	3	3	3	3	3	3	2	3	2	3	3	3	3	3	3	3	3	3	2	2	2	2	2	3	2	4	3	4	2
BANG	3	3	3	2	3	3	3	3	4	2	3	2	5	3	3	4	3	3	3	3	4	4	3	4	4	4	3	3	3	3	3	3	3	4
BENI	3	2	3	3	2	3	2	2	2	2	3	3	3	2	2	2	3	3	3	3	2	1	1	1	2	1	2	1	2	1	9	2	9	1
BHUT	9	9	9	9	9	1	9	1	9	1	9	1	9	1	9	9	9	1	9	1	2	9	4	3	3	4	3	4	3	4	2	2	1	2
BOLI	3	4	5	4	4	3	4	2	3	3	3	2	2	2	2	2	3	2	3	2	2	3	3	2	3	2	2	3	2	2	2	2	2	2
BRAZ	3	2	2	2	3	2	4	2	4	2	4	3	3	3	4	4	3	3	4	3	5	4	5	4	5	4	4	4	4	4	4	4	4	4
BULG	3	2	3	3	3	3	2	3	2	3	3	3	3	3	3	3	3	3	3	3	2	2	2	1	2	2	2	2	3	2	2	3	3	2
BURM	9	3	9	3	9	3	3	4	3	3	3	4	4	4	5	3	5	5	4	4	4	4	4	4	5	5	5	5	5	5	4	5	4	4
BURU	2	2	9	2	9	2	2	2	2	2	3	2	3	3	2	2	4	4	2	2	2	2	5	4	4	4	5	5	5	5	5	5	5	5
CAMB	3	3	3	3	3	4	3	4	4	3	3	4	5	4	9	4	3	4	3	4	3	4	3	4	4	3	4	4	4	4	3	4	3	4
CAME	2	2	2	2	2	2	2	2	4	3	3	2	2	2	2	2	2	2	2	2	2	3	3	4	3	4	3	3	4	4	3	3	3	3
CEAFR	9	9	9	9	9	9	9	9	9	9	9	9	9	9	2	2	2	2	2	2	2	2	2	2	2	3	2	2	9	2	9	2	9	2
CHAD	9	9	9	9	3	3	3	9	5	5	5	5	2	3	4	3	3	3	3	3	4	4	3	4	5	4	5	4	4	4	4	4	4	2
CHIL	4	4	5	3	4	3	4	3	4	3	4	3	4	5	4	4	3	4	3	3	3	3	3	3	3	3	3	2	2	2	2	2	2	2
CHIN	3	3	2	3	3	2	3	2	2	3	3	3	3	2	3	3	3	3	5	5	4	4	4	3	4	3	3	3	4	3	3	3	4	3
COLO	4	3	4	3	5	3	4	3	4	3	4	3	5	4	4	4	5	4	5	4	5	5	5	5	5	4	5	5	5	5	4	5	5	5
COMO	2	2	2	2	2	2	2	2	9	2	3	2	3	2	3	3	2	2	2	2	2	1	2	1	3	2	3	1	9	2	9	2	1	1
CONG	2	2	2	2	2	2	2	2	2	2	2	2	2	2	3	3	2	2	2	2	2	2	2	1	2	2	3	4	4	4	3	3	3	3
COST	9	1	9	1	9	1	2	1	2	1	9	1	9	1	9	1	9	1	9	1	9	1	9	1	2	1	9	1	1	1	2	1	2	1
CUBA	3	3	3	3	3	3	3	3	3	3	3	3	3	4	3	3	3	3	3	3	3	3	3	3	3	3	3	3	3	3	4	3	3	3

	80	81	82	83	84	85	86	87	88	89	90	91	92	93	94	95	96
	a s	a s	a s	a s	a s	a s	a s	a s	a s	a s	a s	a s	a s	a s	a s	a s	a s
CYPR	9 1	9 1	9 1	9 1	9 1	9 1	9 1	9 1	9 1	9 1	9 1	1 1	2 9	2 9	1 1	2 2	2 1
CZEC	3 3	3 3	3 3	3 2	2 3	2 3	3 3	3 3	2 3	3 3	1 1	9 1	2 1	9 1	9 1	2 1	9 1
DJIB	2 2	2 1	1 2	2 2	2 1	9 2	9 1	1 2	2 1	2 2	2 2	3 3	3 3	9 4	4 3	9 2	2 2
DOMR	3 2	9 2	9 2	9 1	3 2	9 1	3 2	3 2	3 2	2 2	2 2	2 2	2 2	2 2	2 2	2 2	3 3
ECUA	9 2	9 2	9 2	9 2	9 2	3 2	4 3	4 3	3 3	3 2	3 3	3 2	3 3	2 3	3 2	3 2	2 2
EGER	2 3	3 3	3 3	3 3	3 3	3 2	9 3	3 3	3 2	2 2	1 1	1 1	1 2	1 1	3 1	2 2	1 9
EGYP	3 1	3 3	3 3	3 3	3 2	3 2	3 3	3 2	3 3	4 3	3 3	4 3	3 3	4 4	4 4	4 4	4 3
ELSA	5 4	5 4	5 4	5 4	5 4	4 4	5 4	5 4	5 4	4 4	4 4	4 4	4 4	4 3	3 3	2 3	3 2
EQ.GUI	9 9	2 2	9 2	1 2	9 9	1 2	1 2	2 2	2 2	2 2	3 3	3 3	3 9	3 3	3 4	3 4	3 3
ERIT	9 9	9 9	9 9	9 9	9 9	9 9	9 9	9 9	9 9	9 9	9 9	9 9	9 9	2 1	2 1	2 1	2 1
ETHI	4 5	4 4	4 4	4 4	3 4	4 4	4 5	4 5	5 5	4 4	4 4	4 4	4 3	4 3	4 4	3 4	4 2
FRAN	2 1	2 1	2 1	2 1	2 1	2 1	2 1	2 2	2 1	2 1	1 1	1 1	1 1	1 1	2 1	2 2	2 9
GAMB	2 1	3 1	2 2	2 1	2 1	2 1	2 1	2 1	2 1	9 1	2 1	2 1	1 1	1 1	2 2	2 3	2 2
GHAN	3 1	9 2	3 3	3 3	3 2	2 2	3 2	2 2	2 2	2 2	2 2	3 2	2 2	2 1	4 2	9 2	1 2
GREE	2 1	2 1	2 1	2 1	2 1	2 1	3 1	2 2	2 2	2 2	2 1	2 1	2 2	2 2	3 2	9 2	3 1
GUAT	5 4	5 4	5 4	5 4	5 4	5 4	4 4	4 4	4 4	4 4	5 5	4 4	4 4	4 4	4 5	4 5	4 4
GUIN	3 3	3 2	3 2	4 1	3 3	3 2	2 3	3 3	3 2	2 2	3 2	2 3	3 3	3 3	3 3	3 3	3 3
GUIN-B	9 9	2 2	2 2	1 2	9 9	2 2	2 2	2 2	2 2	2 2	2 2	1 2	2 9	2 3	2 2	9 2	3 2
GUYA	9 3	9 3	9 3	9 3	3 3	2 2	2 2	1 2	2 2	2 2	2 2	2 2	2 2	2 2	2 2	1 2	2 2
HAIT	4 3	3 3	3 2	3 3	3 3	3 3	3 2	5 3	4 3	3 3	4 4	4 5	4 4	4 4	5 4	2 3	3 3
HOND	4 2	4 3	4 2	4 2	4 3	3 3	3 3	3 3	4 3	3 3	3 3	3 3	3 3	3 3	2 3	2 3	3 2
HUNG	2 2	2 2	2 2	2 2	2 2	2 2	2 2	2 2	2 2	1 1	9 1	9 1	2 1	2 1	1 1	1 2	1 1
INDI	4 3	4 3	4 3	3 3	3 3	3 4	3 3	4 4	4 4	4 4	4 4	4 4	5 4	5 5	5 5	4 5	5 4
INDO	4 3	5 3	4 3	4 3	5 3	4 4	3 3	3 3	3 3	3 3	4 3	4 4	5 3	4 4	4 4	4 4	4 3
IRAN	5 9	4 5	5 5	5 5	5 5	5 5	4 5	5 5	5 5	4 5	4 4	4 4	4 4	3 4	4 4	5 4	4 3
IRAQ	4 4	4 4	4 4	4 5	5 4	5 5	4 4	5 4	5 5	4 4	5 5	5 5	5 5	5 5	5 5	5 5	5 5

	80	81	82	83	84	85	86	87	88	89	90	91	92	93	94	95	96
	a s	a s	a s	a s	a s	a s	a s	a s	a s	a s	a s	a s	a s	a s	a s	a s	a s
ISRA	2 2	2 2	2 2	2 2	3 2	3 2	3 2	3 2	3 2	3 2	2 2	2 2	9 2	9 2	4 2	4 3	4 3
*OT	9 9	9 9	9 9	9 9	9 9	9 9	9 9	9 9	4 4	4 4	4 3	4 3	4 4	4 4	9 4	9 4	9 4
ITAL	2 1	2 1	2 1	2 3	2 1	2 1	2 1	2 2	3 1	2 1	2 1	2 1	2 1	9 2	2 2	2 2	1 2
IVOR	2 1	2 2	9 1	9 1	9 1	9 1	2 1	2 1	1 1	2 2	2 2	2 2	3 3	2 2	2 3	2 3	3 3
JAMA	9 1	9 1	9 1	9 1	2 2	2 2	2 2	1 2	3 2	2 2	2 2	1 3	3 3	2 3	1 3	3 3	1 2
JAPA	9 1	9 1	1 1	2 1	1 1	1 1	1 1	1 1	2 1	1 1	1 1	1 1	1 1	1 1	2 1	2 1	2 9
JORD	3 2	3 2	9 3	9 2	2 2	3 2	3 2	3 2	3 2	3 2	3 2	3 2	2 2	2 2	3 2	3 2	3 1
KENY	9 2	2 2	3 2	3 2	4 3	2 2	3 2	3 3	3 2	2 2	3 3	3 3	4 4	3 4	4 4	4 3	3 4
KUWA	9 9	9 1	9 1	3 1	2 9	3 2	2 2	2 2	1 2	2 2	5 5	4 5	3 9	3 3	3 2	3 2	2 2
LAOS	3 3	3 3	3 3	3 4	3 4	3 4	4 4	3 4	3 3	2 3	2 3	2 2	2 3	2 3	9 2	1 2	1 1
LEBA	9 9	9 9	9 9	9 9	9 9	9 9	9 9	9 9	9 9	3 9	4 4	3 3	4 3	3 4	4 4	4 4	3 3
LESO	2 2	3 2	3 2	2 2	2 2	3 3	3 2	2 2	3 3	2 2	2 2	3 2	9 3	2 3	3 3	2 2	2 1
LIBE	3 3	3 2	3 2	3 3	2 3	3 3	3 3	2 3	3 3	4 3	5 5	4 5	4 5	5 5	5 5	5 5	5 5
LIBY	4 4	3 4	3 3	3 3	3 4	3 3	3 4	4 4	3 3	3 3	3 3	3 3	3 3	3 3	3 3	3 3	3 3
MADA	2 2	2 2	2 2	2 2	9 2	2 2	2 2	2 2	4 3	3 3	2 2	3 3	3 3	9 3	9 2	9 2	9 2
MALAW	2 2	2 2	2 2	3 3	2 3	3 3	3 2	9 9	2 2	3 2	2 3	3 3	3 3	2 2	2 2	2 2	2 2
MALAY	2 2	3 2	9 2	2 3	2 3	3 2	2 2	2 2	2 2	2 2	2 2	3 2	2 2	1 2	2 2	3 2	2 2
MALI	3 3	3 3	3 2	3 2	3 2	9 2	2 2	2 2	2 2	2 2	4 3	4 3	3 3	3 1	3 3	3 1	1 1
MAUR	3 2	2 2	2 2	3 2	3 2	2 2	2 2	2 1	3 2	3 4	4 4	4 4	3 4	2 3	2 2	2 3	1 2
MEXI	3 3	3 3	3 3	3 2	3 3	3 3	3 3	3 3	3 3	3 3	4 3	3 3	3 3	3 4	4 4	4 4	4 3
MORO	3 2	3 3	4 3	4 3	4 3	4 3	3 3	3 3	3 3	3 3	3 3	3 3	3 3	3 3	3 3	3 3	3 2
MOZA	3 3	3 2	3 3	3 5	3 3	4 5	4 5	4 5	3 4	3 4	3 4	3 4	4 5	3 4	3 3	2 3	3 3
NAMI	4 3	3 9	3 9	3 9	4 3	4 4	4 5	4 5	4 4	3 3	2 2	2 2	2 2	9 2	9 2	9 2	9 2
NEPA	3 2	3 2	3 2	2 3	3 2	3 3	3 3	3 3	3 3	3 3	4 3	3 2	3 3	3 3	3 3	2 3	4 3
NICA	9 4	2 3	3 3	2 4	3 4	4 5	3 5	4 4	4 4	3 4	2 3	3 4	3 4	3 4	3 4	3 3	3 3
NIGE	9 2	3 2	3 2	3 1	3 2	2 3	2 2	2 2	2 2	2 2	4 3	2 2	3 3	2 3	3 3	4 2	3 2

	80	81	82	83	84	85	86	87	88	89	90	91	92	93	94	95	96
	a s	a s	a s	a s	a s	a s	a s	a s	a s	a s	a s	a s	a s	a s	a s	a s	a s
NIGIA	2 2	9 2	9 2	2 2	3 9	2 2	3 2	2 3	2 2	3 3	3 3	2 3	3 3	4 4	4 5	4 4	3 4
OMAN	9 2	9 2	9 2	9 2	9 2	9 2	9 2	9 2	9 1	9 2	9 1	9 1	9 9	9 1	2 2	2 2	9 2
PAKI	3 3	4 3	5 3	4 3	3 3	3 3	3 3	3 3	3 3	3 3	4 3	4 3	4 4	3 4	4 4	5 4	4 4
PANA	9 2	9 2	9 2	9 2	9 3	9 2	9 3	3 2	3 3	3 4	3 2	3 2	2 2	2 2	1 2	2 2	3 2
PAP NG	9 9	9 1	9 1	9 1	9 9	9 2	9 2	9 2	4 2	4 2	4 4	4 3	4 9	4 3	3 4	3 3	3 3
PARA	4 3	3 3	4 3	4 3	4 3	4 3	4 3	3 3	3 3	2 2	3 2	2 3	2 3	2 3	3 2	3 2	3 3
PERU	3 2	3 2	4 2	4 3	4 4	5 4	4 4	5 4	5 5	5 5	5 5	4 5	5 5	4 4	4 5	4 4	4 4
PHIL	4 3	4 4	4 3	4 4	4 3	4 4	3 4	4 3	3 3	4 3	4 4	4 4	4 4	4 4	4 3	3 4	3 3
POLA	3 3	3 2	3 3	3 3	3 3	3 3	3 3	3 3	2 2	2 2	2 2	2 2	1 2	1 1	1 1	1 1	9 1
ROMA	3 3	3 2	3 2	3 3	3 3	3 3	3 3	3 3	2 3	4 4	3 2	2 2	3 1	2 2	3 2	2 2	2 2
RWAN	9 9	2 1	3 1	2 1	2 9	9 2	3 2	2 1	2 1	2 2	5 4	5 4	4 9	4 4	5 5	5 5	5 5
SAOTM	2 2	2 2	2 2	2 2	9 2	9 2	9 2	9 1	2 2	2 2	1 1	1 1	9 1	9 1	9 1	9 1	9 1
SAUDI	3 2	9 2	9 2	3 2	3 2	3 2	3 2	3 3	3 2	3 2	3 2	3 2	2 3	3 3	3 2	4 3	3 2
SENE	9 1	9 1	9 2	9 1	2 2	3 1	2 2	3 2	2 2	2 2	3 3	3 3	3 3	3 3	3 2	4 3	3 2
SEYC	9 2	2 2	2 2	9 2	2 2	2 2	2 2	2 2	9 2	9 2	9 2	2 2	9 2	9 1	9 1	9 1	9 1
SILE	9 2	2 1	9 2	3 2	2 2	2 2	2 2	2 2	2 3	2 2	2 2	3 3	4 4	4 4	5 5	4 4	5 5
SING	3 3	3 2	3 2	2 2	2 2	1 2	1 1	2 2	2 2	2 2	2 2	2 1	1 1	1 2	2 1	2 1	2 1
SOMA	3 3	3 2	3 2	3 3	3 3	3 3	4 3	4 3	5 4	5 5	5 5	5 5	5 5	4 5	5 5	5 4	4 5
SAFR	3 3	3 2	3 3	4 2	3 3	4 4	5 5	4 5	4 5	4 4	4 4	5 4	5 4	5 5	5 4	4 4	4 4
SKOR	3 3	3 3	3 3	4 3	3 3	3 3	3 3	3 3	3 2	3 3	3 3	3 3	3 3	2 2	3 2	3 2	3 2
SRILA	2 1	3 2	3 2	5 4	5 4	5 4	5 4	5 4	4 5	5 5	5 5	5 4	5 4	5 4	4 3	4 5	5 4
SUDA	3 2	3 3	3 2	3 2	3 3	3 3	3 4	4 4	5 5	4 3	4 4	4 5	5 5	5 5	5 5	4 5	5 4
SURI	9 2	3 2	3 3	3 3	9 3	3 2	5 5	4 4	2 3	9 2	3 3	9 2	1 2	9 2	9 2	9 2	1 2
SWAZ	2 1	2 1	2 1	2 2	3 2	2 2	2 1	2 2	1 2	2 2	2 2	2 2	1 2	3 2	3 2	2 2	1 2
SYRI	5 4	5 5	5 5	4 4	4 4	3 4	5 4	5 4	4 4	4 3	4 4	4 3	3 3	3 4	4 4	3 3	3 3
TAIW	3 3	3 3	3 2	3 3	2 2	2 2	2 2	2 2	2 3	2 2	2 2	2 2	1 2	2 2	2 2	2 1	1 1

	80		81		82		83		84		85		86		87		88		89		90		91		92		93		94		95		96	
	a	s	a	s	a	s	a	s	a	s	a	s	a	s	a	s	a	s	a	s	a	s	a	s	a	s	a	s	a	s	a	s	a	s
TANZ	2	2	2	2	2	2	9	3	2	3	2	2	2	2	2	3	2	2	2	2	2	3	2	2	1	2	2	2	2	2	3	2	3	3
THAI	3	3	3	3	3	3	9	3	2	3	3	2	3	3	2	3	2	3	2	2	3	2	2	2	4	3	2	3	3	3	2	2	2	3
TOGO	2	2	2	3	2	2	3	3	3	3	2	3	2	3	2	3	2	1	2	2	3	2	3	3	2	3	4	5	3	4	2	3	2	3
TRIN	9	1	9	1	9	1	9	1	9	1	1	1	1	1	1	1	2	1	1	1	2	2	2	2	1	2	2	2	1	2	2	1	1	2
TUNI	3	1	3	2	3	2	3	3	3	3	3	2	3	3	3	3	2	2	2	2	3	3	4	3	3	3	3	3	4	3	4	2	3	2
TURK	4	3	4	3	4	3	4	3	3	3	4	3	4	3	4	3	4	3	4	3	4	3	4	4	5	4	4	5	5	5	4	5	4	4
UGAN	4	4	5	4	4	5	5	5	4	4	5	5	4	4	4	4	4	4	4	4	4	4	4	4	3	3	3	3	3	3	3	4	4	3
UNAE	9	1	9	1	9	1	9	1	1	1	1	1	1	1	2	1	2	1	2	1	2	1	2	2	1	2	1	1	1	1	2	1	2	1
UVOLT	9	2	9	2	9	2	3	3	9	9	9	9	9	9	9	9	9	9	9	9	9	9	9	9	9	9	9	9	9	9	9	9	9	9
URAG	4	3	4	3	4	3	4	3	3	3	2	1	9	2	9	2	9	1	2	2	4	2	2	2	2	2	2	1	2	2	2	2	1	1
USSR	3	3	3	3	3	3	3	3	3	3	3	3	3	3	3	3	2	2	2	2	3	3	3	4	2	9	9	9	9	9	9	9	9	9
ARME	9	9	9	9	9	9	9	9	9	9	9	9	9	9	9	9	9	9	9	9	9	9	9	9	9	2	1	3	2	2	2	2	2	2
AZER	9	9	9	9	9	9	9	9	9	9	9	9	9	9	9	9	9	9	9	9	9	9	9	9	3	5	2	5	3	4	2	4	2	3
BELA	9	9	9	9	9	9	9	9	9	9	9	9	9	9	9	9	9	9	9	9	9	9	9	9	9	2	2	2	1	2	2	2	2	2
ESTO	9	9	9	9	9	9	9	9	9	9	9	9	9	9	9	9	9	9	9	9	9	9	9	9	9	2	9	2	1	2	1	1	1	2
GEOR	9	9	9	9	9	9	9	9	9	9	9	9	9	9	9	9	9	9	9	9	9	9	9	9	4	2	4	5	2	4	3	3	2	3
KAZA	9	9	9	9	9	9	9	9	9	9	9	9	9	9	9	9	9	9	9	9	9	9	9	9	9	1	1	1	1	3	2	1	2	3
KYRG	9	9	9	9	9	9	9	9	9	9	9	9	9	9	9	9	9	9	9	9	9	9	9	9	9	1	1	1	2	1	2	1	2	1
LATV	9	9	9	9	9	9	9	9	9	9	9	9	9	9	9	9	9	9	9	9	9	9	9	9	9	1	1	2	1	2	2	2	2	1
LITH	9	9	9	9	9	9	9	9	9	9	9	9	9	9	9	9	9	9	9	9	9	9	9	9	1	1	1	1	1	1	1	1	1	2
MOLD	9	9	9	9	9	9	9	9	9	9	9	9	9	9	9	9	9	9	9	9	9	9	9	9	4	3	9	3	2	2	2	1	2	2
RUSS	9	9	9	9	9	9	9	9	9	9	9	9	9	9	9	9	9	9	9	9	9	9	9	9	2	3	2	3	4	5	4	5	4	4
TAJI	9	9	9	9	9	9	9	9	9	9	9	9	9	9	9	9	9	9	9	9	9	9	9	9	5	4	4	5	2	4	2	3	3	3
TRKM	9	9	9	9	9	9	9	9	9	9	9	9	9	9	9	9	9	9	9	9	9	9	9	9	1	2	1	1	1	2	2	2	2	2
UKRA	9	9	9	9	9	9	9	9	9	9	9	9	9	9	9	9	9	9	9	9	9	9	9	9	1	2	1	2	2	3	2	3	2	2

	80	81	82	83	84	85	86	87	88	89	90	91	92	93	94	95	96
	a s	a s	a s	a s	a s	a s	a s	a s	a s	a s	a s	a s	a s	a s	a s	a s	a s
UZBE	9 9	9 9	9 9	9 9	9 9	9 9	9 9	9 9	9 9	9 9	9 9	9 9	1 2	2 2	2 2	2 2	2 2
VENE	3 2	2 1	9 2	3 2	2 2	2 2	4 2	3 2	3 2	4 4	3 3	3 3	4 3	4 3	4 4	4 3	4 5
VIET	3 3	3 3	3 3	3 3	3 4	3 3	3 4	3 4	3 3	3 3	3 3	3 3	2 3	2 2	2 3	2 2	2 2
NYEM	9 3	9 3	9 3	9 3	9 3	2 2	9 4	3 3	3 4	3 3	2 3	2 3	3 3	3 3	4 4	4 2	3 2
**SYEM	3 3	3 3	2 3	2 3	2 3	3 3	4 5	3 3	3 3	3 3	9 9	9 9	3 9	9 9	9 9	9 9	9 9
YUGO	3 2	3 3	3 3	3 2	3 3	3 3	3 2	3 3	3 3	3 3	3 3	4 5	3 9	9 9	9 9	9 9	2 9
BOSN	9 9	9 9	9 9	9 9	9 9	9 9	9 9	9 9	9 9	9 9	9 9	9 9	5 5	5 5	5 5	5 5	3 4
CROA	9 9	9 9	9 9	9 9	9 9	9 9	9 9	9 9	9 9	9 9	9 9	9 9	4 5	3 5	2 5	5 5	3 3
MACE	9 9	9 9	9 9	9 9	9 9	9 9	9 9	9 9	9 9	9 9	9 9	9 9	9 2	2 1	1 2	9 1	9 1
SERB	9 9	9 9	9 9	9 9	9 9	9 9	9 9	9 9	9 9	9 9	9 9	9 9	9 5	3 5	5 5	4 5	9 4
SLOV	9 9	9 9	9 9	9 9	9 9	9 9	9 9	9 9	9 9	9 9	9 9	9 9	9 1	9 1	9 1	9 1	9 1
ZAIR	4 3	4 3	4 3	4 3	3 3	3 4	3 4	3 3	3 3	3 3	3 3	4 3	4 4	5 5	4 5	4 4	4 5
ZAMB	3 3	3 3	3 3	3 2	2 2	2 2	3 3	3 2	2 3	2 2	3 3	1 2	3 2	3 3	2 3	2 3	2 3
ZIMB	3 2	3 2	3 3	4 5	5 4	4 5	3 3	3 3	2 3	2 3	2 3	2 2	2 2	2 2	2 2	2 2	2 4

*Amnesty International does not code Israel separately from the Occupied Territories
**North and South Yemen were unified in 1990
a Amnesty International
s State Department

2

New Asylum Regimes or a World without Asylum? The Myth of International Protection

Louis Gentile[1]

Introduction

This chapter is based on a contribution to a conference entitled 'New Asylum Regimes in the World' but it might be more accurate to call it 'Towards a World without Asylum'. For that is the direction in which we are moving, a world in which growing human rights rhetoric is matched by increasing barriers imposed by states to keep out asylum seekers. The problem is compounded by a serious decline in the modest level of human rights protection offered to refugees, all of whom are by definition victims, or potential victims, of human rights violations, who have fled across an international border.[2] Let us not forget that what is at stake is what has traditionally been the only effective form of international protection offered to victims of human rights abuses. The United Nations system created in the aftermath of the Holocaust and the Second World War did not envisage effective intervention to protect the human rights of persons inside their national boundaries even if the UN Charter and other international instruments did make reference to promoting and encouraging respect for human rights and fundamental freedoms, and for intervention in exceptional circumstances to preserve international peace and security.[3] Cold War politics ruled out any effective, practical international intervention to protect fundamental human rights.

In 1998 was celebrated the fiftieth anniversary of the Universal Declaration of Human Rights (UDHR), but those of us who are engaged in the practice of refugee and human rights protection see greater cause for shame and mourning than we do for celebration. The international community has completely failed to protect fundamental human rights. The flame of optimism that briefly followed the end of the Cold War was quickly extinguished as genocide was perpetrated in Bosnia and Rwanda while the international community watched. In the absence of political will even genocide has been allowed to occur, discrediting the United Nations which has deflected much of the blame from powerful member states, who alone have the power and resources to make effective universal human rights protection a reality. In 1997 we experienced a new phenomenon as thousands upon thousands of refugees under UNHCR's 'protection' were hunted down and exterminated in eastern Congo (ex-Zaire), a genocide perpetrated against refugees outside their country of origin and ostensibly under the protection of the international community. What have we learned from this experience and other recent emergencies and what can we change to enhance protection in the future? This is the key question for us.

I speak as a practitioner, having spent much of the past ten years in the field dealing with the victims of human rights violations. I have served with the UNHCR in Turkey, Bosnia, Djibouti, as part of the emergency team deployed to the Republic of Congo (Brazzaville) in June 1997, and with the Canadian Foreign Service in Ottawa and the Philippines. I have seen children decapitated by Bosnian Serb artillery in Srebrenica and wounded and starving children who survived being hunted down like animals while trekking for thousands of kilometres barefoot across the ex-Zaire. In recent years I have witnessed both an intensification of human rights violations in countries of origin and a severe decline in the level of protection and assistance provided to refugees and asylum seekers in countries of asylum. How can we account for this deterioration in international protection in an era when the rhetoric of governments worldwide increasingly acknowledges, and even actively advocates, respect for universal human rights principles?

This may come as a surprise to some but as a UNHCR Protection Officer I see myself first and foremost as a human rights practitioner and advocate and see UNHCR, despite its many faults, as the UN's most active and innovative human rights agency. Therefore what I am proposing is not an academic article in the traditional sense but rather a very frank practitioner's point of view. I would like to speak about four interrelated myths which I believe are seriously undermining universal human rights principles and refugee protection. I will then consider the tragedy in the Great Lakes region of Africa in relation to these myths and conclude with lessons learned from our mistakes and recommendations for future action.

Let me first admit that I do not have research evidence to support the 'four myth' theory that I am about to present to you. I derive my hypotheses from my empirical experience. Moreover if one reads the newspapers or watches television news on a regular basis, or if one follows government foreign and domestic policy statements, whether coming from the North or South, those myths have been encountered on numerous occasions. I will try to explain why I believe they are myths and why they are dangerous. They are the following:

1. the international community has made significant progress in protecting universal human rights since the end of the Second World War;
2. universal human rights principles (including asylum and refugee law) are respected in the developed world but for various reasons are nearly impossible to enforce in the developing world;
3. the international community, particularly through the work of UNHCR and its NGO partners, ensures that most refugees are provided with protection and assistance consistent with acceptable international minimum standards; and
4. the developed world is being overwhelmed by bogus asylum seekers who take unfair advantage of overly generous asylum laws.

I shall attempt to address these myths in greater detail.

Significant progress

It is a comforting idea to assume that we have made significant progress in protecting human rights since the end of World War Two. Certain sub-regions, the EU for example, have been completely transformed in the past five decades. From fascism and war to the European Convention on Human Rights (ECHR), that is quite a journey, and without question a journey in the right direction in the human rights context. Real progress in some regions has been accompanied by very significant advances in international and regional human rights law and international humanitarian law.[4] I will not list the numerous human rights instruments adopted, nor as a human rights lawyer would I attempt to deny their importance.

The human rights problem today is not about establishing principles but about practice, and it is in analysing the human rights situation on the ground, in judging progress in the practical application and respect for human rights principles, that this myth begins to disintegrate. It suffices to read the latest reports from Amnesty International or the US State Department, read today's press, or watch the BBC. Better yet come and see for yourselves what human rights principles mean in this day and age. Come and talk to some of the nearly 23 million people our office is attempting to protect and assist worldwide. Speak with the survivors of genocide, ethnic cleansing and a myriad of horrific methods of torture. If your time and resources are limited you won't have to travel too far. You can visit asylum seekers arbitrarily detained in prisons and detention centres across this country and find out first hand what human rights mean in Europe in 1998. I have spent the better part of ten years working with desperate victims and survivors and I have seen no evidence of practical progress on the human rights front or increasing compassion and tolerance among the privileged. Why is this myth of effective progress dangerous? Because it promotes complacency and inaction. It allows governments and civil society to feel that enough is being done to protect human rights when the reality is quite the opposite.

Uneven respect for human rights

The myth of a world in which some regions have achieved extremely high human rights standards and others are simply incapable for whatever reason of achieving high standards of respect for human rights is increasingly popular. How often have you heard in the context of the Rwandan genocide or the war in the Former Yugoslavia that 'those people have been killing each other for generations' and the international community therefore cannot solve these problems? How quickly we forget. Perhaps my understanding of Western European history is incorrect but I am convinced that if one looks back at the past two thousand years one could easily come to the conclusion that this region, home of the Holocaust, the Inquisition and countless bloody wars, is one condemned to perpetual strife, intolerance and conflict.

This myth is particularly appealing in prosperous, powerful states. It implies that root causes of conflict are exclusively locally generated and that powerful states have no responsibility for causing conflict; for example, by contributing to the proliferation of arms or supporting oppressive regimes. Furthermore, it diminishes the moral and practical imperative for intervention by implying not only that the international community bears no responsibility but also that intervention would be futile in a culture condemned to suffer from perpetual strife.

There is very much an 'us and them' idea perpetuated by this myth, one that reinforces racist and xenophobic elements in developed states.

Finally, it implies that democratic, developed states do not themselves violate basic human rights and do not need to be carefully scrutinised to ensure that they respect accepted human rights principles.[5] Yet the European Court regularly finds that European states have violated various universal human rights principles enshrined in the European Convention on Human Rights. In UNHCR we have seen how European states who claim to make human rights a priority will go to extremes to avoid their responsibilities under the 1951 Convention and 1967 Protocol towards persons fleeing from persecution who turn up at their own borders, how they are willing to detain minors arbitrarily or pervert the spirit of the 1951 Convention definition of 'refugee' to deny protection to those who should be protected.[6] The United Kingdom's new human rights focused foreign policy emphasises the need to enhance the human rights of children but the UK maintains its reservation to the Convention on the Rights of the Child (CRC), effectively denying basic human rights enshrined in the CRC to children who are asylum seekers. The Berlin Wall has come down but another wall has ironically taken its place.

Refugee protection ensured

The third myth, that most refugees in first countries of asylum are provided with acceptable standards of protection and assistance, is one that strikes particularly close to home, and I believe that UNHCR bears responsibility for contributing to its perpetuation, and thereby endangering refugees. In many places where UNHCR operates, and we are present in over 120 countries, UNHCR offers very little protection and our assistance falls far below acceptable international standards. I do not mean to confuse you by deflecting attention from the moral and legal responsibilities of states which are failing to protect and respect the rights of refugees and asylum seekers enshrined in international and regional refugee and human rights instruments. It is the states which ultimately should be held responsible for not living up to those responsibilities but UNHCR also has a particular mandate and must be more vocal about the failure of international protection in the absence of political will. In many places we do not even have access to the people we are mandated to protect and when we do have access we may have one Protection Officer assigned to protect a population of 30,000 or more desperate refugees.[7] We have reached the point where conducting our work often means risking our own lives.[8] As I write the whereabouts of Vincent Cochetel, a dear friend and colleague, remains unknown following his abduction 149 days ago (at the time of writing) from his apartment in North Ossetia. In emergency operations we have lost lives and barring a miracle we are going to lose more.[9]

Refugee children often do not receive even basic primary education, and standards of health care are totally inadequate. Fair and efficient status determination procedures are the rare exception rather than the rule. Most disturbingly, refugees are extremely vulnerable to violations of their basic human rights. Every year refugee women and girls are raped in cities and camps, and refugees are returned to their countries of origin where they are in serious danger of persecution, all in blatant violation of international law.

In 1997 the myth of international protection exploded in our faces. All of our wonderful guidelines and principles went up in smoke as an estimated 200,000 people under our protection were hunted down and slaughtered in the jungles of ex-Zaire. In the absence of political and military support, and for the second time in less than three years, UNHCR was faced with an impossible 'Sophie's choice'; most tragically of all, these massacres were almost certainly the direct result of international inaction during and after the Rwandan genocide. In the aftermath of the April 1994 genocide UNHCR and its partners were confronted with a massive humanitarian crisis in Tanzania and eastern Congo (ex-Zaire). It was clear to UNHCR at the outset that armed elements, including many guilty of the genocide in Rwanda, had entered the camps in ex-Zaire. The UN appealed to member states to provide troops to separate armed elements in the camps from civilians. That request fell on deaf ears and UNHCR was left to choose whether it would aid all those in the camps, including the armed factions and perpetrators of genocide who were not entitled to refugee status under international law, or whether we would leave hundreds of thousands of children to die of hunger and disease. The choice was not one UNHCR should have been forced to make.

In late 1996 and early 1997 the choice was equally stark: leave people to die and be killed in greater numbers or undermine core UNHCR and international legal principles by facilitating de facto *refoulement* in a repatriation movement leading to an uncertain and insecure future in Rwanda. UNHCR chose the latter. The only moral option for the international community in both instances, and even more so in Rwanda itself in April 1994, should have been rapid and effective military intervention to stop the killing and to separate armed elements from civilians in the camps.[10] So to conclude on the myth of effective international protection for refugees, suffice it to say that without effective political will and in the current atmosphere, we are not even confident of our ability to protect the refugee's most fundamental right, the right to life.[11]

Bogus refugees

The fourth and final myth is well known: 'bogus' refugees are flooding the West. Developing countries are being 'overwhelmed' by 'freeloading' asylum seekers. This myth is perhaps the most dangerous of all, contributing to intolerance and xenophobia in asylum states. It ignores the fact that the majority of refugees and asylum seekers worldwide are hosted by poor, developing states and not by the wealthy north. Iran and Pakistan alone host more refugees than all of Europe combined. Djibouti, where I was last posted, is one of the world's poorest countries according to the United Nations Development Programme (UNDP) World Development Index. Yet Djibouti hosts an estimated 100,000 asylum seekers, refugees and displaced persons (equal to roughly 20 per cent of the national population). Less than a quarter of these 100,000 persons receive any assistance from the international community and the bulk of the cost of their subsistence is absorbed by the local population. I do not even mention protection which is practically non-existent with asylum seekers condemned to legal limbo in the absence of functioning status determination procedures. By comparison, the United Kingdom, a wealthy G8 country with a population of approximately 58 million, received a total of 255,190 asylum applications from 1990 to 1997 inclusive (representing less than 5 per cent of the total population).

This myth also ignores what governments themselves accept as a truth, namely, that severe human rights violations take place on a regular basis in the majority of UN member states. Mark Gibney's research (chapter 1) is extremely pertinent in this regard and confirms what we in UNHCR have known for years: that there is a direct and positive correlation between the level and severity of human rights violations in countries of origin and the number of persons seeking asylum in the West from those countries. That is to say, people seem to seek asylum primarily because of insecurity and not for economic reasons.

Finally, it seems to me that there are glaring contradictions between universal human rights principles and the asylum and immigration policies of governments. For example, if a state party to the 1989 Convention on the Rights of the Child is bound to act in 'the best interests' of all children on its territory, can it then return a failed asylum seeker who is a minor to a country where insecurity and inadequate health care and education are the known status quo? Can UNHCR support such returns even if insecurity is removed from the equation? Can governments continue to advocate respect for universal human rights in their foreign policies while ignoring those same principles vis-à-vis asylum seekers on their own territory? Can government development and foreign ministers make speech after speech about the need to extend economic prosperity and basic social and economic rights to the world's most poor while ministers of justice and the interior demonise persons who dare to seek a better life abroad? Is there no contradiction there? Is there no danger?

The message I am conveying paints quite a dismal and pessimistic picture but I remain an optimist despite my experience. As a practitioner I feel obliged to learn from the mistakes we have made and to make recommendations to enhance refugee and human rights protection in the future. I am convinced that we can significantly reduce the level of human rights violations and restore credibility to the term 'international protection' by adopting and achieving the following recommendations.

Conclusions and recommendations

1. Political will on the part of governments is the key element required to punish those who violate international norms and to prevent or stop human rights violations and armed conflict.
2. Those who commit war crimes and crimes against humanity must be held accountable for their crimes and there can be no impunity for violators. A strong, and independent International Criminal Court is an absolute necessity.
3. The list of crimes within the Court's jurisdiction should be expanded to include obstruction of humanitarian operations, the recruitment and participation of children under 15 in armed conflict, sexual assault, and attacks against humanitarian personnel.
4. A well-armed and trained Rapid Reaction Force must be available to the United Nations to prevent and deter conflict and genocide, apprehend indicted war criminals and separate armed elements from civilians during humanitarian operations. Such a force must

be exceptionally well trained in international humanitarian and human rights law.

5. Governments should support the Optional Protocol to the Convention on the Rights of the Child, raising the minimum age of all forms of recruitment and participation in conflict to 18 years.
6. All governments should ratify all of the international human rights and international humanitarian law instruments and remove outstanding reservations to those instruments.
7. UNHCR and other humanitarian actors should do nothing to undermine humanitarian and human rights principles. If forced to do so to preserve human life in the absence of political will, UNHCR and all humanitarian agencies must state clearly and accurately how actions or operations undermined humanitarian principles. For example, in the case of the mass repatriation from eastern Zaire to Rwanda UNHCR should be clear in admitting that this movement constituted *refoulement* according to its own definition of that term.
8. Providing humanitarian assistance to human rights abusers and armed elements carries an enormous cost as it perpetuates insecurity within camps, undermining the protection of the most vulnerable and placing all in the camp in grave danger of attack. It also threatens the principle of asylum regionally as it leads to genuine fears, with refugee flows being associated with violence and insecurity.
9. Despite enormous progress, and efforts to train personnel, better emergency preparation and contingency planning are required within UNHCR to respond to crises rapidly and effectively. This will not be possible without significant support from donor states.
10. On the fiftieth anniversary of the Universal Declaration of Human Rights all states should reaffirm their commitment to the right of asylum consistent not only with Article 14 of the UDHR, and the applicable international and regional refugee instruments, but also consistent with universal human rights principles including the best interests of the child principle enshrined in the Convention on the Rights of the Child.

If we can achieve this ambitious agenda perhaps we will be able to enter the new millennium having paid a worthy tribute to the millions of victims we shamefully failed to protect in the twentieth century.

Notes

1. The views expressed in this article are those of the author, a UNHCR staff member, and not necessarily shared by the United Nations or UNHCR. The help of colleagues is gratefully acknowledged, but the article remains a personal point of view. Mr Gentile currently serves as the Refugee Law Training Officer in the UNHCR Branch Office for the United Kingdom and the Republic of Ireland.
2. See 'Refugee' definitions found in the 51CSR, 67 Protocol, 1969 OAU Refugee Convention.
3. Articles 1 and 55 of the UN Charter, for example.
4. See *Collection of International Instruments and Other Legal Texts concerning Refugees and Displaced Persons,* vols 1 and 2, UNHCR, Geneva, 1995.
5. Although it must be conceded that European states have recognised the need for independent scrutiny to uphold accepted human rights standards in adopting the ECHR and subjecting their policies to the scrutiny of the European Court of Justice in Strasbourg.
6. For example, in Germany persecution by non-state agents is not considered to be persecution within the meaning of the 1951 CSR, contrary to UNHCR and other expert and government opinion. The United Kingdom, in contrast, has recently written to UNHCR clarifying its position on non-state agents of persecution, which is consistent with UNHCR standards.
7. In Djibouti, I was the only Protection Officer responsible for a refugee population in excess of 40,000 spread over three rural camps and the capital city. Having such limited protection presence is not at all unusual, and current cutbacks will exacerbate this situation further.
8. I also include all our operational partners in the term 'we', particularly the NGO community, ICRC, and UN and NATO military forces who take enormous risks to provide basic levels of protection and assistance to vulnerable populations.
9. UNHCR local staff are the most vulnerable, often being left behind to run operations after the evacuation of international staff because of security concerns.
10. During the genocide of April 1994 the United Nations Assistance Mission for Rwanda (UNAMIR) was reduced rather than increased.
11. The tragedy in the Great Lakes is one that deserves much greater depth of analysis, and it is not my intention here to provide a complete history of the crisis even from the start of the genocide in 1994. I merely hope to illustrate how vulnerable refugee protection and human rights principles are to deter massive human rights violations effectively or to respond rapidly to stop genocide, in the absence of political will and international mechanisms.

3

Temporary Protection and the Bosnian Crisis: a Cornerstone of the New European Regime[1]

Danièle Joly

Introduction: temporary protection à l'Européenne

Temporary protection *à l'Européenne* arose in the context of profound changes in the asylum regime which had developed after the Second World War but it also constitutes a cornerstone of the new regime unfolding.

While an array of restrictive measures demonstrated an utmost reluctance to accept more refugees in the European Union (EU), a major crisis exploded on its doorstep. After procrastinating the EU yielded to the pleas of the UNHCR and agreed to take in refugees from former Yugoslavia on a temporary basis. In the last analysis it proved impossible for the EU to ignore totally the war in former Yugoslavia and its masses of displaced people resulting from the worst massacres in Europe since the Nazi period. *Real* politics led the UNHCR to come up with a scheme which EU states were ready to consider. This solved their dilemma. The major protagonists in the formulation of temporary protection (TP) in Europe are thus the UNHCR and the EU. Other fora also have views and attempt to influence the course of events but with less effect.

The UNHCR called an international meeting on humanitarian aid and for victims of the conflict in the former Yugoslavia on 29 July 1992 and proposed a comprehensive response. The conflict was raging and there were already hundred of thousands of displaced people. TP constitutes one of seven components in this comprehensive plan which will be examined later. The basic elements of TP as presented at that meeting are the following:

> It should include, at a minimum, admission to the country where such protection is being sought, respect for the principle of non-*refoulement* and basic human rights (the elements of which are further outlined in ... [ExCom Conclusion 22 (XXXII)] and repatriation when conditions so allow in the country of origin.
>
> (UNHCR, 1992, p. 4)

The circumstances bringing about TP

A number of factors contributed to make TP a possible and desirable option to the respective protagonists. From the point of view of refugee protection agencies including the UNHCR, temporary protection seemed to be a *pis aller* (the least 'worst' solution), as no other initiative was taken by most European states to receive refugees from former Yugoslavia. It was clear that no generous offer of asylum or resettlement was forthcoming as had happened with the Hungarian crisis in 1956 or the Indo-Chinese refugee movement in 1979. It was also blatant that the humanitarian need was critical. TP was developed in Europe to respond to a specific crisis, bound by time and place. It became thus an acceptable option, other than the Geneva Convention, not so much because the refugees involved did not meet the Convention criteria (many did, as stated by UNHCR and other agencies), but because of the specificity of the situation. UNHCR presented three main reasons underpinning its proposal: the urgent character of the crisis, its temporary nature, and the mass character of the movement, potentially threatening to overburden asylum procedures in reception countries (UNHCR, 1993). The urgent and mass quality of this refugee movement were for all to be seen; as for its temporariness, it had to be assumed as a sine qua non as temporary protection could only be justified if a long-term solution was posited by the agency acting on behalf of refugees; as resettlement was not on offer, only return conditional on a swift solution to the crisis was to be envisaged.

For EU states, TP became a possible and desirable option because it provided an answer to their dilemma between a policy to reduce refugee numbers on their territory and the pressures to accept former Yugoslavs. The magnitude of the war and its atrocities exploding onto the media had indeed led to a general feeling among the European populations that something had to be done. Another factor which played a part is the geographical proximity of the crisis which made it more difficult to ignore. Moreover, the few states which had received the bulk of the refugees could not cope with any more and were pressurising EU states to 'share the burden around'. A formula had to be found, but nothing more than a minimalist one. The EU found that the requirement of *non-refoulement* was not too difficult to meet as long as it was not accompanied by the usual standards of protection awarded Convention refugees. These people would in no way come to stay. Moreover, the low standard of minimum treatment initially recommended by UNHCR may have helped to reduce the fear of cost outlays and made it clear that integration measures were neither required nor envisaged. In other words, if one cannot keep refugees out, the next best solution seems to be to receive them for a limited period and send them home as soon as possible. TP was acceptable also because it bypassed the Geneva Convention so that the states retained complete control over who would be accepted and because it was accompanied by return as the only outcome considered. This TP proposition enabled governments to satisfy the strands of public opinion which advocated a humanitarian policy vis-à-vis the refugees and those who spoke against immigration (Kjaerum, 1993).

Since the implementation of temporary protection in a variety of ways throughout Europe for former Yugoslavs, the question arises about the future of this precedent. TP has begun to acquire a life of its own, independent of the situation that gave birth to it, and it would be difficult to tie it solely to the events in former Yugoslavia as a case *suigeneris*. When new crises happen it would be difficult for the parties concerned not to call upon this experience, and they have realised that it constitutes an important stake. A new concept has entered the European scene and its tenets will have a strong impact on asylum and on future populations of refugees in Europe. It provides a potential blueprint for events to come and it is being discussed on the basis of the implementation already in place. This continues to be confirmed: on 5 March 1997 the European commission sent the Council a proposal for a joint action based on Article K.3(2)(b) of the Union Treaty concerning temporary protection of displaced persons. On 27 May 1999 the Council adopted conclusions on displaced persons from Kossovo. And the European Council, at its special meeting in Tampere on 15 and 16 October 1999, acknowledged the need to reach an agreement on the issue of TP for displaced persons on the basis of solidarity between member states. In 2000 the European Commission submitted a proposal for a 'Council Directive on minimum standards for giving temporary protection in the event of a mass influx of displaced persons and on measures promoting a balance of efforts between Member States'. An enhanced discussion is taking place on this issue among all fora involved with refugees. As this debate proposes models for other situations that may call for similar measures, each protagonist attempts to arrive at a definition that will serve its agenda, whether it be for instance to further restrictive trends or to expand and consolidate the situation of refugees. In the first place one needs to look at situations which may deem to justify the use of TP rather than the Geneva Convention. On the basis of the experience with former Yugoslavia, and taking on the views of various fora, several pointers can be identified.

Large numbers of displaced people (or in other words mass outflows) was one of the major factors put forward by UNHCR to justify TP. This had been stipulated much earlier on (in 1981) for situations outside Europe whereby UNHCR requested that states 'in situation of large-scale influx ... should always admit them [the refugees] at least on a temporary basis' (UNHCR, 1981, p. 2). At the time of the former Yugoslav crisis UNHCR added that TP is a practical means 'avoiding the imposition of an undue load on the already overladen asylum procedures in receiving States' (UNHCR, 1993, p. 1). What must be determined, however, is when one can begin to speak of mass outflow and who will identify it. An emergency situation is another UNHCR criterion: it sees in TP 'a response to the emergency' (UNHCR, 1993, p. 1). It is implicit that UNHCR will play a central role in determining such situations.

It is semantically logical that temporary protection ought to be used for temporary crises or, in UNHCR's words, 'whenever safe return to the country of origin can be envisaged within a reasonable period' (UNHCR, 1993, p. 7). Not only must one ask here when and who but also how one can know. For the UNHCR an answer to this question is sought in 'international efforts to achieve solutions to the situations causing their flight' (1993, p. 7). However, such an evaluation cannot be based on hard facts and presumptions of events which follow their own course. The conflict in former Yugoslavia is a case in point and calls for greater caution in the future.

Civil war or generalised violence situations have also been advanced as a criterion. The UNHCR makes it clear at a later stage that the cause of the flight has to be taken into account:

> However liberally its terms [of the Convention] are applied, some refugees fleeing the civil wars and other forms of armed conflict that are the most frequent immediate causes of refugee flight fall outside the letter of the Convention ... with no specific element of 'persecution'.
>
> (UNHCR, 1994c, p. 15)

The UNHCR makes it clear that those are in need of and deserving of international protection and humanitarian assistance. Paradoxically TP ushers in general official recognition from the EU that bona fide refugees exist who are not necessarily included in the Convention definition and who deserve protection. This is stated in the Commission's proposal for a Directive (2000, p. 26) which refers to

> the preparation of a common policy on asylum including common European arrangements for asylum ... open to those who, forced by circumstances, legitimately seek protection in the European Union!

It is clear that the proposal refers to much broader categories of refugees than conventional refugees, that is, those who are forced by circumstances to seek protection. TP was used also for other groups in some European countries and in the USA. The European Union, while quoting the UNHCR, declares that it is prepared to admit on a temporary basis people displaced because of reasons such as 'armed conflict or civil war' (Council of Ministers, 1995, p. 1); this formula definitely indicates that TP might be used to replace de facto/humanitarian status. This is precisely one aspect causing concern among NGOs such as ECRE which notes that the reference to causation rather than the existence of a mass influx, and the mention of harmonised action 'when, **for instance** [ECRE's emphasis], there is a mass influx', might imply that TP will be used for asylum seekers outside the context of a mass influx (ECRE, 1996a). This is why ECRE insists that criteria justifying the adoption of TP must emphasise the mass and emergency nature of the crisis, and that its 'temporariness' be ensured or helped by an international process to resolve it.

The Council of Europe does not seem to be worried about the EU formula as it deems TP useful in situations of mass influx as well as for asylum seekers 'whose applications have been rejected', that is, as a replacement of humanitarian status, in order to 'avoid the refoulement' (Arnold, 1996, p. 2). Different governments and fora fall on either side of this debate. In the USA the Immigration Act 1990 introduced TPs on the basis of generalised causes which prevent aliens from returning safely (Frelick and Kohnen, 1995). This is also the case with Denmark's Yugoslavia Act quoting 'war or similar unrest' (Brochman, 1995, p. 14). In contrast, the European Commission (Commission of the European Communities, 1994, p. 25) stresses the 'occurrence of mass influxes' and leaves second place to causes of flight. According to the Commission, mass influx 'means arrival in the

Community of a large number of displaced persons' (2000, p. 30). Mass influx implies also that it originates from the same country or geographical area and that it is not just a gradual phenomenon. But the Commission adds that there can be no 'pre-determined quantitative criteria' (p. 8) for declaring that there is a mass influx. This would be ascertained and decided jointly by a qualified Council majority for each specific situation. As for Norway, for instance, it states clearly that TP will not be used as a general instrument in refugee policy but will be appropriate 'in situations involving mass migration' (Brochman, 1995, p. 52). It takes a lawyer to point out that both the mass character of the refugee movement *and* its causes other than those justifying Convention status are a sine qua non for TP (Kälin, 1996). According to Kälin it is the prima facie granting of status which would constitute an appropriate response to a mass influx of Convention refugees; this would certainly alleviate one concern of the UNHCR and of governments, that is, the risk of overloading asylum procedures in the receiving states. *Il suffisait d'y penser*; this was nowhere notified by the UNHCR or other fora which called upon the 'overladen asylum procedures' argument. The capacity of reception would nonetheless have to be taken into account, but this is one aspect which has not been developed in the context of arrivals from former Yugoslavia in the EU.

Finally, geographical proximity appears to assume some importance. The territory of former Yugoslavia lies on the edge of Western Europe and shares some of its borders with EU member states. The EU envisages possible harmonised action on TP if the EU 'is so close to the region concerned that it could itself be considered as belonging to the region of origin' (Council of Ministers, 1995, p. 2). Will it then in future apply to the borders of the EU, Central Europe, Europe as a whole, or can it be considered for the Mediterranean shores outside Europe? The last is not to be discarded 'if help and adequate protection are not available in the region of origin' (Council of Ministers, 1995, p. 2). The EU itself thus does not reject the possibility of using TP for groups of diverse regional and national origin. But it makes it clear, as do the UNHCR and the Commission, that protection must first be sought and secured as near the place of origin as possible. This is countered by the Inter-governmental Consultations which describe TP as

> particularly appropriate where large numbers of refugees or asylum-seekers and mixed categories of persons have moved relatively short distances, perhaps only into an immediate neighbouring

> State and where there is a real likelihood that they can soon return home.
>
> (Secretariat, 1995, p. 21)

This discussion at least indicates that the matter is not quite settled. While the most unmovable position is that of the EU, there is still room for varying interpretations of the burden-sharing resolution and its application. However, one thing is certain: the number of contributions to the debate on TP and the variety of fora involved demonstrates that TP is firmly entrenched as an important component of the new asylum regime.

Status and instruments

First of all it must be noted that there does not exist an international convention or declaration on temporary protection. There are only UNHCR documents which were drafted for the benefit of countries outside Europe and remain quite succinct (ExCom Conclusion 19 on Temporary Refuge 1980 and ExCom Conclusion 22 1981 on the Protection of Asylum-seekers in situations of large-scale influx) and subsequent UNHCR texts drafted for the situation in former Yugoslavia.

A new status?

The TP created for the benefit of former Yugoslavs can be considered as a new status. A form of TP existed in the 30s (Hathaway, 1984; Joly, 1996) but this was the only status available and not additional to a universal one, 'in parallel to the generous standards of protection provided by the 1951 Convention' (Rudge, 1996a, p. 3): as such it is in Europe a qualitatively new concept today. At the time of writing, UNHCR is putting forward that it is not such a new notion because it is implicit in the protection awarded by Convention status, as enshrined in the cessation clause. This explanation might result from a UNHCR attempt to justify the adoption of temporary protection or to demonstrate coherence and compatibility with the Geneva Convention. In reality the interpretation and implementation of the Geneva Convention in Europe up until the 80s demonstrates the contrary. Convention status had become customarily tantamount to permanent residence and integration. The notion of return was not called upon where Convention refugees were concerned and this constitutes one tenet of the 'old regime'. When the question of return arose it fell upon the refugees themselves to petition European governments and EU institutions to obtain the setting up of return programme (Joly, 1996). This interpretation is confirmed by Kälin's argument that temporary protection made it possible to offer protection to non-Convention refugees without undermining the institution of permanent asylum (Kälin, 1996).

Instruments

The two EU documents on refugees from Former Yugoslavia constitute the first regional instruments on temporary protection; they are also the first (partially) pan-European texts establishing a status for a refugee population. They are, however, not binding but take the form of recommendations or guidelines. It is a mark of the times and of the new asylum regime. Each state keeps entire control over numbers and details of implementation which has led to vast discrepancies throughout the EU and across the rest of Europe. In spite of this, there seems to be a consensus about the desirability of this status as a minimalist solution. Only a few states created specific legislation governing temporary protection as states generally preferred to use other existing statuses sometimes adapted for the occasion, or simply ad hoc measures (Joly, Kelly and Nettleton, 1997). Denmark, the Netherlands and Spain developed a specific legal basis for TP. Belgium prepared one and abandoned it, while Germany could not implement it. Sweden, which did not use any for former Yugoslavs, has set one up for future use. No state initially specified the total duration of the temporary acceptance of the refugees (including the renewals for permission to stay) before another status had to be contemplated. In other words, we are looking at a process which is neither definitive nor static. On the one hand each step of this process establishes a potential model for the future, whilst on the other hand the variations in its implementation give scope for discussion. As a further contribution to this debate there are resolutions and declarations by other institutions about temporary protection quoted throughout this paper: the Council of Europe, the European Commission, the European Parliament, the OSCE (Organisation for Security and Cooperation in Europe), the Intergovernmental Consultations, ECRE and other NGOs.

Non-refoulement

Non-refoulement is the first requirement set by UNHCR for temporary protected refugees (UNHCR, 1981, and UNHCR, 1992). This principle was generally respected, at least once a border was reached. In reality this might be more a state of affairs preceding TP rather than a consequence of its adoption. It could even have been a contributory factor to the acceptance of TP by EU states as it became clear that it was near impossible to return such masses of asylum seekers to their homes in the face of the well-known atrocities taking place there (Secretariat, 1995). Prior to the crisis in Yugoslavia it had become customary in Western Europe to apply much more widely the *non-refoulement* clause than the granting of refugee status.

Access

Access to the receiving countries was not made easier for potential beneficiaries of TP than for other asylum seekers, except for vulnerable groups such as detainees or people in need of medical treatment. In the usual manner, as soon as the number of asylum seekers from the zones of conflict grew, most countries in turn imposed visas (European Parliament, 1996). This measure, combined with fines to transporters in most countries to impede arrivals, and difficulties of access are noted by UNHCR (1994a). If such persons managed to reach a border spontaneously, however, they generally benefited from *non-refoulement.*

One must establish in most countries a clear distinction between 'invited persons' and spontaneous arrival. The former had an easy access to a procedure giving them a form of temporary protected status and concomitant rights. Another aspect of TP for vulnerable groups is that they had access to the procedure in the country of origin or the region of origin. In some cases, the latter can be compared to temporary resettlement from a first country of asylum. A common difficulty they encountered was how to get out of the zone of danger into safety. Moreover, in most cases, the first country rule applied which led to dispersal of families and a near impossibility of being regrouped. It was not possible to apply for protection in more than one country as the EU document stipulated that people had to be coming 'direct from combat zones' (Council of Ministers, 1992, p. 2). Nonetheless Kälin quotes as one benefit of TP the fact that it 'allows for suspending such provisions' (the 'safe third country' clauses), permitting more of a burden-sharing (Kälin 1996, p. 11).

As there was in practice *non-refoulement* throughout the EU for designated groups of former Yugoslavia, the delivery of a visa was tantamount to giving access not only to physical presence in a reception country but also to temporary protection. As a consequence the contradiction is rendered more blatant between the recognised need for protection of these groups and the imposition of visas to prevent their access to it.

Some countries felt the necessity to mitigate the visa requirement; Denmark, for example, established a foreign service mission in the conflict area which came to be known as the 'Zagreb office' (Brochman, 1995). This brings us nearer to the possible models presented by the Inter-governmental Consultations for processing in the region or country of origin (Secretariat, 1994).

Group determination

Another characteristic of this new status is that it relies on a positive group determination, mostly on a national combined with a vulnerability basis. Group determination was prevalent in the 30s and early 40s but the Geneva Convention was introduced precisely to avoid the shortcomings of such a formula which failed to cover all those in need of protection. This is the one that held sway in Europe during the 'old asylum regime'. Temporary protection changed those parameters.

The UNHCR proposed the following broad criteria:

> Persons who have fled from areas affected by conflict and violence
> Persons who have been or would be exposed to human rights abuses [including as a result of campaigns of ethnic or religious persecution]
> Persons who owing to their specific situation have felt compelled to flee as a result of the conflict.
>
> (UNHCR, 1993, p. 2)

The last was subsequently changed and broadened to 'Persons who for other reasons specific to their personal situation are presumed to be in need of protection', so that it also included those whose need for protection was based on objective circumstances other than place of origin alone (UNHCR, 1994b, p. 2).

The EU resolution first established a criterion based on the area of origin, 'former Yugoslavia', and brought in further qualifications on two grounds:

- The state of conflict in the actual place of origin if they come 'direct from combat zones' (Council, 1992, p. 2)
- Vulnerability for those who 'have been in a prisoner-of-war or internment camp and cannot otherwise be saved from a threat to life or limb; are injured or seriously ill and for whom medical treatment cannot be obtained locally; are under a direct threat to life or limb and whose protection cannot otherwise be secured; have been subjected to sexual assault, provided that there is no suitable

means for assisting them in safe areas situated as close as possible to their homes' (Council, 1993).

For the first time in a regional instrument women have been identified as a group worthy of protection if they have been subjected to sexual assaults. In its resolution on burden-sharing the EU reiterates the above categories in other 'situations of armed conflict or civil war' (Council, 1995, p. 1). In a subsequent document, the Commission stresses group determination based on 'country or geographical area' (2000, p. 14).

In practice, different EU countries adapted and interpreted the guidelines in their own way, some limiting TP to Bosnians or a few of the nationalities from former Yugoslavia, others extending it to all nationals from former Yugoslavia. Most gave places to vulnerable groups. Moreover, the status awarded differed not only between two countries but also sometimes within the same country according to the refugees' mode. The Commission points out that states broadly adopted one of the two following approaches: those which have introduced special, often nationality related temporary protection mechanisms, clearly defining the beneficiaries, and others which chose a more vague approach 'based on the general principle that the beneficiaries would be those who do not fulfil the requirement of Article I of the Geneva Convention, but whose return to the country of origin would otherwise cause special hardship' (Commission, 1996, p. 3). It designates the first approach as being more straight forward but fails to pronounce itself on which it supports.

Both the European Parliament and the Council of Europe advocate wider all-embracing criteria, the former speaking of persons fleeing generalised violence who may not fall within the specific definition of refugees (Arnold, 1996), while the latter includes humanitarian refugees fleeing regions beset by war, civil strife or natural disasters such as from Rwanda, Afghanistan, Liberia, Somalia, Sudan and those defined by the UNHCR but to which it takes care in adding the new category of people fleeing from 'natural or ecological' disasters (Arnold, 1996, p. 3). The broadest definition is to be found in the United States Immigration Act 1990 as it comprises persons kept away from their state of origin because of

- ongoing armed conflict that poses a serious threat to personal safety;
- environmental disaster such as earthquake, flood, drought, or epidemics, in which the foreign state is unable to handle the return of its nationals;

– or, any other extraordinary and temporary conditions that prevent aliens from returning safely.

(Frelick and Kohnen, 1995, p. 343)

This status has at times applied to Salvadorans, Somalians, Lebanese, Liberians, Kuwaitians, Bosnians and Rwandans, often with a cut-off date with regard to their arrival or application. One puzzling aspect concerns the national groups who benefited from this measure as their inclusion appears to have been arbitrary.

One human rights lawyer, in contrast, argues that beneficiaries of TP should be persons who are not covered by the Geneva Convention definition but come under the OAU Convention and Cartagena Declaration, warning against the Resolution on burden-sharing which includes all (Kälin, 1996). This is what evidently happened where former Yugoslavs are concerned as many countries did not give an opportunity to Geneva Convention refugees to obtain the relevant status. This takes us into the arena of the relationship between TP and the asylum procedure.

Temporary protection and the asylum procedure

In most EU countries TP could not run concurrently with the standard asylum procedure and TP-protected persons had their application frozen, postponed or not considered at all. The relationship to the procedure has changed over time in most countries. As TP was prolonged a kind of norm arose through practice in several European countries that there was a time limit to temporariness and TP persons were given access to the Convention asylum procedure or to a humanitarian status. UNHCR initially did not insist on access to the procedure and EU states welcomed this view in their 1992 Conclusion on former Yugoslavia (Council, 1992). At the same time, however, ECRE had requested from the beginning that TP persons should have access to the asylum procedure if they so wished, but this was often perceived by the authorities in most countries as non-acceptable. Even in some instances where TP refugees had access to the procedure, however, they were put off applying for refugee status as they would then have lost the relative advantages awarded by TP status and become assimilated to asylum seekers. The Commission's proposal for a directive remains ambiguous on this issue: it lays down the 'absolute requirement' that access to the procedure be granted to any beneficiaries of TP (2000, p. 21), but adds in a subsequent paragraph 'at least at the end of the temporary protection' (p. 21) which seems to qualify considerably the absoluteness of the requirement. Reading through the document, it can be inferred that TP and an application for asylum cannot run concurrently (p. 21). The question of access to the procedure or at least of a regularisation of TP persons' situation became more acute as time went by and furthermore when the issue of return arose.

The Council of Europe stresses the importance of providing for an examination of applications for asylum in parallel to TP 'in the shortest possible time and at the latest within a given lapse of time' without giving an indication of the time limit, although it quotes the two years' deadline in Denmark and three years in Norway (Arnold, 1996, p. 8). The Commission states unequivocally that it must not exceed two years (Commission, 2000). The European Parliament is forthcoming, positing a general agreement that 'four years is too long and it ideally should last only two years. After this time alternative solutions should be considered; the provision of permanent status being clearly the most appropriate solution' (European Parliament, 1996, p. 11). This position was already advocated by a human rights lawyer in 1993, who stated unequivocally that if repatriation did not 'take place after a period of two years, the situation of the refugee should be normalised' (Kjaerum, 1993, p. 15). This is also the view expressed by ECRE (Rudge, 1996b). While return was not on the agenda, UNHCR (UNHCR, 1994a) had asked governments to consider three possibilities for the regularisation of TP refugees: recognition as Convention refugees, granting to all or certain groups a humanitarian status, if not a set of ad hoc measures as close as possible to Convention status. When return comes onto the agenda, according to the European Parliament, it is essential that all those receiving TP at least have access to the normal asylum procedures prior to repatriation (European Parliament, 1996).

Return

It is a view shared by UNHCR that the optimum solution for an existing refugee problem is the voluntary return of refugees in good conditions. The war ended and the UNHCR officially lifted temporary protection in December 1996. The next course of events logically would have been the return of refugees to their place of origin. Return was the order of the day and raised three main questions: when, how, where? Social reality demonstrated that conflicts were continuing and that not all TP persons were able to return. They were therefore to be accommodated on a longer term basis in the country of exile. A crucial issue which was stressed when TP was implemented was the concern not to give unofficial support or recognition to ethnic cleansing. The

Dayton Agreement was based on those premises: refugees must be able to return to their place of origin. In practice this prompts a dilemma about what must be done if that place of origin is an area dominated by one ethnic group where refugees from another group want to return. What if the latter are threatened in their life and security? It was precisely what was happening (ECRE, 1996b). Will host countries then force refugees to return nonetheless to an area which is not their place of origin but where the same ethnic group is ruling, thus confirming ethnic cleansing? This option would contravene the spirit of the Dayton Agreement but not its legal requirements as third parties are not bound by them. In contrast, it would perfectly fit the EU interpretation of Article 1A of the Geneva Convention on internal flight alternatives/relocation. One other option is to give TP persons a permanent status in the country of exile (Convention status or a humanitarian status). Consequently, while temporary protection could be construed as a replacement of humanitarian status as discussed above, in another sense it presupposes the existence of such a status as it cannot be assumed that all TP persons would necessarily be able to return or qualify under the Convention.

Unlike Convention refugees, TP persons could fall under forcible repatriation orders, and some countries (such as Germany and Switzerland) have implemented it. One may need to establish a clear semantic distinction between 'return' which is voluntary and 'repatriation' which can be imposed. So far the two terms have often been used interchangeably with an adjective indicating the distinction. There seems to be a general agreement that the best possible option is voluntary return. Yet even some liberal sources of opinion such as the Council of Europe, while stating that voluntary return is the basic principle, accept that 'returns other than on a voluntary basis must not be ruled out', with an exception for certain categories such as Convention refugees, victims of torture, traumas caused by war, rape, etc. (Arnold, 1996, p. 9). UNHCR proposed that states should make it possible for the refugees from former Yugoslavia to prepare their return and that repatriation should be implemented in an orderly manner, proposing several formulae setting out the phases of repatriation:

1. Internally displaced persons as a priority, then refugees from neighbouring states, then those from other countries.
2. First returnees to their home area where their ethnic group is the majority, then those who wish to relocate within new areas where

their ethnic group is the majority, and last those to areas where returnees now constitute the minority.
3. Return of childless adults or adults where spouses or children are still living in the former Yugoslavia, followed only later by return of families (quoted in CERE, 1996).

It appears that states have not been rushing the departure of their TP refugees.

The importance of a good return programme is unanimously accepted. More generally the CSCE (1993) promotes the creation of programmes to assist the return in dignity not only of refugees but also of foreigners who do not qualify for permanent immigration. Some of the EU countries have already had some experience in organising return programmes for refugees or asylum seekers. Germany in 1990 prepared a reintegration and reemigration plan for asylum seekers, such as Sri Lankans (Federal Ministry of the Interior, 1990). Other instances are those of countries taking back their own nationals against financial compensation from the host country (Italy/Albania, Germany/Rumania, Poland/Czech Republic) (Muus et al., 1993). Scandinavian countries have set up return programmes for Chilean refugees; in 1992 the Norwegian government introduced a programme for former Yugoslavs, building on the established support scheme for Chilean refugees which included benefit payments, a travel grant, health insurance for one year, development aid in the society of origin beneficial to the whole local society, and a two-year period for the returnees to change their mind if they could not make good in their home country (as long as they had a settlement permit) (Brochman, 1995). Similar programmes are being set up for the former Yugoslavs in other Scandinavian countries.

A number of fora and documents insist on the safeguards which need to be an integral part of a return programme. ECRE emphasises that States should grant to a returning refugee the legal right to return to the host country within six months (CERE, 1996, p. 1). This measure in fact seems to constitute an incentive for the refugees to attempt a return. ECRE also stresses the need to support 'le retour volontaire des réfugiés en toute sécurité, dans la dignité et ... accompagné de moyens suffisants pour le retour à une vie normale' (CERE, 1996). As stated here security is not deemed sufficient but dignity is also becoming a sine qua non concomitant of return in the discourse of agencies and individuals concerned with the interests of returning refugees. The Commission itself appears to have taken up this formula of return in 'adequate conditions of safety and dignity' in its Explanatory Memorandum to a Proposal for a Directive (2000, p. 3). However, this involves a complex combination of conditions which pertain to the legal, material and emotional domain. In a normative document, Hathaway et al. (1996) set out the general premises underpinning a successful repatriation. A set of guidelines is also advanced by Kälin:

> 1. Repatriation will not succeed if it is not yet a safe and feasible return. Second, [it] may be seriously hampered if refugees are not encouraged to explore, without penalisation the feasibility of return. Finally, repatriation is meaningless without reintegration, and reintegration requires careful bridge-building between returnee and stayee communities.
>
> (Kälin, 1996, p. 15)

The return phase of the former Yugoslavs' TP saga is undoubtedly a pivotal one. On the one hand return is seen by some as the acid test of temporary protection (Secretary of the Inter-governmental Consultations, quoted by Rudge, 1995). On the other hand it is not at all straight forward as the map of the homeland has de facto changed and no access is possible for a good number of refugees to what was their former place of residence. From the experience of TP for former Yugoslavs and from the multifarious practices implemented arise possible models for the future on this status.

Standards of treatment

The hallmark of TP is that it did not offer integration programmes; in several instances it even involved measures which were aimed to prevent integration. This feature is again characteristic of the new asylum regime. Return was the objective and the reception programme of TP persons reflected this orientation. Despite this general feature there were in practice multiple variations throughout Europe. Broadly and almost across the board, the level of social rights was not as good for TP persons as that of Convention or even humanitarian status refugees (barring those where they were awarded Convention or a Scandinavian humanitarian status). On the whole TP persons enjoyed slightly better rights than asylum seekers although not in every aspect. Various countries display different modes of implementation of these reduced rights and it may happen that in a single country there are sometimes discrepancies according to the modalities by which the person was admitted. In one country (France) the prohibition of *refoulement* created a paradoxical situation which enabled the people concerned to stay but without any status accompanied with social rights. The Commission (2000) is proposing to resolve this conundrum, stressing the need both for a residence permit for the entire duration of the protection and for well-defined rights.

The initial standards set by the UNHCR in 1992 remained unbelievably low, in accordance with EXcom 22 (UNHCR, 1981) which had been devised for the benefit of poor non-European countries. Indeed in the countries where those had been implemented, that is mostly on the African continent, such requirements placed the refugees on a similar level to that of the local populations in several respects. In Europe this is far from being the case and it can be argued that Western European countries could afford a better standard of treatment from the onset. Moreover, even if UNHCR requirements could be deemed satisfactory for a couple of months, its proposals demonstrate in the best of cases an incredible lack of foresight. More than one year later the UNHCR expressed the carefully couched view that there was a need for a review of standards (UNHCR, 1993). As years went by the UNHCR put forward a polite request for an improvement stating that 'when the period of temporary protection has to be prolonged, improved standards of treatment *might* be called for' [my emphasis] on the grounds that 'unlike asylum-seekers, whose claims were not yet examined, the need of the person concerned for international protection was already established' (UNHCR, 1994a, p. 2). But surely the latter argument was valid from the beginning? Finally, it was in 1995, that the UNHCR called for standards 'close to that to which recognised refugees are entitled' (UNHCR, 1995a, p. 3), including family reunification, employment, education and a certain degree of integration over a protracted period of time.

The UNHCR position has attracted sharp criticisms from various quarters including lawyers, some of whom accuse the organisation of having given 'tacit approval' to the use of TP 'as an opportunity or excuse to restrict refugee rights' (Hathaway et al., 1996, p. 32). Concern is also voiced by ECRE with regard to the impact of TP on the treatment of refugees in general: 'what we are witnessing is the downgrading of the entire European asylum system to the lesser protection level afforded by TP' (Rudge, 1996a, p. 8). Whether the UNHCR lent itself to such a situation or was pressganged into it, the trading of protection for former Yugoslavs against more precarious rights appears to be confirmed by one intergovernmental mouthpiece: 'enhancing the rights of beneficiaries so much that the stay would become more permanent. This could diminish both the capacity and the willingness of States to provide such protection' (Secretariat, 1995, p. 16).

Two types of arguments are being put forward to support an improvement of standards which may overlap in practice but do not in legal terms. The first one is the time factor, summarised by the Council of Europe into 'the longer the stay, the more extensive the rights' (Arnold, 1996, p. 7) for humanitarian reasons which seem generally accepted. The second one is based on the quality of the presence-/residence in the host country deriving from international instruments. In particular the Convention is said to have carefully constructed a refugee regime that bestows rights as a function of the refugee level of attachment to the asylum state (Hathaway et al., 1996) and shows a gradual improvement of treatment according to simple presence, lawful presence, lawful residence (not necessarily permanent), domicile or habitual residence (Kälin, 1996). In addition lawyers also find grounds for an improvement of standards in the International Covenant on Civic and Political Rights (ICCPR) and the International Covenant on Economic, Social and Cultural Rights (Hathaway et al., 1996), arguing for instance that it is in no way a case of 'public emergency which threatens the life of the nation' as required for emergency suspension of rights under the ICCPR (Hathaway et al., 1996, p. 35). ECRE proposes that TP should only be implemented if it is accompanied by training and educational programmes, a right to family reunification, a guarantee of decent living conditions, social benefits and opportunities for gainful employment, identity papers and travel documents as afforded to other refugees (ECRE, 1994). The arguments put forward by NGOs towards an improved temporary protection status appear to have been taken up by the Commission which proposes minimum standards of treatment and the delivery of documents (Commission, 2000).

Family reunion

One crucial question is that of family reunion, which was generally not granted, even when several members of the same family had obtained protection in different parts of Europe. One could argue that it is the one area which should have priority in the range of rights awarded. These people were not asylum seekers whose genuineness still had to be proven. They were recognised persons in need of protection and many had suffered untold persecution. One of their main concerns would be close members of their family left behind, and the possibility of bringing spouse and children to safety is almost a necessary condition to maintain or recover psychological balance. The importance of family life is stressed by the European Convention on Human Rights and Fundamental Freedoms and it is possible to speak of a violation of article 8 if family reunion is not allowed in the reception country while it cannot be achieved in any other country (Kjaerum, 1993). The European Parliament points out that the right to family reunification derives directly from the right of residence (European Parliament, 1992). According to ECRE there should be no difference for Convention refugees, de facto and TP refugees where family reunification is concerned (Rudge, 1996b).

At the same time the lack of facilities for family reunion is a political tool as it constitutes one essential element of the anti-integration programme, that is, this is the best way of ensuring that people will return as was spelt out clearly by the Inter-Governmental Consultations. Many states feel that 'a more generous policy on family reunion is likely to undermine the temporary nature of any scheme by making returns more difficult' (Secretariat, 1995, p. 16). The concern to limit numbers might be another factor explaining states' reluctance to accept family reunion. However, in reality the additional fear of attracting too many if family reunion was made available does not seem to have been vindicated: in Scandinavian countries when this was rendered possible, the number of arrivals remained far below what could have been expected (Brochman, 1995). According to the Commission's proposal for a directive, separated family members who remained in the place of origin or in another member state should be able to be reunited (Commission, 2000).

Other important features of reception are access to education and employment, which in many cases were not available. Language classes in the language of the host country were at times simply prohibited as even the education provided to children was delivered in the language of the country of origin. Travel and identity documents were often not delivered so that it was near to impossible for the refugees to meet members of their family or community who resided in another asylum country. One is to ask the question as to what would have happened if the EU states 'Convention on the Crossing of External Borders' had been implemented which makes it possible for even asylum seekers to travel freely within the EU for a limited period provided that they declare themselves to a competent authority on arrival. Temporarily protected persons are not mentioned in that draft convention; would they not benefit from the same right? The Commission covers these issues in its proposal for a directive and stipulates that temporarily protected persons must have access to suitable accommodation, assistance in terms of social welfare and means of subsistence, necessary medical care and access to education and vocational/further training for minors and adults. It stresses that their right to work must be on a par with Convention refugees (Commission, 2000, p. 33). A special mention is made of appropriate medical or other assistance for persons with special needs (including those who have undergone rape, torture or other serious ill-treament).

Finally, one area to be considered is the attitude of civil society vis-à-vis the TP refugees, its organised sectors, the media and public opinion. Contrary to the fears of government public opinion seems to have been more favourable to TP persons from former Yugoslavia than to asylum seekers generally in most countries. This may result from a combination of factors. Is it because host populations had been reassured that those people were not going to stay, because they were European, because the knowledge of the terrible atrocities taking place in their homeland brought up reminiscences of the Nazi extermination? At the end of the day, there was no generalised nasty backlash from native populations. On the contrary, in Denmark for instance where TP people had been kept separate from the population, local initiatives actually proceeded to integrate them (Brochman, 1995).

This much reduced level of social rights had been accepted by UNHCR on the basis of a short stay in the country of protection. However, the duration of the conflict was prolonged and several countries began to make adjustments to these as time passed. The debate now revolves around not only what level of rights but also over what period of time. One must be careful not to conflate the calculation of time scales for standard of treatment with what is considered as reasonable for a temporary protection status. The two debates must be treated separately. For instance, it might appear acceptable to award a temporary protection status for two years before a more durable status is granted, while separation from one's children, spouse or parents (for a child) for two years might seem an eternity or the least unreasonably long. The same might be said for the right to work, to education and to identity documents.

Comprehensive action

A comprehensive approach in connection with refugee issues had been written and spoken about considerably but without much action to further it until recently. Non-governmental bodies in particular have emphasised for a long time the need to act on root causes, human rights violations and others. Governments of the EU also mentioned it in their programme on asylum submitted to the Maastricht summit (Joly, 1994). However, such an approach only entered the realm of the possible after the end of the Cold War as the latter precluded international consensus on this question. As early as 1990 a German official document developed a comprehensive approach (Federal Ministry of the Interior, 1990) which encompassed many of the aspects implemented at a later date for the former Yugoslav crisis. In the same year Sweden also established similar guidelines in a working paper developing a 'Comprehensive refugee and immigration policy' (Swedish Ministry of Labour, 1990).

With the crisis in former Yugoslavia a comprehensive action became not only possible but also necessary for a variety of reasons, not the least being the refugee movement which ensued. We had already witnessed how a mass refugee flow could cause the implementation of particular policies towards the country of origin, in Vietnam and more spectacularly in Haiti as this motivated direct military action by the USA. Such intervention was even more spectacular in Kossovo in 1999. The EU programme for comprehensive action (Joly, 1994) which looked very remote in terms of priorities was urged into implementation by the unremitting escalation of the conflict in former Yugoslavia and the masses of displaced people who resulted from it. The guiding principle of this comprehensive action is to be found in the EU 1992 Conclusion, stating that displaced people should be encouraged to stay 'in the nearest safe areas to their homes' (Council of Ministers, 1992, p. 1). This implied a series of measures designed to achieve this aim. Those were reasserted in 1995: highlighting as 'top priority' measures to restore peace in conflict situations where people are being displaced, the EU recommended that aid to the civilian population caught up should mainly be provided on the spot in particular by creating safe areas and security corridors and by providing humanitarian aid (Council of Ministers, 1995, p. 1). In this context TP is envisaged only as a last resort when other possibilities of protection have been exhausted.

The EU had responded to an appeal launched by the UNHCR which had outlined the components of this comprehensive response as:

1. respect for human rights and humanitarian law (in former Yugoslavia)

2. preventive protection, that is, to prevent and contain displacement by providing protection and assistance *in situ* and reduce the factors which compel displacement
3. humanitarian access
4. special humanitarian need in the case of a life-threatening condition for which no treatment can be organised locally
5. temporary protection
6. material assistance for neighbouring reception countries of refugees
7. return and rehabilitation (UNHCR, 1992).

As a consequence funding was provided for humanitarian aid in the countries of origin. Action was developed to secure access for humanitarian organisations and to obtain the release of detainees in prisoner or concentration camps. Material assistance was sent to neighbouring reception countries with the aim of helping them to offer a relatively durable solution rather than constitute a transit country.

Internationally protected zones were established in the midst of conflict zones, the so-called 'safe havens'. These have become highly controversial if not totally discredited after the tragic events of Srebrenica. It is not clear whether they would be used again but they have become a target for criticism (Arnold, 1996). The notion of 'safe haven' has sometimes been understood very critically as deriving from the right to remain concept which might be equated with the negation of the right to seek asylum (Hathaway et al., 1996) or, more sinisterly, the right to die in one's country.

Economic sanctions against the countries which continued hostilities were put in place. Mediation and diplomacy were intended to bring pressure to bear on the forces at war in the region. The strategic aim of that action was to put an end to the conflict in order to remove the causes of further refugee flows and enable the return of TP persons. The Owen and Vance plans were designed for that purpose but failed to score much success. The only action which had an impact was the direct military intervention initiated by the USA as European states proved unable to act.

The return programme itself constitutes the final stage, whereby social and economic aid will be awarded to countries for reconstruction if they take back the refugees. Rehabilitation projects are also set up for the returnees but which include the population *in situ* so as not to create rivalries and jealousies.

A consensus seems to have arisen on the question of a comprehensive approach spanning from NGOs to governments. Referring to the need for a global refugee policy ECRE speaks of an 'accepted wisdom' (Rudge, 1996b, p. 3). Governments such as the Norwegian and the Swedish ones write it in their official policies (Brochman, 1995). The Inter-governmental Consultations also join in this concert of views. The UNHCR itself appears to have adapted its mandate for the benefit of a global approach to the problems of coerced displacement and protection comprising asylum, the promotion of conditions in countries of origin, the protection of individuals in their own homes and their own countries, and calls for the development of 'new tools of protection' which include 'humanitarian diplomacy ... closer working relationships with the military both in the context and peace-keeping or peace-making operations, logistical support for humanitarian assistance, and the physical protection of refugees and displaced persons' (UNHCR, 1994c, p. 10). However, this slippage of the UNHCR mandate and its 'tools of protection' runs the risk of leading to the neglect of asylum and protection; this has caused widespread concern best expressed by Goodwin-Gill (1996).

Burden-sharing was supposed to be part of the comprehensive plan. This is one important feature of TP and to an extent it led a number of European countries to accept a limited number of refugees. However, the discrepancies in numbers remained exaggerated; for instance Germany received about 300,000 and the UK less than 10,000 (Joly, Nettleton and Kelly, 1997). The EU agreed to a resolution on burden-sharing but it was heavily debated, amended and controverted internally (Council of Ministers, 1994b) before arriving at a fairly innocuous public text, which failed to add much to the existing situation. It retained the following criteria: the contribution made to the resolution of crises, military resources, local protection, humanitarian assistance, all economic, social and political factors that may affect capacity. This resolution does not apply to admissions prior to its publication. Another initiative contributing to burden-sharing is the proposal to set up a European Fund for refugees which could be used in large-scale influx, put forward by the European Parliament (Wiebenga, 1995) and supported also by the Council of Europe (Arnold 1996). This mechanism has been incorporated in the Commission's proposal for a directive (Commission, 2000).

Although there is a general understanding that a global/comprehensive approach is necessary, problems arise with regard to its content. The crucial issue is that of the balance between different components of this comprehensive policy. There is a real risk that a policy driven by the political will to limit numbers of arrivals in host countries, over-emphasising measures directed at assistance in the country/region of origin, may lead to grave gaps in asylum and protection. Another issue pertaining to the tackling of root causes is the danger that action will be considered too late, only after flows of refugees are perceived as a threat, rather than as a preventive strategy.

This comprehensive action and its experience may teach a few lessons for the future. It is imperative that the issue of safe havens be reexamined. Governments have not commented at length on their shameful failure and have failed to initiate a serious critique of the concept. When a new refugee crisis could be foreseen in Kosovo, prompt and mass military intervention was not accompanied but followed by a similar approach to the one in Bosnia – where refugee outflows are concerned, comprehensive action was again reactive. More questions need be asked, however, on the efficiency of action to reduce the factors of conflict leading to refugee movements or on how to put an end to it. It is not as easy as might be presumed. Preventive action would be called for but it does not appear that governments are capable of complying with this requirement. The reconstruction and rehabilitation for return are being tested currently: the situation in former Yugoslavia is a particularly delicate one as one may wonder to what extent the conflict has ended and to what extent the rehabilitation programme runs the risk of confirming ethnic cleansing.

The fora and institutions involved

The question of temporary protection has attracted the involvement of most institutions and fora concerned with asylum in Europe: the Council of Europe, ECRE, NGOs and International NGOs, the OSCE, the European Parliament, the European Commission, the Intergovernmental Consultations, the EU, individual governments and the UNHCR. All have issued declarations, resolutions or positions. While two main partners have set it up, that is the UNHCR and the EU, it appears that the EU is the one which calls the tune. The UNHCR has been called upon as consultant in EU discussions on asylum issues but is sworn to secrecy and is increasingly absorbed under the influence of the EU. One cannot help thinking that the UNHCR could have placed the stakes higher where the standard of treatment for TP persons is concerned. In effect many countries have awarded more than the minimum requested by the UNHCR. It could also have insisted on a minimum of parity and harmonisation between receiving countries.

Conclusions: a new asylum regime

I have argued in this chapter that a new asylum regime is unfolding with temporary protection as its cornerstone. As a confirmation of this hypothesis it is worth quoting the UNHCR which posits temporary protection as 'a feature of whatever approach is adopted' while it welcomes it as an asylum strategy in the context of addressing prevention, protection and solutions on a comprehensive regional basis (UNHCR, 1994c, p. 22). According to the Council of Europe, TP must be considered as an integral part of a comprehensive approach to restore peace and prosperity in countries stricken by war (Arnold, 1996). The new regime and in particular its TP component are not always considered in a negative manner. It has been put forward that TP closes 'protection gaps' between the binding principle of *non-refoulement* and the discretionary character of asylum, between the protection of Convention refugees and humanitarian refugees (Kälin, 1996). TP is also seen as a solution to the tensions between the needs of refugees and the migration control objectives of governments under certain conditions, in a normative document proposing a model for the structuring and implementing of TP (Hathaway et al., 1996). And yet it remains difficult to envisage that governments will be ready to set up a favourable system of temporary protection truly beneficial to the refugees in a planned and preventive manner. Recent history seems to demonstrate that they are only ready to act when a refugee movement is about to congregate on states' borders. NGOs and academics are concerned about the crisis of the protection regime and one author speaks of its 'impending fundamental breakdown' (Hathaway et al., 1996, p. 4). Numerous voices have expressed their preoccupation about the downgrading of protection (such as Rudge, 1996a; Goodwin-Gill, 1996).

Can one say that temporary protection is now an integral part of the asylum regime? EU initiatives appear to confirm this. Willing or pressured consensus is unfolding on this question. Most fora concerned have somehow accepted TP for differing reasons. From the point of view of agencies defining refugees' interests it seems clear that the golden age of Convention refugee status and its concomitant advantages for refugees are over; therefore some form of protection is deemed preferable to none at all. For governments TP is written into a new regime concerning migration into Europe. The plan is to recruit temporary contract workers, with no intention of integrating them whatsoever and to send them back home as soon as the contract is over; if necessary, rotas can be established to bring in new groups. It is not the case that governments want zero immigration as a French minister (Charles Pasqua) declared years ago; in 1996 Michel Debré corrected this phrase stating that he did not believe in zero immigration and adding that what was needed was 'zero irregular immigration' ('immigration irrégulière zéro') (*Le Figaro*, 7 November 1996) paired with managed immigration. In 2000 a French politician (Francois Juppé) stated that immigration was necessary on account of the ageing autochthonous population. This approach is also adopted by the European Commission (1994), specifying that controlling migration flows does not necessarily imply bringing them to an end, but that it means migration management. Governments are aware that they need a certain mode of immigration to meet the needs of the economy and thus incorporate this into their plan. A slippage keeps occurring in official documents between labour migration and asylum which did not happen under the old asylum regime (Commission, 1994). We are increasingly witnessing the setting up of integrated asylum and labour migration policies which run the risk of conflating the two domains, as testified by internal government documents; one such example is a Swiss text which explains the objectives of a migration policy as *inter alia*:

> Disposer d'une offre suffisante de main-d'oeuvre qualifiée et non-qualifiée sur le marché du travail ... Protéger les personnees persecutées pour des raisons politiques – Octroyer une aide sur place aux étrangers ayant besoin de protection, ainsi que dans la région touchée – Recourir à l'admission provisoire des étrangers ayant besoin de protection comme dernière solution humanitaire.
>
> (Arbenz, 1995, p. 95)

> [To have access to a skilled and non-skilled labour force on the labour market ... To protect persons persecuted on political grounds – To award help to foreigners in need of protection in situ and in the affected region – To resort to the temporary admission of foreigners in need of protection as a last humanitarian solution.]

This slippage is pervasive and can be found even in UNHCR texts (Casella, 1995). But governments also believe that the post-war experience of immigration has made them wiser and are intent on blocking any laissez faire allowing for gradual regroupment and settling down of the immigrants. There is a major difference of substance with the previous immigration policy of the 60s, which brought in foreign labour, in that the current approach applies also to asylum in the 90s. This is why temporary protection was a breakthrough for European governments. States want to regain absolute control over decisions on who can come in and temporary protection allows them just that. 'For many participating states (France, Germany, Italy and the UK) temporary protection is a question of State sovereignty' (Secretariat, 1995, p. 19). This is a strange paradox at a time when states are lowering internal borders to the EU but such measures apply to 'third country nationals'.

As a necessity, to further this aim, new asylum instruments cannot be binding conventions any longer but mere loose declarations and guidelines. Again the states of Western Europe draw away from any kind of universal definition and prefer group-specific criteria which are those adopted for former Yugoslavs as they allow a tighter control of beneficiaries. This also ties in with a non-integration programme, even if some of the measures can be considered as non-humanitarian, in order to deter long-term perspectives of settlement and encourage return (i.e. no family reunion), as was stated unambiguously by the Inter-governmental Consultations (Secretariat, 1995). Finally, the comprehensive action approach adopted satisfies NGOs and governments as it can alleviate the crisis and be beneficial for the refugees but also serves the interests of governments who do not want to have to take in more displaced populations. Moreover, it is a sine qua non for a regime whose foundation and only or preferred long-term solution is return. Return is now hailed by all and sundry as the optimum durable solution for refugees. This conclusion is arrived at through different routes. Governments and the EU adopt it because they do not want to keep refugees over any lengthy periods of time; for that matter, they do not want to integrate any new migrant either and it makes part of the new immigration cum asylum regime in Europe. Sociologists and NGOs argue in favour of return because it appears to be the least traumatic long-term option rather than permanent uprooting and dislocation; it is also frequently the wish of the refugees themselves if they can return in satisfactory conditions. However, this presumably was true of previous movements of refugees. Why is it becoming now a premise of refugee policies? UNHCR may adopt it both because it is in the interest of refugees and because it may help to convince reluctant governments to accept refugees on their territory on the basis that they are not going to stay. Hopefully this new approach will never lead to forcible returns with perhaps tragic consequences.

Several parameters of the new regime are like this allegory from Jean Cocteau's film *La Belle et la Bête*: a present from the Beast to Belle, a magnificent pearl necklace in her hands, turns into an ugly piece of string as soon as her nasty sister holds it. Key notions which were promoted by refugee NGOs have now been appropriated by governments such as 'harmonisation of asylum policies' or 'a comprehensive approach to refugees'. And it is a strange paradox that this is the point at which they cease to be beneficial to refugees.

However, having tabled the key components of the new regime the last word has not yet been said about it. It is not sealed and delivered but it is in the making. Despite the fact that the governments of the EU and the EU as an institution call the tune on central features of the new regime and indeed they reach a consensus with non-EU governments such as the USA, while they also influence Central and Eastern European countries, social reality challenges their action and other fora also attempt to do so. The detail and balance of the new regime are being contended sharply. For instance, the length of the conflict in former Yugoslavia and to this day unresolved aspects of it have forced governments to consider other options than the absolute and strict return policy. In addition, NGOs are disputing every detail of the new regime: the standard of treatment of TP persons, the harmonisation of TP, the criteria and circumstances justifying its use, its relationship to other statuses, the return programmes, the comprehensive action involved. It seems that the Commission's proposal for a Council Directive has taken on board several of the points made by NGOs. Even public opinion intervenes to influence the modalities of TP, as in Denmark where local populations and local power went much beyond the national official policy. The variations in the implementation of TP, throughout Europe, give scope for a debate on the 'best' model and are being used to the full by agencies for refugees.

References

Arbenz, Peter (1995) 'Rapport sur une politique suisse en matière de migrations', May.

Arnold, Mrs (1996) Preliminary draft report on temporary protection of persons forced to flee their country. Committee on Migration, Refugees and Demography, Parliamentary Assembly Council of Europe, Strasbourg: 18 September.

Brochman, Grete (1995) *Bosnian Refugees in the Nordic Countries: Three Routes to Protection,* Oslo: Institute of Social Research, March.

Casella, Alexander (1995) *The Theory and Practice of Mass Information: a Method to Regularise Unwarranted Population Movements, to Promote Voluntary Repatriation and to Support Peace-keeping Operation,* Geneva: UNHCR, February.

CERE (Conseil Européen sur les Exilés et les Réfugiés) (1996) *Position prise par le Conseil Européen pour les Réfugiés et les Exiles sur la question des réfugiés de l' ex-Yugoslavie*, Avril.

Commission (1994) *Communication from the Commission to the Council and the European Parliament on Immigration and Asylum policies*, Brussels, 23/02.

Commission (1996) *Temporary Protection: a Subject for 'Common Action'?*

Commission of the European Communities (2000) *Proposal for a Council Directive on Minimum Standards for Giving Temporary Protection in the Event of a Mass Influx of Displaced Persons and on Measures Promoting a Balance of Efforts between Member States in Receiving Such Persons and Bearing the Consequences thereof*, Brussels, 24.5.2000, COM(2000).

Council of Ministers (1992) *Conclusion on People Displaced by the Conflict in the Former Yugoslavia*, 10518/92, London, 30.11/1.12.

Council of Ministers (1993) *Resolution on Certain Common Guidelines as regards the Admission of Particularly Vulnerable Persons from the Former Yugoslavia*, Copenhagen, 1 June.

Council of Ministers (1994a) Note from the Presidency to Migration Working Party (Admission) of Steering Group (Asylum and Immigration) Draft Council Resolution on burden-sharing with regard to the admission and residence of refugees, Brussels, 1 July.

Council of Ministers (1994b) Report from the Presidency to Permanent Representatives Committee/Council (JAI). Burden-sharing with regard to the admission and residence on a temporary basis of displaced persons, Brussels, 17 November.

Council of Ministers (1995) Council Resolution of 25 September 1995 on burden-sharing with regard to the admission and residence of displaced persons on a temporary basis, *Official Journal*, 262, 07/10/95.

CSCE Office for Democratic Institutions and Human Rights (1993) CSCE Human Dimension Seminar on Migration, including Refugees and Displaced Persons, Consolidated Summary, Warsaw, 20–3 April.

ECRE (1994) *A European Refugee Policy in the Light of Established Principles*, London: ECRE, April.

ECRE (1996a) Comments from ECRE on the 1995 'Burden-sharing' resolution and decision adopted by the Council of the European Union, London: ECRE.

ECRE (1996b) *Position on Refugees from the Former Yugoslavia by ECRE*, update December.

European Parliament (1992) *Resolution on European Immigration Policy*, Resolution A3-0280/92, 18 November.

European Parliament (1995) 'Resolution on the Communication from the Commission to the Council and the European Parliament on Immigration and Asylum policy', *Official Journal*, C103, 24.7.1977, p. 1.

European Parliament (1996) *Temporary Protection: the Protection of the Refugees from the Former Yugoslavia by the Member States*, draft.

Federal Ministry of the Interior (1990) Report by the Inter-ministerial Working Group on a 'Refugee Concept', Bonn, 25 September.

Frelick, Bill and Barbara Kohnen (1995) 'Filling the Gap: Temporary Protected Status', *International Journal of Refugee Law*, 8, 4, pp. 339–64.

Goodwin-Gill, Guy (1996) 'Refugee Identity and the Fading Prospect of International Protection', Conference on Refugee Rights and Realities, Nottingham, 30 November.

Hathaway, James (1984) 'The Evolution of Refugee Status in International Law: 1920–1950', *ICLQ*, 33, pp. 348–80.

Hathaway, James et al. (1996) 'Towards the Reformulation of International Refugee Law: a Model for Collectivised and Solution-oriented Protection', Consultative Workshops in London and Washington, 4 and 11 October.

Joly, Danièle (1994) 'The Porous Dam: European Harmonisation on Asylum in the Nineties', in *International Journal of Refugee Law*, 6, pp. 159–93.

Joly, Danièle (1996) *Haven or Hell? Asylum Policies and Refugees in Europe*, Basingstoke: Macmillan – now Palgrave Macmillan.

Joly, Danièle, Lynette Kelly and Clive Nettleton (1997) *Refugees in Europe: the Hostile New Agenda*, London: MRG.

Kälin, Walter (1996) *Towards a Concept of Temporary Protection*, study commissioned by UNHCR, Bern, 12 November.

Kjaerum, Morten (1993) 'Temporary Protection in Europe in the '90s', in CSCE Expert Seminar on Migration including Refugees and Displaced Persons, Warsaw, 20–4 April.

Muus, Philip et al. (1993) *Reception Policies for Persons in Need of International Protection in Western European States*, Geneva: UNHCR, September.

Refugee Policy Commission Ministry of Labour (1995), 'Swedish Refugee Policy in a Global Perspective', summary of a report to the Swedish Government by the Parliamentary Refugee Policy Commission, June.

Rudge, Philip (1995) Interview, 21 November.

Rudge, Philip (1996a) Rights of persons under temporary protection Parliamentary hearing on temporary protection for people forced to flee their country. The Committee on Migration Refugees and Demography Parliamentary Assembly, Council of Europe, Paris, 12 April.

Rudge, Philip (1996b) *Foreign Policy for Refugees and Migration: Efforts within Europe concerning Migration*, Bern: *ECRE*, 6 November.

Secretariat of the Inter-governmental Consultations on Asylum, Refugee and Migration Policies in Europe, North America and Australia (1994), *Working Paper on Reception in the Region of Origin*, September.

Secretariat of the Inter-governmental Consultations on Asylum, Refugee and Migration Policies in Europe, North America and Australia (1995), *Report on Temporary Protection in States in Europe, North America and Australia*, Geneva: August.

Swedish Ministry of Labour (1990) A *Comprehensive Refugee and Immigration Policy: Directives for a Government Committee*, working paper for the informal consultation on long-term perspectives and policies, Nyon, 13–14/9.

UNHCR (1979) (Executive Committee – 30th Session) Ex Com. Conclusion 15 No. 15 (XXX) Refugees without an asylum country.

UNHCR (1980) (Executive Committee – 31st Session) Ex Com Conclusion 19, No. 19 (XXX1) Temporary Refuge.

UNHCR (1981) (Executive Committee – 32nd Session) ExCom Conclusion, No. 22 (XXXII) Protection of Asylum Seekers in Situations of Large-scale Influx.

UNHCR (1983) (Executive Committee – 34th Session) ExCom Conclusion 30, No. 30 (XXXIV) The Problem of Manifestly Unfounded or Abusive Applications for Refugee Status or Asylum.

UNHCR (1992) A comprehensive response to the humanitarian crisis in the former Yugoslavia. International meeting on humanitarian aid for victims.

UNHCR (1993) Informal Meeting on Temporary Protection, Background Note, Geneva, 21 January.

UNHCR (1994a) Background Note: Informal Meeting of Government Experts on Temporary Protection, Geneva, 23 March.

UNHCR (1994b) Background Note: Informal Round Table on Temporary Protection in the Broader Context, Diyonne, 30 June.

UNHCR (1994c) Note on International Protection (submitted by the High Commissioner), Geneva, 7 September.

UNHCR (1995a) Information Note: Informal Meeting of Government Experts on the Implementation of Temporary Protection, Geneva, 20 April.

UNHCR (1995b) The Scope of International Protection in Mass Influx, I. Introduction, Sub-Committee of the whole on International Protection 26th meeting, EC/1995/SCP/CRP.3, 2 June 1995.

UNHCR (1996) Working paper for the development of a policy package in Europe, Geneva, June.

Wiebenga, Jan (1995) Report on the Communication from the Commission to the Council and the European Parliament on Immigration and Asylum Policies. Committee on Civil Liberties and Internal Affairs, European Parliament, 29 June.

Note

1. This chapter is an updated version of 'Temporary Protection within the Framework of a New Asylum Regime', *International Journal of Human Rights*, 2, 3, Autumn 1998, pp. 49–76 .

4

Lessons from the Kosovo Refugee Crisis: Innovations in Protection and Burden-Sharing

Michael Barutciski and Astri Suhrke

Introduction

The Kosovo refugee crisis that developed in the wake of NATO's air strikes against the Federal Republic of Yugoslavia in late March 1999 presented an extraordinary challenge of asylum. While the refugees were readily admitted to Albania, the initial blockage at the Blace border crossing to the former Yugoslav Republic of Macedonia nearly became a disaster when tens of thousands of people were trapped in the open for several days, initially denied both protection and assistance. The dramatic events at Blace concealed a more fundamental challenge. In extreme form, Blace represented the apparent conflict between the rights of refugees and the interests of states that in the last decades of the twentieth century had undermined traditional asylum in Europe, North America and much of the developing world as well.

This chapter will examine the nature of the challenge and the adequacy of the solutions that were developed.[1] The challenge was to persuade a host country, Macedonia, to admit a massive influx of refugees that the government initially rejected. The eventual solution was based on a 'burden-sharing' scheme involving transfer of refugees to other countries, both in the region and outside. While the two innovative programmes (called 'humanitarian transfer' and 'humanitarian evacuation') solved the immediate protection problem, both the programmes and the way they were handled were controversial.

Legal-maximalists versus pragmatists

At the time, critics – including human rights activists and many UNHCR staff – argued that the Macedonian government must unconditionally admit the refugees. Setting sharing as a precondition was feared to compromise the principle of unconditional asylum and further accelerate the restrictive policies of states towards refugees. That Macedonia's initial denial of asylum could set a precedent was a matter of particular concern because the political conditions that eventually made sharing schemes possible in the Kosovo case were unlikely to be frequently repeated. Others argued that the Macedonian position was a political fact that had to be recognised, and that a flexible response in this case was necessary to avert a humanitarian disaster at the border. Transfers and other forms of sharing promised to increase the number of refugees who would be given protection; that it appeared as a precondition for asylum was immaterial.

The first view may be called legal-maximalist in recognition of its position in international refugee law (see below). In moral philosophy, it reflects a Kantian perspective of universal rights and obligations. The second view is steeped in a utilitarian and pragmatic tradition. It was articulated by states most concerned to find a solution to the impasse at the border. Not only might the Blace spectacle, and repeated instances of *non-entrée* to Macedonia, jeopardise the lives of the refugees, but also the massive population pressure at the border so frightened the Macedonian government that it threatened to withdraw its support for NATO's military campaign in Kosovo. This in turn alarmed leading NATO countries, above all the United States, whose officials advocated immediate measures to reduce the asylum burden on Macedonia.

The pragmatic and the legal-maximalist approach clashed – at times spectacularly – as states and international organisations tried to deal with the Kosovo refugee crisis. In addition, there were ambivalence and at times contradictions in the position of UNHCR, reflecting on the one hand concern for principled adherence to traditional forms of refugee protection and on the other pressures to find immediate solutions. The various tensions in the international response to the refugee crisis probably served neither the refugees nor the development of a coherent and effective refugee regime.

We shall argue that there is a third approach that in some measure reconciles the opposing camps. The essence of the argument is that (1) there is a legal case for not considering first asylum as an unconditional obligation on all states in all refugee situations; (2) there is a moral-political case for encouraging states to share refugees for whom they feel they have – or arguably do have – a special responsibility; and (3) recognition of such exceptional cases will strengthen the international refugee regime. The exceptional case where burden-sharing is imperative, we shall argue, is when vulnerable states are faced with a mass influx of refugees that may export the conflict and lead to serious destabilisation.

The Kosovo case

The nature of the challenge

For the Macedonian government, the refugee inflow raised fundamental issues of national security. The country's short political history has been marked by divisions among its majority Slav population and minority Albanian population. A new coalition government that included the more nationalist representatives of both the Slav and Albanian populations was formed only a few months before the NATO bombing campaign. The ethnic Albanian refugees from Kosovo had grievances regarding their status in Yugoslavia that resembled those of ethnic Albanians in Macedonia whom they now joined. While the exact number of ethnic Albanian citizens in Macedonia remains controversial, the sudden refugee presence – almost 350,000 arrived within nine weeks – represented close to 20 per cent of the total population and had a serious effect on the country's delicate ethnic balance.[2] Proportionally, it is as if the UK were confronted with the sudden arrival of ten million refugees on its shores. The situation increased the risk that Macedonia would be dragged into the conflict. It was also not clear if or when the refugees would return to Kosovo. Although it was argued that NATO could not afford to lose this war – and would persist until the refugees could return – it was recognised that a new Palestinian-type situation could be in the making.[3]

Joint UN humanitarian contingency plans prepared during the summer of 1998 recognised Macedonia's reluctance to admit refugees.[4] The government's publicly announced ceiling of 20,000 refugees was accepted as a plausible planning target, although it was assumed that, if matters deteriorated, more would be admitted, probably after a delay at the border.[5] Yet for years local media and politicians had been saying that the border would be closed in the event of a mass refugee flow from Kosovo. The only feasible option publicly discussed was to transport refugees in a 'humanitarian corridor' from the border to neighbouring Albania. Nonetheless this option was not incorporated in UNHCR planning because its standard policy was to call for asylum in the country of first arrival. UNHCR's Executive Committee (EXCOM) had concluded already in 1981 that the principle applied to mass arrivals as well as individual asylum seekers: in EXCOM conclusion no. 22 (1981), member states affirm that

> [i]n situations of large-scale influx, asylum seekers should be admitted to the State in which they first seek refuge and if that State is unable to admit them on a durable basis, it should always admit them at least on a temporary basis ... In all cases the fundamental principle of non-refoulement – including non-rejection at the frontier – must be scrupulously observed.[6]

At the annual meeting of EXCOM that preceded the Kosovo emergency outflow, member states further concluded that asylum must be unconditional. Conclusion no. 85 (1998) establishes that

> access to asylum and the meeting by States of their protection obligations should not be dependent on burden sharing arrangements first being in place, particularly because respect for fundamental human rights and humanitarian principles is an obligation for all members of the international community.[7]

Considerations specific to the Kosovo case reinforced the disinclination to plan for transfers from Macedonia to other countries, particularly neighbouring Albania. While the Albanian government in principle welcomed transfers, UNHCR's previous experience with the relatively small Kosovo caseload during the summer of 1998 suggested that providing assistance and protection in Albania was not easy.[8] The UN contingency planners, moreover, operated on the principle of voluntary transfers and had assumed that, given the difficult conditions in Albania, few if any refugees would want to be relocated there. More fundamentally, UNHCR and other UN humanitarians did not make plans to cope with a mass refugee flow in early 1999 because they believed that NATO air strikes would not lead to a mass outflow of refugees but, rather, would rapidly pave the way for a political settlement of the conflict.

Crisis strikes

In retrospect, the 'Day One' phase of the emergency appears short and decisive. It started on the weekend of 27–8 March, when tens of thousands of refugees entered northern Albania. By the middle of the week a parallel crisis was unfolding at the Blace border crossing between Kosovo and Macedonia. By the following weekend, 3–4 April,

'Day One' was drawing to a close in the sense that initial guidelines for the humanitarian response had been formulated, principal decision-making structures were in place and a division of labour was emerging.

Until a few days earlier, the Macedonian government had generally admitted Kosovo Albanians. By 30–1 March, however, a qualitatively different scene developed at the border. Macedonian border guards slowed the entry by meticulously checking arrivals, causing long lines of vehicles with refugees to form, at times stretching back 10 km. Then the trains packed with refugees started to appear. By 1 April, six trains carrying some 25,000 refugees had arrived. More followed.

Like most governments faced with a sudden, massive influx of refugees, the Macedonian authorities nearly panicked. The government insisted that the refugees be allowed in only on a transit basis, and that their status and eventual physical location must be clarified prior to entry. The Macedonian government wanted international assistance and assurances that at least some refugees would be transferred elsewhere. In the meantime, new arrivals were contained in the Bleak field on the Macedonian side of the border, without shelter and only minimal assistance.

The spectacle attracted intense international attention for days, creating strong incentives for states and organisations concerned to find a solution. In a matter of days, Blace was indeed unblocked. The critical package was finalised over the weekend of 3–4 April. NATO forces stationed in Macedonia in connection with the unfolding Kosovo conflict built camps for the refugees, thus ensuring a framework for controlled entry as the government demanded. The United States took the lead in promising economic assistance and a programme to share refugees, initially suggesting that it would take 20,000. The government of Norway, which also held the chairmanship of the OSCE, called the Macedonian government directly on 3 April and offered to take 6,000 refugees. At the same time, the US embassy in Skopje facilitated Macedonian plans to transfer some of those trapped at Blace to Albania, and extracted a promise from its ally, Turkey, to take 20,000. The World Bank weighed in with a massive aid programme of 40 million dollars to assist Skopje.[9]

By 6 April, the Bleak field was empty. Several thousand refugees had been moved to camps built literally overnight by NATO forces, and plans for further relocation were underway. Another several thousand were evacuated by the government, with US assistance, in a controversial transfer operation to Turkey, Greece and Albania.

Nobody questioned that the people arriving at the border were refugees needing protection: the issue was identifying who was responsible for providing protection. The position of UNHCR during the first days of the crisis was that Macedonia was obliged under international law to admit the refugees, since not doing so would be to drive them back into the hands of hostile Serb forces and constitute *refoulement*. While UNHCR was willing to discuss sharing schemes, this was not initially seen as part of a package, and not presented to Skopje as such. Rather, the position was that the refugees had to be admitted, and sharing discussed in a second phase. In other words, first asylum had to be unconditional.[10] UNHCR only agreed to de facto conditionality when the US and other actors were preparing a package that linked admission to sharing schemes with third countries. Even then, the evacuation programme remained a source of dissension within UNHCR, with some staff seeing it as undermining UNHCR's efforts to promote unconditional asylum.[11]

Apart from principled concerns relating to precedence and eventual repatriation (see below), UNHCR's position reflected a sense of political realism. Until the NATO air campaign and subsequent exodus occurred, the European states clearly preferred that Kosovo refugees remain in the immediate Balkan neighbourhood.[12] Apart from the lone offer from Norway, this was the dominant European position during the first days of the crisis as well.[13] Since any sharing would have to involve the EU, it might seem quixotic for the High Commissioner to start down that road until the states themselves were prepared to participate. The initial reluctance of states to help reduce the refugee burden on Macedonia is also indicated by the nature of the first US offer to share, which was to transfer Kosovo refugees to Guantanamo, the US-leased military base in Cuba. Strongly criticised by human rights activists, the proposal was soon abandoned in favour of admission to the US mainland.

Yet it is striking that even when a sharing programme was under way, UNHCR appeared a hesitant participant. This was evident both in relation to the evacuation programme out of the region's Humanitarian Evacuation Programme (known as HEP), and above all in relation to transfers to the Albania Humanitarian Transfer Programme (known as HTP). In both cases, as we shall see, the US appeared as the main protagonist, calling for rapid resumption of the evacuation programme when it seemed to stall in the second half of April,[14] and strongly criticising UNHCR for condemning Macedonia's *non-entrée* policy, both during the first Blace crisis and in later incidents. Under pressure from the US government, UNHCR eventually committed itself to proceed with evacuations out of the region and produced guidelines for the innovative humanitarian evacuation programme that involved airlifts.

Circumstances relating to management and operational plans reinforced the legal-maximalist element in UNHCR thinking. For the first days of the emergency, UNHCR's role at the Macedonian border was basically handled by the staff from the Pristina office that had been evacuated several days earlier. The staff were pulled out of a long IDP operation within Kosovo and were largely unfamiliar with the particular complexities involving Macedonia's concerns. Their main preoccupation was to secure asylum for their now severely traumatised caseload from Kosovo.

As we have seen, in 1998 UNHCR contingency planners had not incorporated the idea of a 'humanitarian corridor' from Macedonia to Albania, largely in deference to the principle of first asylum. Similar concerns were evident during the 'Day One' phase of the crisis. At that time, moreover, it seemed too late for a corridor. Albania was struggling to cope with the first wave of the exodus from Kosovo, and there was little excess capacity to receive refugees under safe and orderly conditions.[15] As a result, the corridor idea was only briefly discussed among UNHCR's leadership during the first Blace crisis, and was rapidly discarded.

UNHCR's position on first asylum had another dimension. The agency has repeatedly stressed in recent years that keeping refugees in their region of origin allows for an easier implementation of the preferred durable solution of voluntary repatriation. When confronted with the large outflow from Kosovo, both the High Commissioner and European governments restated this view in the early phases of the emergency.[16] UNHCR's first protection guidelines issued during the crisis similarly reaffirmed: 'The basic position remains that, in so far as it is possible to do so, the situation should be dealt with on a regional basis, keeping refugees as close to their country of origin as may be done in safety'.[17]

The United States rather than UNHCR took the initiative in assembling a package of aid to Macedonia that in fact, if not in name, constituted conditionality of asylum. The US embassy in Skopje played an early and central role in this process, reflecting its status as a key post in US policy towards the Balkans.[18] It was also involved in the hasty evacuations in which refugees were moved directly from the border to Turkey and Albania.

Reasons of policy and relative power explain the US role. Unlike UNHCR, Washington had multiple interests in the conflict, which shaped its response to the refugee crisis. Foremost among these was to secure Macedonia's cooperation to host troops from NATO countries during the escalating conflict with Belgrade. For the Macedonian government, to align with NATO during the war with its neighbour entailed obvious risks. When the refugee crisis increased the potential costs of collaboration, key figures in the government threatened to criticise publicly the air strikes and ask NATO forces to leave the country. These developments, which took place during the first days of the emergency, made the US Embassy double its efforts to solve the asylum crisis at the Blace crossing.

Strategic factors relating to the war lent urgency to the refugee challenge in other ways as well. Having launched the air strikes as a solution to the vexing Kosovo conflict, NATO was accused of having triggered a humanitarian crisis instead. To answer its critics, it was important for NATO – above all the US and the UK, which took the lead in the air campaign – to minimise the refugee spectacle at the border and prevent the human disaster that loomed. Single-dimensional humanitarian concerns were also significant. This was not only the largest refugee crisis in Europe since World War II, it unfolded in ways that recalled the most ignominious aspects of European history. The Blace crisis touched basic humanitarian sentiments that also received strong institutional backing, in the US and elsewhere.[19]

The combination of strategic and humanitarian concerns ensured that the Kosovo refugee crisis received extraordinary attention from the powerful Western states. This rapidly resulted in a solution based on burden-sharing involving both evacuation of refugees out of the region and to neighbouring countries. Within days, thousands of refugees had been evacuated to Turkey, Germany and Norway.[20] Eventually over 90,000 persons were moved out of the region during the 11-week emergency.

Formulas for sharing: HTP and HEP

The humanitarian evacuation programme (HEP)

By the end of the emergency, almost 92,000 refugees had benefited from HEP in 29 host countries. The scale and speed of such an evacuation were unprecedented. Overall, HEP contributed positively to the protection of the refugees by alleviating the burden on a reluctant host state that feared destabilisation. Yet there were problems of implementation.

The justification and purpose of HEP were marred by some lack of clarity. To one human rights group that believed the refugees should be resettled, HEP seemed a hasty resettlement exercise.[21] While UNHCR's official statements clearly and consistently distinguished HEP from its other programmes, the lines became blurred between the concepts of resettlement, humanitarian evacuation and temporary protection. This was evident in UNHCR field reports even late in the emergency:

> Although in writing HEP and resettlement have always been considered two separate issues pursuing different objectives, in practice until now genuine resettlement cases have been dealt with under the HEP scheme as this was the most speedy way to take the refugees out of the country.[22]

This blurring of concepts was owing largely to inconsistencies in government positions on HEP. While most participating European governments saw HEP as an emergency form of temporary protection, traditional immigration states outside Europe in practice treated HEP as a resettlement operation.[23] The latter consequently replaced their resettlement programme quotas with HEP. This left UNHCR field staff with little choice but to include some resettlement cases in the HEP arrangement.

A broader implication concerned different reception conditions in host third countries. Contrary to the ad hoc temporary protection[24] arrangements concerning Bosnia-Herzegovina,[25] UNHCR quickly stipulated relatively precise refugee rights and obligations in the host country of destination for HEP.[26] The fact that the duration of the emergency was short and that repatriation occurred less than three months after the mass outflow ensured that the obligations of the 1951 Refugee Convention concerning prolonged stays were not necessarily applicable to this particular caseload. Although refugee evacuations in and out of the region sometimes resulted in an unclear administrative status accorded in host countries, these ad hoc administrative measures generally did not result in violations of international refugee law.[27]

Yet the immigration status of the beneficiaries of HEP who have not been repatriated continues to be a bureaucratic headache for the authorities of some receiving countries. This is particularly problematic when it is combined with the differing statuses accorded to previous refugee arrivals from Kosovo and caseloads from other conflicts or continents. The differentiated treatment of refugees has even led to tensions between the Kosovo caseload and other refugees from 'less popular' conflicts.[28] This is difficult to defend in terms of the non-discrimination clause found in the Refugee Convention and such problems will be likely to complicate the development of refugee policy in the near future.[29]

Other unclear aspects of HEP related to voluntariness and criteria for selection. While the 1951 Refugee Convention does not necessarily require refugee movements or relocations to be voluntary as long as the principle of *non-refoulement* is respected,[30] general human rights standards suggest forced movement of refugees to third countries can be problematic. In operational terms as well, involuntary evacuations by aircraft represent a political nightmare. Voluntariness presumes a measure of knowledge on the part of the refugees. Informed decisions by refugees contemplating evacuation are dependent on the availability of information concerning socio-economic rights and political conditions in the country of destination. Although such criteria may impose slight delays on the emergency nature of the programme, it is a necessary trade-off in order to get refugees to volunteer for an option that may leave them with a form of refuge on a distant continent.

In the Kosovo case, UNHCR operated on the principle of consent, if not full and free choice of country.[31] However, the lack of systematic information about the various HEP destinations, and the existence of a wide variety of destination countries with varying reception conditions, was problematic. The ability of refugees to decide on evacuation, moreover, was further reduced by selection and screening procedures that appear to have depended largely on queues that ensured a 'first-come first-serve' practice. Closely related was confusion about the criteria for selection. Was the principal objective of HEP to quickly off-load refugees from Macedonian territory? If so, criteria of vulnerability relating to protection should not be primary. Yet, this entailed a dilemma for humanitarian actors: an emergency operation focusing solely on the quickness of the off-loading process could theoretically be conducted most effectively by selecting refugees indiscriminately and leaving vulnerable refugees behind. Similarly, if HEP was to serve temporary protection needs, immigration criteria related to permanent resettlement would be irrelevant. Yet, a mixture of all criteria was evident in the operation of the programme and expectations. Time pressures led to deficient communications and exacerbated the confusion. Some actors were simply unsure whether refugee selection for HEP was dependent on vulnerability and family ties.[32] Some critics complained that HEP discriminated against refugees in host families by targeting camp refugees; the answer was to emphasise its role as an efficient off-loading process vis-à-vis the host asylum state rather than as a mechanism to address the needs of the refugee population at large. The desperate humanitarian situation, and the fact that HEP was largely perceived by refugees and the local population as 'a rapid way of obtaining tickets to the West',[33] led to abuse. According to one NGO, 'UNHCR concedes that refugees have bought and sold places on departing planes, and falsified their identities'.[34] A number of illegal camp entries involving non-camp refugees and locals created security problems. The local police may have played a role in aggravating this problem, which led to greater frustration among camp inhabitants. UNHCR recognised the misuse of HEP by desperate refugees and consequent loss of some donor government confidence:

> As an increasing number of countries has activated or increased their quotas, refugees in some instances appear to be favouring some destinations over others. Information is presently being disseminated to the refugee population in the camps through pamphlets and other means to remind them that this is a temporary evacuation programme. While departures are voluntary and links to destination countries are taken into account if possible, in principle they do not have a choice as to the country of destination.[35]

Regardless of official statements discouraging shopping around for a country of destination, the reality on the ground was characterised by significant abuses of this nature as identified by UNHCR:

> Originally conceived as a rapid evacuation programme, it has turned into a cumbersome process with distinct criteria per country of destination. At the same time, with increased quotas having been activated by a number of countries, refugees are choosing their country of evacuation. This has reportedly resulted in high no-show rates, both for interviews and, worse, at the time of embarkation.[36]

Misuse of programmes to move refugees out of a conflict region is familiar from earlier cases, notably the large resettlement programmes for Indo-Chinese refugees. There is another, more subtle drawback which also applies to HEP. In terms of universal refugee protection standards, extra-regional evacuations may harm refugees generally in the sense that they encourage governments to develop effective selection systems and quotas which could ultimately undermine and replace the availability of protection for individual or spontaneous asylum seekers. Indeed, HEP probably allowed some governments to score public relations points by appearing 'humanitarian' in receiving a limited number of 'popular' refugees. The fact that governments are free to grant permanent residence to beneficiaries of HEP complicates this approach from a multilateral point of view. While this may suit particular donor states in the short term, in that it quickly integrates evacuees within their immigration policies, it introduces wide discrepancies in the standards and results in a programme that is essentially difficult to coordinate because of the differing reception conditions.

Humanitarian transfer programme (HTP)

As mentioned above, to deal with the initial crisis at the border the Macedonian government had made arrangements with Albania and Turkey (facilitated by the US) in order to transfer refugees from the border directly to these two countries. There was widespread criticism of these government-organised transfers from international media sources. The criticisms related to the abusive conditions under which the transfers were carried out: there were allegations that families were involuntarily separated and sent to unknown destinations. The embassies that were sympathetic to Macedonia's concerns chose more discreet forms of intervention that focused on ensuring the humane treatment of refugees who were to be transferred in the following days. Nevertheless, the negative international media coverage of these transfers eventually made HTP a politically awkward option that had considerable public relations consequences for the image of Macedonia.

Given the abuses associated with the initial transfers, UNHCR's reluctance to participate in this form of burden-sharing is understandable. On some occasions, UNHCR personnel on the ground even attempted physically to block the departure of buses that were engaged in these transfers.

While the denial of asylum by Macedonia that motivated the transfer option concerned UNHCR as a matter of principle and practice, first asylum, as we have seen, was already made conditional by the internationally supported HEP. It is clear that refugee transfers to Albania were favoured by asylum-weary European states that preferred to have the refugees contained in the immediate region. They consequently encouraged this option.

When conditions for receiving refugees in Albania later improved, objections to HTP were made even more difficult to explain. In fact, by early May, when NATO made it clear that there were empty camps in

Albania waiting for refugees to be transferred, delays and blockages at the Blace border post were to a certain extent unnecessary and could have been avoided. On 5 May, NATO announced:

> With the in-flow of refugees over the FRY-FYROM border exceeding the outflow to other countries it is the intention to transfer large numbers of refugees from FYROM to SE Albania ... The initial movement of refugees from FYROM, to take advantage of the present spare capacity in existing camps, should begin as soon as possible.[37]

Yet it is striking that significant transfers never occurred and that UNHCR was not able to encourage this option. As pointed out by UNHCR at the end of May: 'Transfers from Macedonia to Albania are not proceeding at a rate necessary for this scheme to make any noticeable impact on the situation at the Blace border crossing, or in the overcrowded camps.'[38]

Part of the problem that may explain the reluctance of UNHCR personnel to engage actively in HTP relates to the degree of voluntariness or consent required for these movements. Although bus transfers are operationally quite distinct from airlift evacuations, they raise similar problems of voluntariness addressed above in the HEP analysis. UNHCR's policy on this critical issue was not clear, as evident in the following statement: 'The extent to which voluntariness of departure should be integral to the transfers is a vexed one from a doctrine point of view and a factor complicating the operation of the programme.'[39] Initially, all evacuations (including transfers) were supposed to be voluntary: 'The decision to depart to a third country is entirely voluntary.'[40] Several weeks later, this standard was changed to a form of implicit consent in the case of HTP: 'Preferably all persons evacuated to Albania should agree to go. At the very least, they should not object and, should they do so, this should be respected.'[41]

The actual implementation of this standard was never tested thoroughly, as few refugees consented to the UNHCR-sponsored transfers.[42] As pointed out by the High Commissioner, 'transfers to Albania are a convenient option, but must be carried out only if refugees do not object – and most do'.[43] Given the Department of International Protection's eventual broad encouragement of HTP[44] and positive assessment of its feasibility,[45] it seems puzzling that this option was not pursued more actively in the later phases of the emergency.

One reason explaining the unenthusiastic implementation of HTP is that personnel in the field believed that the application of this option directly at the border would jeopardise the first asylum principle on which they insisted. In this context, it is likely that any objections made by refugees arriving at the border were not in fact seriously assessed in terms of their reasonableness by staff unwilling actively to support HTP.[46] During one reported border incident, for example, UNHCR staff 'intervened and informed the refugees that the decision to go to Albania must be free and voluntary and emphasised that they had the right to asylum in Macedonia'.[47] The differing criteria applied by personnel in the field is reflected in an internal document which stipulates that the 'transfers should be voluntary because UNHCR cannot be associated with forcible relocation'.[48]

More important, HTP was fundamentally weakened by the parallel existence of HEP. Any reluctance on the part of the refugees to move to Albania was made even greater by the availability of evacuations to Western countries. Similarly, it was not by chance that quotas for some countries in the region remained unfilled while quotas for other countries were quickly filled.[49] In this sense, it is possible to see HEP as having undermined HTP in terms of protection policy options.[50]

The problem encountered by UNHCR in Macedonia was that by insisting on obtaining protection in the first country of asylum, there was an increase in the risk of having refugees stuck in a no-man's-land at the border (that is, obtaining no asylum). The fact remains that refugees were blocked repeatedly in a no-man's-land at Blace for days while several camps were left empty in Albania because the refugees were never transferred even though there seemed to be appropriate camp conditions. This situation involves a difficult ethical choice in which international actors can insist on voluntariness in refugee movements and risk not getting asylum, or accept lower standards in order to get more asylum.

Implications of the Kosovo model

The approaches of the legal-maximalists and pragmatists point to tensions among the various norms and principles that have shaped international refugee policy in recent years. Unconditional first asylum is a position that is consistent with the EXCOM conclusions cited above and is generally considered a basic norm of refugee protection. Yet this position can be challenged on legal grounds in terms of the actual obligations found in the 1951 Refugee Convention and 1967 Protocol.

In this context it is important to distinguish between political recommendations and legally binding norms. The EXCOM conclusions are not legally binding norms in the sense of immediately enforceable binding commitments. The legally binding protection principles are codified in treaties signed by states. Given the consensual nature of treaty law, we cannot expect states to assume an obligation to allow refugees admission into their territory if there is a serious threat that this would lead to national destabilisation. The most basic principle in international refugee law, *non-refoulement,* should be read in this perspective, otherwise the law risks becoming irrelevant to policy-makers confronted by refugee emergencies. This realisation helps explain the drafting imprecision regarding the moment at which *non-refoulement* applies (that is, before or after the border has been crossed?) and the inclusion of an exception to *non-refoulement* based on national security reasons in paragraph 2 of the 1951 Refugee Convention's article 33.[51] Although the scope of this exception can be debated, it is relatively clear that the *non-refoulement* principle in treaty law has been left deliberately imprecise in certain situations. This ambiguity has allowed political leaders increased flexibility when dealing with concrete problems related to mass inflows so that they do not find themselves hampered by unworkable international principles.[52] The inclusion in the Refugee Convention of a clause authorising provisional measures in cases involving national security[53] is another example of the pragmatic dimension of the principles codified in international law. The principles are more realistic (or in tune with legitimate state concerns) than is often suggested by human rights advocates.

Nevertheless, the paramount purpose of the Convention is to protect refugees. It is worth emphasising that the Convention does not oblige states to provide asylum for people who satisfy its refugee definition: it simply prohibits *refoulement* to dangerous territories. The most basic form of protection found in the Convention, *non-refoulement,* can be offered in the country of first asylum or in any third countries (including neighbouring states) that are capable of providing refuge. As states and international bodies are explicitly or implicitly making the connection between security and refugee flows in order to restrict admission of asylum seekers, it is necessary to ensure that any reference to the accepted exceptions in the Convention is done in order to promote burden-sharing and not to defend *refoulement.*

Once it is accepted that a host country is too vulnerable to accept a mass influx of refugees, the options available in terms of refugee protection seem to rely on international burden-sharing arrangements as provided for in the Refugee Convention's preamble. The forms of possible sharing concern the costs of the operational response and provision of territorial asylum in safe countries. As UNHCR is mandated to protect refugees regardless of whether a frontline state claims an exception to protection duties, this suggests a duty to engage in contingency planning for burden-sharing in probable cases of this kind. The argument presented by human rights advocates suggesting that respect for refugee law principles 'can in no way be contingent upon the implementation of a responsibility sharing programme'[54] does not reflect the current state of international law.

Yet burden-sharing by transferring refugees to safe third countries is not only a complicated transaction with some dubious aspects in terms of rights, equity and justice, it is also historically a rare occurrence. Recent efforts to formulate regional or global arrangements for burden-sharing in institutionalised and planned form have produced meagre or no results.[55] Burden-sharing appears as a lofty principle that receives general but non-binding support from states, and which is realised only on an ad hoc basis in exceptional cases. This record suggests that efforts to promote burden-sharing have to be selective rather than general, and have to focus on the exceptional cases where such sharing is imperative for humanitarian reasons and plausible in political terms. What are these cases?

The principal case before the Kosovo Conflict involved the Indo-Chinese refugees, who largely were transferred to third countries but – in contrast to Kosovo – were all under resettlement programmes rather than programmes generally related to temporary protection. What the two refugee situations have in common, however, is striking, especially if we compare the Malaysian and Macedonian responses. In both cases (1) the influx was sudden and very large, (2) the refugees were ethnically related to a significant minority in the receiving state, (3) the host government feared a large inflow would destabilise the internal ethnic balance, and (4) as a result temporarily or definitely denied asylum to some of the arrivals. In both cases, the refugees were fleeing from a conflict where the United States was directly involved, and Washington initiated burden-sharing arrangements to accommodate the rights of the refugees and the interests of the asylum states. In the Indo-Chinese case, first asylum became dependent upon resettlement in a quite direct manner. Conditionality related to burden-sharing, in other words, was all but formally recognised.

The two cases suggest some key characteristics of refugee situations where burden-sharing seems possible, namely: situations of mass inflows where the first asylum state credibly threatens to deny asylum with reference to recognised national vulnerabilities, and where outside states have special interests in the particular refugee population.

These are the kinds of refugee situation where humanitarian agencies, and particularly UNHCR, could usefully explore burden-sharing arrangements as part of their routine contingency planning for refugee crises. As the Kosovo case indicates, doing so would seem to require a change of attitude in UNHCR towards recognising the conditionality of asylum and the benefits, in some cases, of advance exploration to plan for burden-sharing. Planning of this kind would not necessarily have a self-fulfilling prophecy by encouraging states to shirk their general obligations of *non-refoulement*, as UNHCR has argued in defence of its disinclination to plan for burden-sharing in the Kosovo case.[56]

As noted above, there are legal arguments for viewing international protection rather than asylum in the first host country as the overriding objective. In terms of ethics and politics, a case can likewise be made for the imperative of burden-sharing in some cases. The exceptional case, as we have suggested, is when a mass influx can reasonably be said to threaten the stability or security of the first asylum state and, as a result, represents a likely exportation of violent conflict. Whether such situations should technically be considered a threat to international peace and security is of secondary importance given the growing recognition in the United Nations that internal conflict is also a matter of common concern. In these situations, the international humanitarian agencies can appeal to both the general and the special interests of states for assistance: the presumed general interest of all in managing violent conflict, and the special interests of some in the region in question. In ethical terms, the counterpart lies in general and special obligations.

There is a presumed general obligation for the responsibility to protect refugees. The 1951 Refugee Convention (as modified by the 1967 Protocol) represents in this sense a clear manifestation of universal Kantian ethics. But there are also special obligations (or duties). In moral philosophy, these are generally understood as special duties towards 'families, friends, clients, compatriots', in other words, a narrower circle of beneficiaries than the universe of 'all', with whom we have less direct ties.[57] The moral basis of these special duties is our responsibility, at least in some measure, for the situation of those in the more narrow circle. If we extend this notion to refugee situations,[58] it is evident that some states are more deeply involved in some refugee-producing conflicts than others and, historically, some of those states have recognised the humanitarian duty-part of their role by taking extraordinary measures to assist the refugees. These states would be the ones to call upon in the first instance during contingency planning for the humanitarian consequences of violent conflict or interventions.

Contingency planning for burden-sharing in exceptional cases need not, of course, involve evacuation out of the region of the HEP variety. Transfers within the region to neighbouring countries might be equally if not more likely. The point is that prior planning for such sharing schemes are likely to maximise protection and avoid near-disasters when unwanted refugees are trapped in inhospitable border areas or – as in the Malaysian case – towed out to sea.

Such innovation – or what we called 'a third approach' at the outset of this chapter – admittedly abridges the principles of universalism that in theory underpinned the international refugee regime as it developed after World War II. In practice, however, it is evident that these universal and profoundly liberal principles were observed by states only to the extent that they were seen to entail exceptional and limited obligations, and/or that the refugees were particularly welcome for political and economic reasons. Thus, for about four decades of the present refugee regime, the Cold War ensured that applicants from communist countries were relatively few (since exit was formally denied). Moreover, those who came were generally welcome as they reinforced the foreign policy interests of Western states to outshine their communist rivals. Until the early 1970s, moreover, economic expansion in Western states could readily absorb new labour. The progressive tightening of first asylum which occurred in Europe and, unevenly but recognisably, also in North America reflected the fact that asylum seekers came from 'third world' countries that did not have exit prohibitions and were more marginal to the Cold War rivalry. The main exception – the generous welcome in North America and Western Europe to Indo-Chinese refugees – generally proves the point.

The challenge of asylum in a post-Cold War world of greatly enhanced mobility and mass inflows of refugees is entirely different. Attempts by states and refugee advocates to explore new regimes, notably through sharing schemes, is a recognition that practice may be adjusted in order to realise the protection that the Refugee Convention holds out. The eventual flexible response to the Kosovo crisis had such an effect. The response was premised on the notion that a viable protection policy requires some reconciliation between the rights of refugees and the interests of states. Incorporating this assumption in contingency planning for refugee protection might help to pre-empt *refoulement* or *non-entrée*.

Bibliography

Amnesty International (1999) *Former Yugoslav Republic of Macedonia: Humanitarian Evacuation and the International Response to Refugees from Kosovo*, June.

Amnesty International (1999) *Former Yugoslav Republic of Macedonia: the Protection of Kosovo Albanian Refugees*, May.

Barutciski M. (1996) 'The Reinforcement of Non-Admission Policies and the Subversion of UNHCR: Displacement and Internal Assistance in Bosnia-Herzegovina (1992–94)', *International Journal of Refugee Law*, 8, 49, pp. 76–80.

'The Crisis in Kosovo from a Humanitarian Perspective', *TALK BACK: the Monthly Newsletter of the International Council of Voluntary Agencies (ICVA)*, 1, 2, June 1999, http://www.icva.ch/cgi-bin/browse.pl?doc=newsletter0699.

Gibney M. J. (1999) 'Kosovo and Beyond: Popular and Unpopular Refugees', *Forced Migration Review*, 5, August, pp. 28–30.

Gibney M. J. (1999) 'Liberal Democratic States and Responsibilities to Refugees,' *American Political Science Review*, 93, 1 March, pp. 169–81.

Goodin, Robert E. (1985) *Protecting the Vulnerable*, Chicago: University of Chicago Press.

ICVA (1999) *TALK BACK: the Monthly Newsletter of the International Council of Voluntary Agencies (ICVA)*, 1, 2, June.

NATO (1999) *Establishment of New Refugee Reception Centres Korce SE Albania: Recce Report*, NATO Doc. K3000/ARSPPP/99, 5 May.

Select Committee on International Development, (1999) *Third Report – Kosovo: The Humanitarian Crisis*, London: House of Commons, 15 May.

Suhrke, A. (1998) 'Burden Sharing during Refugee Emergencies: the Logic of Collective versus National Action', *Journal of Refugee Studies*, 11, 4, pp. 396–414.

Suhrke, A. et al. (Febuary 2001) *The Kosovo Refugee Crisis: an Independent Evaluation of UNHCR's Emergency Preparedness and Response*, www. unhcr. ch/eval.

UN Economic and Social Council, *Report of the United Nation High Commissioner for Refugees*, UN Doc. E/1994/41, 6 MAY 1994.

UNHCR (1998) *Emergency Contingency Plans for the Former Yugoslav Republic of Macedonia*, updated version of May.

UNHCR (1999) Memorandum, *DIP Mission to Albania and FYROM: 18–25 May*, 1 June.

UNHCR (1999) *Humanitarian Evacuation of Refugees from FYROM: Initial Guidelines for Identification of Evacuees during Phase One*, 5 April.

UNHCR (1999) *Moving Kosovars to Albania: a Specific Form of Humanitarian Evacuation*, 3 May.

UNHCR (1999) *Protection Guidelines: Kosovo Situation*, Geneva, 9 April.

UNHCR (1999) *Protection Guidelines: Kosovo Situation – Revision 1*, 30 April.

UNHCR (1999) *Statistical Overview of Asylum Applications Lodged in Europe by Citizens of the Federal Republic of Yugoslavia: January 1998 to February 1999*, Geneva, 2 April.

UNHCR/Skopje (1999) *Guidelines for the Humanitarian Evacuation Programme of Kosovar Refugees in the Republic of Macedonia*, 12 April.

UNHCR/Skopje (1999) *Updated UNHCR Guidelines for the Humanitarian Evacuation Programme of Kosovar Refugees in Former Yugoslav Republic of Macedonia*, June.

Notes

1. The chapter draws heavily on data collected by the authors for an evaluation of UNHCR's response to the Kosovo refugee crisis, commissioned by the agency. See A. Suhrke et al., *The Kosovo Refugee Crisis: an Independent Evaluation of UNHCR's Emergency Preparedness and Response*. www. unhcr. ch/eval, Febuary 2001.
2. Of the 350,000, some 90,000 of the total were evacuated to third countries.
3. The possibility was discussed, for instance, at a New York meeting of the UN Secretary-General, the Assistant High Commissioner for Refugees and the ICRC on 7 April.
4. 'It is expected that political and thus protection issues (question of open borders, refoulement, access to and status of refugees) will constitute the biggest challenges in a possible refugee emergency whereas assistance and logistics should not pose major problems.' UNHCR, *Emergency Contingency Plans for the Former Yugoslav Republic of Macedonia*, updated version of May 1998.
5. 'The influx scenario is based on the assumption that the Government will allow access to new arrivals from Kosovo and that the majority could be accommodated with Macedonian families of Albanian ethnicity.' Ibid.
6. Paragraphs II (A) 1 and 2.
7. Paragraph (p).
8. Albania's transition from a Stalinist regime to market forces was accompanied by near anarchy and a civil war in 1997. UNHCR had struggled to assist a small refugee inflow from Kosovo of some 25,000 in 1998. After shooting incidents and looting of its warehouses, the agency was forced to close down its sub-office in Northern Albania by the end of the year.
9. The programme was prepared at an inter-agency meeting in Washington on Saturday 3 April and formally announced on Monday 5 April.
10. It is indicative that UNHCR received the first, formal offer of sharing from Norway already on Tuesday, 30 March, in response to the accumulation that was starting at the Blace border crossing. It was not accepted until Friday morning, that is, when thousands had been trapped in the cold, muddy field for two days. Not until Sunday, 4 April, did the High Commissioner publicly call for burden-sharing of refugees as a possible solution to the asylum problems in Macedonia. The High Commissioner's Special Envoy arrived in Skopje on 3 April, by which time the package concept was already well advanced. UNHCR's leadership at that point supported the idea.
11. Returning from a field visit in late May, the head of the Division of International Protection in UNHCR stated that: 'Humanitarian Evacuation Programme (HEP) in Macedonia is a source of dissension among the protection staff. Non-HEP protection staff question the compatibility of HEP with our core function to promote the right to seek asylum in a Convention signatory State.' Memorandum, 1 June 1999.

12. The number of asylum seekers in Europe from former Yugoslavia had increased 200 per cent from 1997 to 1998, and the vast majority were Kosovo Albanians. *A Statistical Overview of Asylum Applications Lodged in Europe by Citizens of the Federal Republic of Yugoslavia: January 1998 to February 1999*, UNHCR, Geneva, 2 April 1999. Members of the consultative forum on asylum, ICG (Inter-Governmental Consultations) had met on 23 March, on the eve of the Kosovo refugee crisis, and the tone had been defensive-alarmist. Italy, for instance, urged UNHCR to keep Kosovo Albanians in the region, and called for 'humanitarian containment' in case of a new outflow.
13. Early west European efforts were mainly directed towards keeping the refugees in the region. The British Foreign Minister proposed a 'security zone' on the Kosovo–Macedonian border as an alternative to the Blace field. The German government promoted plans to transfer refugees from Macedonia to Albania and offered Tirana financial aid to build camps. This was the main purpose of the visit of the German Minister of the Interior to Tirana on 3–4 April. The French government, for its part, announced that relocating refugees out of the region would merely assist the Serb policy of 'ethnic cleansing'. A meeting of EU justice and home affairs ministers in Luxembourg on 7 April stressed as 'the main principle' that Kosovo refugees should be given protection in the region rather than being admitted to EU states. To this end, the ministers also approved a German proposal to reduce the pressure on Macedonia by facilitating the transfer of refugees to Albania. Kosovo evaluation, Suhrke et al., *Kosovo Refugees Crisis*, pp. 8–9.
14. Letter from the Secretary of State to the High Commissioner dated 17 April 1999: 'UNHCR and the rest of the international community must ensure that the burden on frontline receiving states is manageable. The United States is working with Macedonia to keep borders open and with NATO to expand current camps and to build new ones, but these efforts will only go so far. I know that UNHCR and others prefer a regional solution to this refugee crisis, as do we. The reality is, however, that the absorptive capacity of Albania and Macedonia has been stretched to the limit, the stability of the region as a whole is threatened, and refugees are suffering. We must therefore move ahead with plans to temporarily relocate refugees in third countries, and I have urged many countries to activate their pledges to host refugees as soon as possible.'
15. Arguably, some of the capacity which was mobilised to transport refugees around the world could have been applied to rapidly improve reception conditions in that country. In contrast, the first influx to Albania created a sense of overflow and pressure on the local infrastructure that imposed certain limits.
16. 'The [UK] Government has always maintained that the vast majority of these refugees wish to stay in the region and this was confirmed during our visit to Macedonia and Albania. Clare Short said, "The dearest wish of the overwhelming bulk of the refugees is to return, and to stay in the region and join up with their family members" ... We agree that for the vast majority of refugees their care in the region is both the most practical and their preferred option.' Select Committee on International Development, *Third Report – Kosovo: the Humanitarian Crisis*, London: House of Commons, 15 May 1999, para. 75.

17. UNHCR, *Protection Guidelines: Kosovo Situation*, Geneva, 9 April 1999.
18. The US Ambassador to Macedonia, Christopher Hill, had the Kosovo portfolio as well and participated regularly in the negotiations led on the US side by Richard Holbrooke.
19. For instance, the head of the division dealing with refugees in the state department (PRM), Julia Taft, joined the US Deputy Secretary of State, Strobe Talbott, on a special mission to Albania and Macedonia during the first week of April. Both were central in defusing the Blace border crisis.
20. Out of a total of 7,972 evacuations for the period 6–11 April 1999, Germany had taken 4,420 refugees, Turkey 2,941 refugees and Norway 515 refugees. UNHCR/Skopje, *Guidelines for the Humanitarian Evacuation Programme of Kosovar Refugees in the Republic of Macedonia*, 12 April 1999, p. 3.
21. Amnesty International believed that since the Albanians fleeing Kosovo were refugees according to the 1951 Refugee Convention, this 'would imply that they should be entitled to the rights elaborated in that Convention, and, consequently, that the evacuation of refugees from Macedonia should properly be treated as the resettlement of Convention refugees.' Amnesty International, *Former Yugoslav Republic of Macedonia: the Protection of Kosovo Albanian Refugees*, May 1999, p. 16.
22. Report filed by a senior protection officer, Skopje, 12 June 1999.
23. The information is based on meetings at the US Embassy in Skopje (21 September 1999) and with the Canadian Immigration Department (22 October 1999).
24. The first two HEP guidelines mention that the operation is organised for the purposes of 'temporary safety'. The last guidelines omit the adjective 'temporary'.
25. 'Such temporary protection includes admission to safety, *non-refoulement* and treatment in conformity with international humanitarian standards.' UN Economic and Social Council, *Report of the United Nations High Commissioner for Refugees*, UN Doc. E/1994/41, 6 May 1994, para 147.

    Even when temporary protection was prolonged for more than two years, the same minimal treatment continued, although it was never made more precise beyond a vague reference to compliance with 'international humanitarian standards'. See the section entitled 'Reduced rights of temporary protection', in Michael Barutciski, 'The Reinforcement of Non-Admission Policies and the Subversion of UNHCR: Displacement and Internal Assistance in Bosnia-Herzegovina (1992–94)', *International Journal of Refugee Law*, 8, 49, 1996, pp. 76–80.
26. The Protection Guidelines of 9 April 1999 provide that the minimum standards of treatment include: protection from *refoulement*, preferably with a legal or other form of enforceable basis for remaining in the country of protection; respect for basic human rights and dignity, including access to means of subsistence (access to work or social services, or international assistance), shelter, health care, clothing and, depending on the length of stay, some form of education for children; the ability to join families when different members are enjoying protection in different countries (i.e. not family reunification in the sense of bringing family members from Kosovo to country of protection, but if, for example, some family members are in Germany and some in Switzerland, they should be allowed to reunite

together in one or the other of those countries). The last provision is slightly reworded in the revision of 30 April 1999. None of the three sets of HEP guidelines produced during the emergency mention reception conditions in the host countries.

27. However, the following passage is likely to open UNHCR to severe criticism from jurists on the grounds that binding legal obligations in treaty law cannot be suspended without an explicit clause authorising such a derogation. 'Where Kosovar refugees are not provided with access to asylum procedures, they should at a minimum enjoy a form of temporary protection, in fact if not in name. In these exceptional circumstances, *the application of the Convention could be temporarily suspended,* albeit with the clear understanding that the Convention must have a place in determining protection needs at the time of return' (emphasis added). UNHCR, *Protection Guidelines: Kosovo Situation – Revision 1,* 30 April 1999.
28. Information communicated by NGOs operating in Oxfordshire, England. See also, 'The Crisis in Kosovo from a Humanitarian Perspective', *TALK BACK: the Monthly Newsletter of the International Council of Voluntary Agencies (ICVA),* 1, 2, June 1999 http:// www.icva.ch/cgi-bin/browse.pl?doc=newsletter0699: 'This has created distortions and resentment. Over one thousand Kosovo refugees in one camp, in Bihac (Bosnia) demolished their camp and set off back to Macedonia in the hope of being able to benefit. They were persuaded to come back by UNHCR officials.' See also Matthew J. Gibney, 'Kosovo and Beyond: Popular and Unpopular Refugees', *Forced Migration Review,* 5, August 1999, pp. 28–30.
29. Article 3: 'The Contracting States shall apply the provisions of this Convention to refugees without discrimination as to race, religion or country of origin.'
30. Article 33(1) of the Convention: 'No Contracting State shall expel or return ('refouler') a refugee in any manner whatsoever to the frontiers of territories where his life or freedom would be threatened on account of his race, religion, nationality, membership of a particular social group or political opinion.' Internal movements are circumscribed by article 26: 'Each Contracting State shall accord to refugees lawfully in its territory the right to choose their place of residence to move freely within its territory, subject to any regulations applicable to aliens generally in the same circumstances.'
31. 'While departures are voluntary and links to destination countries are taken into account if possible, in principle they do not have a choice as to the country of destination.' UNHCR/Skopje, *Updated UNHCR Guidelines for the Humanitarian Evacuation Programme of Kosovar Refugees in Former Yugoslav Republic of Macedonia,* June 1999.
32. See, for example, Amnesty International, *Former Yugoslav Republic of Macedonia: Humanitarian Evacuation and the International Response to Refugees from Kosovo,* June 1999, p. 4: 'It is evident that many of the problems incurred in the running of the HEP had much to do with the pressure of doing things quickly – which meant that proper systems of identifying those refugees most in need of being evacuated were never established.' The same report goes on to state at p. 9 that 'UNHCR targeted the most vulnerable refugees and those with special needs as priority for evacuation, and concentrated on submitting those cases to governments'.

33. See UNHCR (Policy Research Unit), *Camp Security in Macedonia*, July 1999.
34. 'Crisis in Kosovo from a Humanitarian Perspective'.
35. UNHCR, *Updated UNHCR Guidelines*, June 1999.
36. UNHCR Memorandum, DIP Mission to Albania and FYROM: 18–25 May, 1 June 1999.
37. NATO, *Establishment of New Refugee Reception Centres Korce SE Albania: Recce Report*, NATO Doc. K3000/ARSPPP/99, 5 May 1999.
38. UNHCR Memorandum, *DIP Mission to Albania and FYROM: 18–25 May*, 1 June 1999, para. 3.1.
39. Ibid.
40. UNHCR, *Humanitarian Evacuation of Refugees from FYROM: Initial Guidelines for Identification of Evacuees during Phase One*, 5 April 1999.
41. UNHCR, *Moving Kosovars to Albania: a Specific Form of Humanitarian Evacuation*, 3 May 1999.
42. 'UNHCR has struggled to prevent any forcible movements from the border to Albania, while encouraging the refugees to move south of their own accord. This has not been easy. UNHCR officials say that voluntary means "raising no objections", and they also say that the refugees are being given every chance to register objections. It is not clear, however, whether anyone who objects can automatically remain. What, for example, of refugees who want to return quickly in the event of a settlement? Would this constitute a reasonable objection? So far the issue has not been forced. Only 600 refugees have agreed to move to Albania', 'Crisis in Kosovo From a Humanitarian Perspective'.
43. Background paper submitted by the High Commissioner to the High Level Meeting on the Kosovo Crisis, 13 May 1999, para. 4.
44. 'Transfers should be implemented broadly in accordance with the DIP guidelines, which stipulate that non-objection rather than voluntary application should determine who goes, with reasons for objection being subject to some assessment as to their reasonableness.' UNHCR Memorandum, *DIP Mission to Albania and FYROM: 18–25 May*, 1 June 1999, para. 3.3.
45. 'Albania has a border contiguous with Macedonia, meaning movement is quick and easy, and Albania imposes no quota nor selection criteria for accepting Kosovars.' UNHCR, *Moving Kosovars to Albania: a Specific Form of Humanitarian Evacuation*, 3 May 1999.
46. The reluctance of some UNHCR staff to participate in HEP was well known: 'UNHCR will be asked by [the government] to identify those willing to move and assist the government with transportation and logistics. In view of the [government's] position on humanitarian evacuation and perception that UNHCR is unhelpful, this is an unlikely scenario.' *Humanitarian Transfer of Kosovo Refugees from Macedonia to Albania*, updated on 10 May 1999. An internal e-mail message dated 14 May 1999 highlights a similar point: 'We are noticing US impatience with UNHCR's lack of enthusiasm for "mandatory movements" to Albania.'
47. Note for the file: Albania transfer incident at Blace, 23 May 1999. This incident in which UNHCR even used the media to pressure the government is confirmed in a separate note to the file prepared by the Emergency Co-ordinator on 24 May 1999.

48. *Humanitarian Transfer of Kosovo Refugees from Macedonia to Albania*, updated on 10 May 1999. 'Crisis in Kosovo from a Humanitarian Perspective'. A more realistic approach that was expressed around the same time by the Director of the Europe Bureau: 'In my view the best thing would be to aim for [transfers] of the new arrivals to Macedonia, if they are to come. Once in the border areas and desperate for shelter we will tell them that the camps in Macedonia are full but that we have place for them in camps in Albania with UNHCR presence and that UNHCR will take them to these camps. I believe that many refugees will simply get on the bus and agree to go to Albania. This would be what we call a non-forcible movement. It would not be based, however, on a voluntary choice of between Macedonia and Albania.'
49. 'Turkey unfortunately is not a very popular destination, in spite of decent accommodation being provided. Since the movements have to be voluntary and rightly so, we have increasingly problems in filling flights to Turkey and regularly flights are cancelled due to lack of takers as so many other countries do offer possibilities.' Internal UNHCR Europe Bureau e-mail message, 14 May 1999.
50. 'We have tried [transfers] to Albania from camps in Macedonia and surprise, surprise hardly any takers (only family reunification so far) especially when 27 countries (and some attractive countries) are fighting to take refugees to their countries.' Ibid.
51. Article 33 of the 1951 Refugee Convention: (1) No Contracting State shall expel or return ('refouler') a refugee in any manner whatsoever to the frontiers of territories where his life or freedom would be threatened on account of his race, religion, nationality, membership of a particular social group or political opinion. (2) The benefit of the present provision may not, however, be claimed by a refugee whom there are reasonable grounds for regarding as a danger to the security of the country in which he is, or who, having been convicted by a final judgement of a particularly serious crime, constitutes a danger to the community of that country.' Although this last provision refers to the threat posed by individuals, the destabilisation context suggests that the individuals represent a threat because of their membership of a larger group. Other interpretations of this provision would require a restrictive explanation of the moment at which *non-refoulement* applies (i.e. only after the border is crossed) in order to preserve the overall coherence of the Convention in situations of destabilisation. The latter approach appears to have been favoured by the drafters who discussed these issues at the Conference of Plenipotentiaries on the Status of Refugees and Stateless Persons, Summary Record of the Sixteenth Meeting (held at the Palais des Nations, Geneva, on Wednesday, 11 July 1951, at 3 p.m.), UN Doc A/CONF.2/SR.16, 23 November 1951. See particularly the exchanges between Mr Petren (Sweden), Mr von Trutzschler (Federal Republic of Germany), Mr Rochefort (France), Mr Larsen (Denmark), Mr Zutter (Switzerland – 'States were not compelled to allow large groups of persons claiming refugee status to cross its frontiers'), Mr Theodoli (Italy – 'a State could not commit itself not to expel or return large groups of refugees who presented themselves on its territory, and who might endanger public security'), Baron van Boetzelaer (Netherlands – 'the Netherlands was somewhat

diffident about assuming unconditional obligations so far as mass influxes of refugees were concerned, unless international collaboration was sufficiently organised to deal with such a situation').

52. See, for example, the particularly restrictive interpretation given of the *non-refoulement* principle by the US Supreme Court in *Sale v. Haitian Centers Council, Inc.*, 509 US 155 (1993).
53. See article 9: 'Nothing in this Convention shall prevent a Contracting State, in time of war or other grave and exceptional circumstances, from taking provisionally measures which it considers to be essential to the national security in the case of a particular person, pending a determination by the Contracting State that that person is in fact a refugee and that the continuance of such measures is necessary in his case in the interests of national security.'
54. Amnesty International, *Former Yugoslav Republic of Macedonia*, p. 20.
55. See Astri Suhrke, 'Burden Sharing during Refugee Emergencies: the Logic of Collective versus National Action', *Journal of Refugee Studies*, 11, 4 (1998) pp. 396–414.
56. See Suhrke et al., *Kosovo Refugee Crisis,* Appendix D: '[T]he evaluation suggests that UNHCR should have given more and earlier attention to the probability that the refugees would not be admitted to a potential country of asylum, and that alternative protection strategies should have been explored. UNHCR is concerned that contingency planning which assumes that states will not comply with their responsibilities to receive and host new arrivals, particularly in mass influx situations, runs the risk of becoming a self-fulfilling prophecy.' The logic of this response is somewhat akin to not having a lifeboat on board because it would undermine the passengers' faith in the seaworthiness of the ship.
57. Robert E. Goodin, *Protecting the Vulnerable,* Chicago: University of Chicago Press, 1985, p. xi.
58. For a lucid application to asylum policies, see Matthew J. Gibney, 'Liberal Democratic States and Responsibilities to Refugees,' *American Political Science Review*, 93, 1 (March 1999), pp. 169–81.

5
Asylum in Europe: Underpinning Parameters

Dennis de Jong

Introduction

In this chapter, I shall illustrate how European cooperation in the fields of asylum and immigration works in practice. I shall do so on the basis of a case study, that is, the 'crisis' concerning immigration from Iraq and the neighbouring region, as it was dealt with by the EU in late 1997 and early 1998.

In the course of 1997, Germany, the Netherlands, Greece and Sweden noticed a sharp increase in Kurdish asylum applications from Turkey and Iraq. In the Netherlands, for example, the total number of asylum applications rose from an annual 22,000 to 34,500 during 1997, about a third of which consisted of Iraqi asylum applications.

Asylum applications tend to be unevenly distributed among EU member states. In 1997, Germany received 52 per cent of all applications, the Netherlands 8 per cent, Greece 1 per cent and Sweden 2 per cent. The distribution of Iraqi applications was different, but equally uneven: Germany received 40 per cent of these applications, the Netherlands 27 per cent, Greece 11 per cent and Sweden 9 per cent.[1] This means that 87 per cent of all Iraqi applications were lodged in only 4 of the 15 EU member states. All of these states were confronted with a consistent increase in the numbers of Iraqi applications and felt that their asylum procedures had come under pressure because of these developments.

This situation seemed ideal to test Europe's ability to show solidarity with regard to asylum and immigration policies, so that in dealing with increases as outlined above the member states concerned would be supported by the EU as a whole. In the remainder of this chapter I shall examine whether those member states have indeed been supported by the EU as a whole, and whether the consultations in the context of the EU have produced results that are in line with Europe's international obligations, especially under human rights law, and are humanitarian in nature.

The EU action plan on the influx of migrants from Iraq and the neighbouring region

Since mid-1997 the countries facing increased immigration from Iraq and the neighbouring region raised the subject matter in the various competent EU bodies. Originally, these negotiations took place in the third pillar, that is the Justice and Home Affairs (JHA) part of the European Union. At its meeting on 9 and 10 October, the JHA Council recognised the seriousness of the situation and decided to create a special Multi-Disciplinary Group (MDG) to examine the various elements of the issue.

From the very beginning, there were all kinds of institutional concerns. In particular, it was felt that a discussion on the political aspects of the Kurdish problem would go beyond the competence of the third pillar. This would be the prerogative of the second pillar, that is, the Common Foreign and Security Policy (CFSP) part of the European Union. Although the mandate of the MDG was broad enough to cover all the ground, what remained unclear was to which body the MDG should then report. Fortunately, most of these institutional debates were held between the members of permanent representations, who tend to have a more distanced view as to national bureaucratic implications. This meant that eventually a way forward was found that would guarantee an integrated approach: the MDG would report to Coreper (the Committee of Permanent Representatives), although the K4 Committee, which coordinates JHA matters, and the Political Committee, which coordinates CFSP matters would be fully informed and consulted, whenever necessary.

Based on the work of the MDG, the General Affairs Council, at its meeting of 26/7 January 1998, adopted the EU Action Plan on the influx of migrants from Iraq and the neighbouring region.[2] For an issue that had only come up in the course of 1997, this can be regarded as relatively swift action from the EU. Not only had the member states concerned succeeded in placing the issue on the political agenda, but their efforts had also produced a comprehensive action plan.

The plan consists of the following:

A. Improved analysis of the causes and origins of the influx
B. Development of contacts with the government of Turkey and with the UNHCR
C. Ensuring that humanitarian aid makes an effective contribution
D. Effective application of asylum procedures
E. Preventing abuse of asylum procedures
F. Tackling the involvement of organised crime
G. Combating illegal immigration
H. Ensuring coherent and coordinated implementation, monitoring and review.

The structure of the plan thus reflects a good attempt to define a comprehensive or integrated approach to the issue. First, a serious effort is made to detect the reasons behind immigration from Iraq. Secondly, possibilities for reception in the region are explored. Thirdly, the asylum dimension of the issue is recognised. Fourthly, measures are prepared to tackle aspects related to illegal immigration.

Yet, reality is not as rosy as the picture shown above. There are occasional defects in the action plan itself, but, far more importantly, its implementation showed a marked shift into the direction of JHA and from then on it remained biased towards an over-emphasis on elements relating to illegal immigration. As for the text of the action plan itself, its title departs from its stated purpose: although the plan recognises the asylum dimension of the problem, the title just refers to the 'influx of *migrants*', thus creating the impression that the issue is primarily an immigration problem. Secondly, due to a certain reluctance of the Political Committee to tackle the main cause of the influx, that is, the problem of Kurds in Turkey, Iraq and other countries in that region, the plan contains no specific recommendations to this effect. The problem with CFSP decision making is that, if there are differing views on issues, decision making tends to become paralysed. The General Affairs Council does not exert the same amount of pressure on COPO as the JHA Council does with respect to the K4 Committee. Admittedly, the situation of the Kurds has been a problem for decades, and it is unlikely that the EU would suddenly find a solution. The CFSP could at least have invested some time and energy in trying to come up with creative ideas to revitalise the dialogue. It was not that such ideas were unavailable: some experts emphasised that, in order to de-escalate the conflict, it could be of great interest to support the region economically, thus making the Kurdish population less dependent on the leaders of the various factions, who tend to earn their income through criminal activities. A mere recommendation to update the analysis of the political, economic and humanitarian situation is insufficient.

Real imbalances arose with the implementation of the plan. As was to be expected, the second pillar did not take the matter very seriously and nothing was produced in that context. Perhaps the only tangible result that was reached in this respect was the European Commission change of policy, which now declared its readiness to sustain humanitarian aid to the region while it was already on the verge of being eliminated.

With regard to the asylum aspect, there were three main policy approaches:

- reception in the region
- financial burden sharing
- improvement of the implementation of the 1990 Dublin Convention on Responsibility Sharing.[3]

The idea of reception in the region was seriously considered. Unfortunately, the region was rather closely defined and did not include member states of the European Union itself. This, of course, enormously complicated any kind of implementation. The Islamic Republic of Iran, the Caucasian region and Syria could not possibly be considered as safe areas for Kurdish refugees. As for Turkey, the situation was more complex: on the one hand, Turkey has been accused of persecuting Kurds in the east of the country and has maintained a geographical reservation to the 1951 Geneva Convention, limiting its scope to European refugees; on the other hand, Turkey has allowed UNHCR to offer protection to Iraqi Kurds inside the country.

Evidently UNHCR was in a difficult position, being faced with increasing pressures from the European Union to seriously consider Turkey as a safe haven for Kurdish refugees. UNHCR's local office in Ankara was of the opinion that EU pressure towards Turkey could be useful, if this were to lead to a situation where Turkey would take a number of practical steps aimed at facilitating the work of UNHCR. Such steps could include, for example, the abolition of the requirement that only asylum applications which were lodged within eight days of entry into Turkish territory would be taken into consideration. Also, it could be envisaged that Turkey would commit itself to respect the outcome of UNHCR's examination process. This way, there would be a guarantee for those who were recognised by UNHCR as refugees, to the effect that Turkey would not repatriate them. As a long-term solution, pressure could perhaps lead to the lifting of Turkey's geographical reservation to the 1951 Geneva Convention. The official position of UNHCR was far more cautious, however: it was felt that increased pressures on Turkey might have the opposite effect and might even endanger the on-going UNHCR activities in Turkey.

Despite UNHCR's reluctance, the first drafts of the action plan did contain explicit references to the measures referred to above. However, in late 1997 the relations between the EU and Turkey had become cumbersome after the rather restrictive conclusions expressed by the European Council regarding Turkey's candidature for membership of the European Union. Many member states feared that formulating demands or even requests in the field of refugee protection would only exacerbate tensions between the EU and Turkey; hence it was decided to include only a very general reference to the need for a dialogue with the Turkish government 'with the aim of identifying and implementing specific means of improved cooperation'. The UK Presidency tried to implement this part of the action plan through a series of direct contacts with the Turkish authorities at the level of the chairman of the K4 Committee. However, in order to avoid any sensitivities, discussions concentrated on the fight against illegal immigration, as this was perceived as the only area where, under difficult political circumstances, Turkey would be ready to cooperate. The whole idea of reception in the region was therefore tacitly dismissed.

Paragraph 8 of the action plan contains a provision on financial burden-sharing:

> In relation to asylum-seekers and displaced persons who have arrived on the territory of the European Union, the Commission, together with Member States, to consider the most appropriate use of relevant EC funding to improve reception conditions.

As the provision refers to 'relevant EC funding', there were no additional budgetary means provided for this particular objective. This meant that existing budget lines had to be used. On 27 March 1998, the Council adopted two Joint Actions:[4] the first concerned the financing of specific projects in favour of displaced persons who have found temporary protection in the member states and asylum seekers and included a total budget of 13 million ECU. The second concerned the financing of specific projects in favour of asylum seekers and refugees and included a total budget of 3,750 million ECU. Although the action plan is not listed among the instruments which the projects should implement, the Commission has made a sincere attempt to give priority to those projects which were related to the influx of immigrants from Iraq and neighbouring countries. It is not possible, however, to maintain that through this funding the financial burden of member states facing most of the influx was seriously alleviated. Even if all the projects had been related to the influx of immigrants from Iraq and neighbouring countries, the overall amount of 16,750 million ECU is hardly significant compared to the actual costs involved. However, perhaps more important than the financial contribution itself was the consensus reached at European level that some kind of financial burden-sharing was appropriate under these special circumstances.

As I said before, the idea of concentrated reception within the European Union was never given any serious consideration. This is remarkable, as the travel routes of Kurdish immigrants were clearly established, with Greece as the normal point of entry into the EU. To a certain extent, though, the attention given to the implementation of the Dublin Convention can be seen as an attempt to establish this. After all, in accordance with this convention, generally the country of first entrance is responsible for the examination of the asylum applications. If the Dublin Convention were to be effective, Greece would have been responsible for most of the caseload.

I believe that it is this very consequence of the Dublin Convention which is also the reason for its failure: member states with long external borders would carry the largest responsibility, not only for border controls per se, but also for the examination of asylum applications of those reporting at the border or on their territories. The rationale behind all of this was that if external border controls were to be at a uniform level, there would be no major influx of asylum applicants. This may be true in situations where the neighbouring country has ratified the Geneva Convention and offers proper protection to refugees. But, especially for southern European states, there are no such neighbours. If an asylum seeker reports him- or herself at the Turkish/Greek border, Greek authorities cannot just leave the person at the border and send him back to Turkey, on the grounds that they could find protection in Turkey. Under the present circumstances, as described above, there is no guarantee that Turkey would effectively award this form of protection. This means that Greece would be responsible for the substantive examination of asylum applications, even if they were lodged at the border.

In reality, it never came to that: most asylum applicants would be in transit through Greece and from there mostly travel through Italy as illegal immigrants, without lodging an asylum application. Once they had arrived in the country of destination (Germany, the Netherlands, or Sweden), they would lodge an asylum application without giving any information about their travel route. Asylum applicants would maintain, for example, that they had travelled in the back of a lorry, and that they had had no idea where they were until they had finally got out. Most of the implementation discussion concerning the action plan has centred on this particular aspect of the problem: most northern member states felt that the burden of proof under the Dublin Convention was too high. If it was a well-established fact that the normal travel route went through countries like Greece and Italy, they felt that there should be no need to prove this in each and every case, or at least this general pattern should count as supplementary means of proof. This, however, was completely unacceptable to southern European States who were well aware of the implications for their national caseload.

Eventually, this entire discussion resulted in an addition to the draft Eurodac-Convention concerning fingerprinting. So far, the convention foresaw only the fingerprinting of asylum applicants, but this was extended to third-country nationals who have been found to enter the territory of member states illegally. It is doubtful whether this will really help countries of destination: most illegal immigrants do not get caught upon their entry into the territory of a member state, so that a comparison of fingerprints will not provide any 'hits' in their case. Only illegal immigrants who have been stopped at the border will figure in the Eurodac database, provided that the border guards effectively take their fingerprints. However, a member state which catches illegal immigrants, is also responsible for their return to their country of origin; normally speaking, those who are caught should therefore not be in a position to travel through to other European member states. Altogether it can be assumed that the majority of cases would therefore remain as they are now.

I believe that all these difficulties could have been avoided if a different approach had been taken. Instead of insisting that the Dublin Convention had been formally ratified by all member states and had to be implemented, affected member states could have reaped much more success with a sincere approach, admitting that they wanted to put the burden on Greece and possibly Italy. Recognising that the major case-load would have to be dealt with by these two countries, member states could have had a frank discussion on some form of compensation. Technical as well as financial assistance might then have been organised, not only through EU mechanisms, but also on a bilateral basis. This could have been the prelude to a real discussion on responsibility sharing.

The Dublin Convention will have to be renegotiated in the context of the Treaty of Amsterdam: it is one of the subjects mentioned in Article 63 of the consolidated version of the Treaty establishing the European Community (hereafter called EC Treaty). This means that there will have to be a new instrument, most likely a regulation of the EC, and it is to be expected that the basic question of fairness of the present criteria of the Dublin Convention will come to the fore in that context. I very much doubt that peripheral states will continue to accept the basic principle that the state of entry is the main responsible state. It is therefore regrettable that the action plan has not provided the opportunity for a discussion on these matters based on a real-life and urgent situation. Since this has not happened, I am rather pessimistic about the possibility of concluding the negotiations on an EC regulation within the prescribed period of five years.

The remaining part of the action plan concerns the fight against the involvement of organised crime and of illegal immigration as such. Concerning the fight against organised crime, the recommendations of the action plan urge the European Drugs Unit (nowadays Europol) to analyse the situation and to provide the basis for an examination by member states of the scope for joint law enforcement projects in this area.

As for the fight against illegal immigration, a range of measures is proposed. A number of recommendations concerns the issuing of visas: exchange of information and consular cooperation, as well as the specialised training of staff at embassies and consulates in the region. The second set of measures relates to pre-frontier assistance and training, in particular, concerning false documents. Thirdly, the importance of consistent and effective border controls is emphasised, and the training and exchanges between officials of member states and third countries involved is envisaged. Fourthly, the action plan urges member states to introduce and implement carrier's liability legislation. Finally, return and readmission possibilities are mentioned, the local circumstances permitting.

These are all practical measures, and the negotiations with Turkey, as mentioned above, tended to concentrate on this particular aspect of the problem. This approach has been much criticised, as it was felt that it did not fully take into account the fact that many Kurdish 'immigrants' were fleeing a region where they do not feel safe. In other words, by defining the problem as one of illegal immigration, the asylum aspect might easily be forgotten. It must be admitted that, as a consequence of stepping up the efforts of Turkish border guards, it has become more difficult for displaced persons from the region to reach Europe. With the lack of certainty that Turkey might offer protection against *refoulement* itself, this would imply that persons in need of international protection might not receive it.

Of course, this has not been the intention of governments, although it has become the consequence of their policies. Member states perceived the influx from Iraq and the neighbouring region as being of a mixed composition: apart from genuine refugees or displaced persons, the influx consisted to some extent of economic immigrants. For the latter category, an increased effort to combat illegal immigration was deemed highly appropriate. The fact that there seemed to be far less concern with the effect this might have on the possibility for genuine refugees and displaced persons to leave the region and seek shelter in Europe can be explained by the decision-making process itself. Asylum and illegal immigration are dealt with in different groups within the Council structure. Whereas the Asylum Group of the Council was fully engaged in discussions concerning the implementation of the Dublin Convention, the Migration Group made far more progress with the development of practical measures against illegal immigration. From these expert groups, the various proposals went directly to the K4 Committee. This committee generally lacked sufficient expertise to have strategic discussions, even though its mandate includes the coordination of activities of the various expert groups. The main preoccupation of members of the K4 Committee was to ensure that there would be enough measures taken to show to governments that the EU had taken an active stand on this. They were far less interested in finding strategic solutions or maintaining the balance between the need for protection of refugees and displaced persons on the one hand and the fight against illegal immigration on the other .[5]

Lessons to be learned from the Iraqi crisis

The discussions concerning the action plan have demonstrated that for governments the distinction between asylum and immigration is not as clearcut as it may be for lawyers. Although all member states have subscribed to the 1951 Geneva Convention, and Article 63 of the EC Treaty explicitly refers to this convention, governments tend to think more in terms of protection to be awarded to people once they have already entered the territory. They are far less concerned with the need for refugees to actually reach Europe. As a consequence, policies aimed at combating illegal immigration take over, when it comes to the protection of Europe's external borders and the routes leading to them. The EU condemns time and again the role of traffickers, even though ever more genuine refugees need to call upon such intermediaries to reach Europe in the first place.

But even within Europe, the protection of asylum applicants and displaced persons is under pressure. Especially, budgetary implications of high numbers of asylum applicants are politically significant. Add to this the uneven distribution of the asylum caseload among member states, and it becomes evident that member states are prone to exploit or undermine Dublin-type arrangements to shift the burden to each other.

In my opinion, the protection of refugees and displaced persons can only be maintained if progress is made in the development of some kind of responsibility sharing, first within the EU, and subsequently at a worldwide level. The various references to EC funding mechanisms, which are to be found in the action plan, constitute some basis for financial responsibility sharing. The EU programmes for the funding of projects in the fields of border controls, asylum and immigration are still rather modest, but they could be further developed to cover most of the expenditure relating to the reception of asylum applicants, including eventually even costs relating to the examination of asylum applications. It is likely that governments would be less affected by sudden influxes if they knew that budgetary implications were to be borne by the EU.

Instead of trying to develop an EU regulation based on the criteria contained in the Dublin Convention, further attempts could be made to come to an even distribution of asylum applicants among member states. However, this will be far more difficult than developing financial responsibility sharing mechanisms: one of the questions that remains difficult to answer is whether you can force asylum applicants to go to a responsible member state, if they have had no previous ties with that state. After all, the criteria of the Dublin Convention still relate to actions of the asylum applicants themselves, even if it is the mere fact of having transited through that particular state.

The 1951 Geneva Convention does not give the asylum applicant the right to choose his or her country of destination. Article 31, paragraph 1, of this Convention is significant in this respect:

> The contracting States shall not impose penalties, on account of their illegal entry or presence, on refugees who, coming directly from a territory where their life or freedom was threatened in the sense of article 1, enter or are present in their territory without authorization, provided they present themselves without delay to the authorities and show good cause for their illegal entry or presence.

This provision actually requires that refugees ask for asylum in the first country on their route, unless they have been authorised to enter the territory of another country. This principle is reflected in the provisions of the Dublin Convention where generally speaking, the country of first arrival is responsible. However, under a new EU distribution mechanism, it could very well be that they are offered protection not by the first country of arrival, but by another member state. In that case, perhaps paragraph 2 of Article 31 of the Geneva Convention might constitute a legal basis, but I must admit that I find myself here on rather shaky ground:

> The Contracting States shall not apply to the movements of such refugees restrictions other than those which are necessary and such restrictions shall only be applied until their status in the country is regularized or they obtain admission into another country. The Contracting States shall allow such refugees a reasonable period and all the necessary facilities to obtain admission into another country.

This paragraph explicitly takes into account the possibility of a different country offering protection than the country where the asylum application has been lodged in the first place. It is not clear, however, whether this provision sees to the situation where it is not the asylum applicant who opts for protection in another country, but the existence of a system of responsibility sharing.

Even though it is hard, if not impossible, to find a firm legal basis for a forced transfer of asylum applicants from one member state to another, there is no provision to be found in the 1951 Geneva Convention either that would actually forbid this. The most important provision of the Convention, the principle of *non-refoulement* (Article 33), is certainly respected.

An EU responsibility-sharing mechanism might be legitimate vis-à-vis international law, if it had a very clear structure. Although the EU cannot be considered a federal state, the hybrid nature of European cooperation could be reflected by the mechanism under consideration. For example, a system could be designed with first reception near the external borders of EU member states. In special centres, to be funded by the EU and staffed by practitioners from many member states, the first appraisal of the asylum application could be undertaken. If it were to be found that the asylum applicant was in need of international protection, either as a refugee or as a displaced person, he or she could be transferred to the responsible member state. This state would then take care of proper reception and integration policies and would translate the first decision made at the centre of first reception into its national law and practice. Possible appeal procedures would equally have to be governed by the national law of the responsible member state. If the first appraisal of the asylum application were to be negative, there should be an appeal mechanism too. In that case, however, I would consider it inevitable that this ought to be governed by EU law. Even though the reception centre is geographically located on the territory of one member state, the decisions made with regard to asylum applications affect the Union as a whole: in the case of a positive decision, this is most evident, since another member state will often become responsible for the protection of the refugee or displaced person. In the case of a negative decision, the EU interest is that the rejected applicant is returned to his or her country of origin. Again, before such a return can be effected, there should be some kind of appeal procedure. This follows from the Council Resolution of 20 June 1995 on Minimum Guarantees for Asylum Procedures. Even in cases of asylum applications at the border which are found to be manifestly unfounded, the Resolution requires an appeal procedure, although members states may permit an exception to the general principle of suspensive effect. I would suggest that for this appeal procedure a European board should be responsible, composed of judges from various member states.

By Europeanising the first decision concerning the asylum application, the territory of the member states becomes more or less an entity, at least functionally. This would in my opinion provide a legal basis for the forced transfer of asylum applicants to a particular member state. However, is this possible on the basis of the EC Treaty, as it has come out after the Treaty of Amsterdam? Article 68 of the EC Treaty defines the competencies of the Court of Justice in rather narrow terms: it can examine interpretation questions when they are raised in a case pending before a court or a tribunal of a member state against whose decision there is no judicial remedy under national law. The appeals board as referred to above could not be considered as a special branch of the Court of Justice. As yet, there has not been a case before a national tribunal.

There seems to be a way out of this, however. In accordance with Article 63 of the EC Treaty, the Council shall within a period of five years after the entry into force of the Treaty of Amsterdam, adopt minimum standards with regard to the qualification of nationals of third countries as refugees and minimum standards on procedures in member states for granting or withdrawing refugee status. In my opinion, these provisions provide the basis for the development of an intake procedure as outlined above. European law as defined in these instruments should govern the procedure in the centres of first reception, as well as the proceedings of the appeals boards. Strictly speaking, the European Court of Justice cannot examine interpretation questions, as defined by the appeals boards, since these are not 'tribunals of a member state'. But this could be redressed by including in the European instruments mentioned above a special provision, spelling out that, for the purposes of Article 68, the appeals boards should be considered as such.

As for the criteria governing responsibility sharing, a number of options can be distinguished. It could prove useful to divide up the refugees/displaced persons in accordance with their nationality. Each member state would thus be responsible for the reception of persons of a specific nationality. The advantage would be that reception facilities could be adjusted in order to take account of the specific cultural characteristics of each group. In the case of an improved situation in the country of origin, returns could be facilitated, as in principle it would only involve movements from one member state back to the country of origin. In the case of appeals, for example, because the person concerned has received temporary protection, even though he or she considers him/herself to be a refugee, this distribution mechanism would have the advantage of centralising the expertise about the situation in a country or region of origin. However, there are also significant disadvantages: asylum movements are never stable and may vary considerably from one year to another. This would imply that constant adjustments need to be made and that a member state may have to take up more nationalities or less, depending on the actual influxes. However, if responsibilities shift over time, a lot of the advantages mentioned would be lost. In addition, the concentration of specific nationalities in a member state may produce social tensions, and last but not least special exceptions need to be made for asylum applicants with close ties to other member states. In this respect, one could think of applicants with family members already legally resident in another member state.

Another option would be to set a quota for each member state, preferably according to the percentage of the total number of refugees/displaced persons recognised in the centres of first reception. In the past, it has proved almost impossible to fix criteria for such quota-setting mechanisms. The Council Decision of 4 March 1996[6] on an alert and emergency procedure for burden-sharing with regard to the admission and residence of displaced persons on a temporary basis contains a number of such criteria, but they are vague and too numerous to become easily operational. The mechanism that I propose here differs from previous mechanisms since the asylum applications have already been examined in the centres of first reception. Therefore, member states would only be responsible for receiving refugees and displaced persons. One might expect member states to be more lenient when it comes to the formulation of criteria for the transfer of these more limited numbers of people. In return, they would be able to return any spontaneous asylum applicant to centres of first reception. All in all, I would think that this should be politically feasible.

In a recent article,[7] I have developed the thesis that, in order to sustain and improve protection mechanisms under the Geneva Convention, consideration should be given to the possibility of replacing the present system by one of continental responsibility for first reception in the region, followed by global responsibility for resettlement, if the situation in the country of origin does not improve within a reasonable period of time, such as five years. This has the advantage for some of the developing countries offering protection to significant numbers of refugees for longer periods of time, that there would be world solidarity after this period of first reception. At the same time, it would make it possible for European States to declare inadmissible asylum applications from non-European asylum applicants. Instead, they would need to offer protection to refugees in the context of global resettlement programmes. Although in numbers and budgetary implications this approach might lead to similar effects for the member states, it certainly would make the influxes more predictable.

Even if there were to be regional and global solidarity mechanisms as outlined above, there might still be significant numbers of illegal immigrants. It is questionable whether active enforcement policies in this respect are required. Assuming that illegal immigrants will be excluded from general welfare systems (except in emergency situations), they will either have to be supported by friends or relatives, be engaged in illegal employment, or they will make their living through criminal activities or even begging. If friends or relatives support them, their presence on the territory of member states hardly poses any problem. It certainly does not require active investigation methods. When immigrants are engaged in illegal employment, there may be a distortion of the labour market, and this should therefore be counteracted. Instead of focusing on the immigrants, however, it would be preferable to focus on the employers: they make the profits and they often do not respect national social legislation when dealing with illegal immigrants. If governments were to be successful in their policies targeting the employers, illegal employment would disappear over time. It is only when illegal immigrants are engaged in criminal activities or have to resort to begging practices that active state intervention might be helpful. But then it is not phrased as combating illegal immigration as such, but rather as combating crime and begging. In that case, there ought to be no difference between the prosecution of nationals and non-nationals, except that the latter category may well have to face active expulsion measures.

Although illegal immigration certainly is not a good phenomenon, one should not forget that it is mostly prompted by labour-market considerations: when prospective (economic) immigrants know that there will be no job opportunity, they are less likely to come over. But it is the very fact that our economies need additional labour for specific jobs which causes the major pull factor for illegal immigration. Instead of concentrating solely on enforcement, it might be advantageous to start thinking of defining new ways to meet these economic needs. In that case, present immigration policies should be redefined in less rigid terms. Thus, one could consider allowing companies to hire third-country nationals, if they are prepared to make a certain payment in return. This tax could be used for training Europeans, so that the lack of labour supply could be redressed.

Conclusion

The European Union finds itself at a crossroads: the new EC Treaty offers possibilities, as most of the present soft law instruments will have to be translated into binding directives or regulations in the coming five years. Personally, I am not overly optimistic about this process. The unanimity rule still prevails, and there is a lack of strategic thinking, both within the European Commission and certainly within the Council.

A few attempts have recently been made to turn away from traditional approaches and to develop new and more strategic thinking on how to deal with immigration and asylum issues. During the second half of 1998, the Austrian Presidency launched a strategic paper. This has been criticised, as some of its paragraphs could be interpreted as undermining the 1951 Geneva Convention. The initiative itself was a step forward, however, as it forced the Council to look at immigration and asylum policies in perspective, that is, including their interrelationship.

Secondly, on 7/8 December 1998, the Council set up a High Level Working Group (HLWG) on Asylum and Migration, 'to establish a common, integrated, cross-pillar approach targeted at the situation in the most important countries of origin of asylum-seekers and migrants'. Although its mandate is rather broad, the HLWG has concentrated its activities on joint country reports. It has, however, the potential for developing more integrated approaches, including elements of foreign policy and humanitarian assistance.

Thirdly, the European Council met in Tampere, in October 1999, to discuss progress in the fields of Justice and Home Affairs in the context of the new situation arising under the new EC Treaty. Immigration and asylum issues figured prominently on the agenda. In order to broaden the debate, a group of academics called 'AGIT' produced an extensive policy document with a wide range of proposals. Although this report has no particular status within the EU, it might be used by individual member states and the Presidency or the Commission, to raise the discussion to a level where more strategic decisions could be taken.

Despite these recent developments, I am afraid that the majority of instruments to be adopted by the Council will be of a traditional nature, more or less copying existing soft law instruments, perhaps reducing the parts that may give rise to liberal interpretations. All member states are aware of the fact that the European Court of Justice may give authoritative rulings about the interpretation of any such instruments and it is therefore to be expected that member states would prefer leaving things out, than having to accept vague, ambiguous wording. The Amsterdam Treaty often speaks of minimum standards: this implies that at national level member states can be more generous. Of course, they will not often be so in practice, since they would fear pull effects if they were. But it will be a good argument to kill any attempts to make European instruments anything more than a reflection of the lowest common denominator.

In order to change this, the European Commission and the European Parliament (EP) have an important role to play: the Commission will undoubtedly be expected to produce most of the proposals, even though member states retain their shared right of initiative until five years after the entry into force of the Treaty of Amsterdam.[8] I would sincerely hope that the Commission does not choose the relatively easy path of copying existing soft law instruments. Of course, some of this work will have to be done, but when it comes to responsibility sharing I expect no results whatsoever from a draft regulation based on the Dublin Convention. A new mechanism as outlined above would then be a possible alternative. Although the EP does not yet have the right of co-decision in these matters, it does have the weapon of the budget. It has been the EP which created existing budget lines for asylum and immigration and it will be up to the EP to expand these lines, so that real financial burden-sharing becomes possible. By narrowly defining the criteria for these budget lines, the EP can exert major political influence.

Outside the EU institutions a constant input from both non-governmental organisations and academics remains of utmost importance: not hindered by political restraints, they can point to the longer-term solutions which are essential to offer protection to those in need of it.

Notes

1. Figures derived from UNHCR's Statistical Unit.
2. Even though the Action Plan has not been officially published, the text is available on the EU/JHA homepage: http://ue.eu.int/jai.
3. Convention determining the State Responsible for Examining Applications for Asylum Lodged in One of the Member States of the European Communities, 14 June 1990, OJ C 254 (19 August 1997).
4. OJ L 138 (9 May 1998).
5. Although especially the Nordic countries urged the committee to pay attention to the asylum aspect, this did not result in anything more than paying lip service to the need to respect the 1951 Geneva Convention. No delegation seemed extremely concerned with the possible effects of measures against illegal immigration on the plight of displaced persons and refugees.
6. OJ C 80/1 (1996).
7. 'The Legal Framework: the Convention relating to the Status of Refugees and the Development of Law Half a Century Later', *International Journal of Refugee Law*, 5, 10, 4, 1998, pp. 688–99. For a similar system of world responsibility

sharing, see James C. Hathaway and R. Alexander Neve, 'Making International Refugee Law Relevant Again: a Proposal for Collectivized and Solution-Oriented Protection', *Harvard Human Rights Journal*, 10, Spring 1997, pp. 115–211.

8. Article 67 of the EC Treaty.

6

Return, Human Rights and International Involvement: Refugees as Social and Political Actors, the Guatemalan Case

Huberto Estrada-Soberanis[1]

Introduction

The condition of refugee is an old historical problem in Guatemala. Since the Spanish Conquest, the Mayan people have lived like refugees in their own country. Today, in other conditions, the war refugees, together with economic migrants support the Guatemalan economy, through support for their families.[2]

The return of refugees has been fraught with difficulties. On 8 October 1992 the government and the Permanent Commission of Refugees signed the first agreement on return.[3] It was the first result of a larger process which began in 1986, when the Guatemalan government initiated the official return. Nevertheless the government proposals established little opportunity to resolve the land problem, its proposals being limited to the traditional legal structure.[4]

On 29 January 1997 the final peace agreement was signed between the Guatemalan government and the Guatemalan National Revolutionary Unity with the United Nations envoy. Thousands of Guatemalans expected much from that process, while the economic crisis and the violence increased.[5] Problems that were raised in the discussions during the peace talks, such as the return process, were part of these expectations. At the time of writing, however, since the signature of the Return Agreement on 20 January 1993, seven years have passed filled with disagreements and difficulties. Despite the government's recognition that return was part and parcel of the first step towards reconciliation, the problem of the refugees' resettlement in their own country has been difficult.[6]

In 1998 the Guatemalan government announced that more than 6,566, Guatemalan refugees still remained in Mexico. They are living in the Mexican states of Chiapas, Campeche and Quintana Roo. However, the United Nations Commissioner for Refugees advances a different set of figures stating that out of 45,000 refugees who escaped from the army to Mexico, 28,400 remained in this country, 59 per cent of whom are children.[7] In 1987, the United Nations High Commissioner for Refugees, Sadako Ogata, said that the return process could be completed in 1999. She also said that the return process had been difficult and that the main commitment of the government was to consolidate the reconciliation process and to resolve the economic and social needs of returned refugees.[8] Nevertheless the government is facing difficulties in the implementation of the peace agreements. Thousands of Guatemalan refugees preferred to survive in Guatemala rather than confront instability and the difficulties of the peace agreements.[9] As in other Central American countries the Guatemalan case has involved the return process of internally displaced persons. They also result from internal war and they face similar problems to those of refugees. For those reasons their claims are considered in related terms.

In the middle of the 1980s, around 40,000 Guatemalans were refugees in Mexico, specially in Chiapas, with support from the Mexican Commission of Support to Refugees and of UNHCR. In September 1986 UNHCR, the Mexican Commission and the Guatemalan governmental Special Commission to Aid Repatriates (CEAR) worked on the return process.[10]

The human rights issue

In Central America the violation of human rights has been a central characteristic of the internal wars. These conflicts involved large territories and towns. Thousands of people were killed and more than two million left their homes for different regions and countries.[11]

In Guatemala the internal conflict has lasted 40 years, and it has roots in the counter-revolutionary movement of 1954. The Guatemalan Civil Society Assembly, as one party involved in the peace talks, defined the main causes of the internal conflict[12] as follows:

- the existence of an unjust agrarian structure
- the extreme poverty
- the state's discrimination against and oppression of the population
- the decay of the social fabric

- the organised violence designed to destroy grassroots organisation
- the lack of effective channels for people's political participation[13]

Among the results of the counter-insurgency strategy are:

- 440 villages destroyed
- 150,000 Guatemalans killed
- more than 100,000 orphans
- more than 150,000 refugees
- one million people internally displaced

The struggle for the defence of human rights has been waged by the popular movement, indigenous organisations and NGOs, but they also faced army repression.

The antecedents

The United Nations High Commission for Refugees (UNHCR) opened a regional office in Costa Rica in 1980 when the consequences of the Central American war began. However, after the victory of the Sandinista movement in Nicaragua, Guatemala became involved in an internal armed conflict. Several peasants also began to come for help in Guatemalan cities.

Two international debates on the refugees' status were held: one of them 1981 in Mexico (Asylum and International Protection to Refugees in Latin America), the other in Cartagena (Colombia: Legal Problems on International Protection of Refugees of Central America, Mexico and Panama). The Cartagena meeting concluded with the declaration which proposed to extend refugee status to people whose security and freedom were in danger as a consequence of violence, foreign invasion, international conflict or any kind of dangerous disturbance. Until then, the UNHCR was not authorised to assist those refugees and the internally displaced were not recognised. The only exception was that of special groups, under the General Secretary's recommendation. In the Central American case, those limitations were significant. For example, in Mexico and Honduras some refugees were not helped because they had no official status. This situation has improved, especially under the action of the United Nations Verification Mission to Guatemala.

It is important to say that during the 1980s the aid and protection for refugees in Central American was limited by regional governments.

The Guatemalan government, for instance, did not allow UNHCR the possibility of observation. Army offensives also included operations in the Mexican refugee area.[14] It was only under the Esquipulas II Agreement that the political environment permitted UNHCR more scope. However, the refugees continued to be perceived by the Guatemalan government as support for the guerrilla movement.

In 1988 the UN approved the Co-operation Special Plan with Central America which included the Development Programme for Displaced, Refugees and Returnees (PRODERE). In 1989 with UNHCR and PNUD support, the International Conference on Refugees, Returnees and Central American Displaced (CIREFCA, Spanish initials) was established. The Central American Conference ended in June 1994. Central American countries and Mexico presented to the international community support initiatives and programmes in favour of displaced people. This situation opened a political space for participation to Central American NGOs.

The struggle of the returned population

Through a tough process which began with their forced escape from their country, the displaced populations achieved, together with popular organisations, recognition of their basic claims in the Agreement of Resettling of population Displaced by the Armed Conflict.[15]

- The category of uprooted people includes all the people affected by the armed conflict who were living either outside or inside the country; it includes refugees, returned and displaced people and members of the Resistance Community Populations.[16]
- The agreements on resettlement establish the participation of the affected population in the design, decision, execution and monitoring of a global strategy of resettling and its projects.
- It recognises extreme poverty as the main cause of Central American conflicts: in Nicaragua the main cause was the counter-revolutionary war.

It is important to note that until the creation of CIREFCA (1989), UNHCR was almost the only source of support and international aid for Central American refugees. It was also a key agent in the creation of CIREFCA. A request to PNUD for the administration of financial resources to each one of the projects was part of the attempts to harness international support.

In contrast with the 1989 situation there were around 150,000 recognised refugees and two million internally and externally displaced people.[17]

Structural problems and solutions

The unequal agrarian structure, extreme poverty, illiteracy and other problems have a historic and structural origin. These problems are also at the root of difficulties in improving the returnee's conditions in spite of land-based projects.[18]

Guatemala is dependent on agriculture yet most of its population is dispossessed of land. The extent of social injustice is brought to light by the fact that the country has the most polarised land distribution in Latin America; 2 per cent of farms occupy 65 per cent of the land and virtually all the remaining 35 per cent is distributed in very small properties (*minifundios,* small land plots). These small properties comprise the majority of the farms, and, as Costello points out, 'Nearly 90 per cent of farms are too small to provide subsistence for their owners.'[19] Most of these poor farmers are indigenous Mayan people, who make up 70 per cent of the country's population.[20] Guatemala is not an industrial country, although there is a certain degree of industrialisation which began during the 1960s and is vulnerable to swings in the world market.[21] Sugar cane, cardamom, beef, bananas and coffee are some of its main exports; by 1995, it had become Latin America's third largest exporter of sugar.

The land structure was a cause of the civil war and still remains without solution. One example is the return process: the government has offered to buy lands for development projects which receive international funds. However, the legalisation process has dragged on and caused problems for the returnees. On 5 February 1998, the Permanent Refugees Commission denounced the government resistance to legalising three rural estates in the South, and in the North West (E1 Peten).[22] Until 1996, most of the 31,787 returnees had been settled in Huehuetenango (14,674), E1 Quiché (10,310), Alta Verapaz (3,081), El Petén (2,456), Suchitepéquez (421) and Escuintla (398), which are all *minifundio* lands with low fertility.[23] The lack of loan funds for peasants' collectives and as technical support are likely to lead to an agrarian crisis as in the Nicaraguan and Salvadoran cases. This threat is worsening the social situation and impedes the achievement of the goals of the peace process. Furthermore, in some resettlement areas, poor peasants are objecting because they also feel entitled to some land rights.

International involvement, globalisation and human rights

Considering the historical experience, as can be seen in the cases of Nicaragua and El Salvador, the world trade institutions and international financial institutions are playing a substantial role in determining the regional environment. Trade and cooperation can support the region's integration into the global economy, but to benefit from this the Central American countries must first improve their internal conditions.

A substantial part of civil society is concerned about the issue of human rights in their various forms. Guatemalan history shows that the absence of the rule of law results from the fact that ruling economic groups have lacked an interest in implementing it. The establishment of the rule of law can help create the conditions for democratisation and improve the economic situation, and can facilitate the creation of a good environment for national and foreign investment. The judiciary system is extremely weak and suffers from waves of corruption at all levels. At the time of writing, the lack of a functioning justice system is more than evident in the increase in economic and other kinds of crimes. The disastrous social and economic situation has contributed to this problem.[24]

Constitutional reforms are required in order to put the peace agreements into effect, and should create a strategic legal framework that reflects the people's needs and their pluralistic will. Such reforms are essential to establish the rights of the Mayan people, who are the country's main cultural and social sector as well as its most important productive force. It is important to point out, however, that constitutional reforms alone are insufficient, and that it is crucial that the rule of law should be backed by legal and administrative tools to ensure its application in all legal areas. To guarantee that it is effectively put into practice, from the local level to the national level, popular participation is vital. The recognition of Mayan law or constumary law is crucial and it is part of the peace agreements. However, there is little interest on the part of the government to implement it.

The limitations of international institutions: the United Nations

In the case of Guatemala, the role of the United Nations and its various agencies, such as the World Bank and the International Monetary Fund, has been determined by historical forces and influenced by US interests. When the Central American peace process officially began, with the Contadora initiative in 1983 and the Arias-Esquipulas peace plan, UN involvement was limited.[25] Now, however, its activity is significant and influential.

Although the role of the UN in peacemaking is of undoubted importance, however, its effectiveness in this role may be limited by contradictory policies deriving from the financial institutions. Countries attempting to overcome civil wars and establish lasting peace are currently dealing with two contradictory processes: the implementation of the peace process and the implementation of structural adjustment.[26] In the case of El Salvador, for example, the two processes have been carried out without adequate coordination; there has been a high degree of contrast between the functions of the UN on the one hand and those of the World Bank and International Monetary Fund on the other. As De Soto and Del Castillo say, 'When the UN itself engaged in peace negotiations early in 1990, it did not think of consulting the IMF or the Bank, notwithstanding the serious financial implications of post-war rehabilitation and reconstruction of the Salvadoran economy.'[27] This problem is especially significant with respect to the agrarian issue, which was one of the main causes of the civil war and is therefore among the most important points in the peace agreements.[28] In El Salvador, however, the process of transferring land as stipulated in the agreements has been affected by measures implemented as part of the structural adjustment process.

It is important to note that the international situation affects UN work in other ways as well, as the organisation is facing increasing budgetary constraints which affect its aid, the fight against poverty, and funds for peace-keeping.[29]

The International Bank for Reconstruction and Development and the International Monetary Fund

The World Bank and the IMF are promoting neoliberal reforms which imply the liberalisation of agricultural trade[30] and the rejection of land reform as an alternative economic development policy.[31] As can be seen in the case of E1 Salvador, the concern of the IMF and the World Bank is principally to ensure the implementation of a structural adjustment programme rather than to contribute to the resolution of the causes of the war.[32] The IMF and the World Bank have undergone important changes since they were first created 50 years ago, but their essential nature as economic institutions has remained unchanged. This fact defines and guides their policy making, and gives them a role quite unlike the UN's peace-keeping role.[33] There have been several difficulties in the implementation of structural adjustment in Guatemala, but it is still underway and the international and regional trends indicate that international financial institutions will continue to promote it. This logical trend has great significance for the process of implementing the Civil Society Assembly's proposals.[34]

Among these difficulties is the fact that the Guatemalan ruling classes have been extremely reluctant to implement economic reforms, which has created a highly polarised social and economic structure. Certain sectors continue to resist the reforms required by the international financial institutions, just as they resisted the social, economic and political reforms of the 1944 revolution, or the rather different reforms proposed by the Alliance for Progress during the 1960s. They have instead chosen to maintain an obsolete system of land structure and a coercive relation to the work force, a relation which reflects and defines their economic projects. It is worth noting, however, that there is also a modernising sector within the bourgeoisie. The contradictions between this sector and the more conservative group might be sharpened by structural adjustment measures, and thus might help open the way for changes.

Continuing the application of the structural adjustment programme implies taking into account IMF conditional practices, especially with respect to the balance of payments, an area in which Guatemala has suffered a chronic imbalance. Most of this imbalance has resulted from a lack of a coherent governmental economic strategy, which has included the lack of agrarian reform combined with macroeconomic reforms. The application of conditions also signifies a reduction of public expenditure, reduced subsidies, price liberalisation, privatisation, and other related measures. These measures will surely alter the process of implementing peace agreements unless there are economic policy agreements and coordination between the UN, the IMF and the World Bank. This is important not only because of Guatemala's internal condition but also because the country is strategically located and thus influential in regional and international processes like the Free Trade Agreement of the Americas and the Uruguay Round.[35]

At this point, it is unavoidable to ask about the potential conflicts between the implementation of proposals similar to those of the Civil Society Assembly in order to guarantee the achievement of peace and the implementation of a severe stabilisation and structural adjustment programme. Are these processes, peace, democratisation and structural adjustment absolutely contradictory? How can the Guatemalan people implement the peace agreements while taking into account the global economic trends and the development crisis?[36]

To find perfect solutions is difficult; nonetheless, some considerations and possible measures may be suggested.

Conclusions and recommendations

- Most of the refugees and returnees are Mayan indigenous people and peasants.
- The refugees have fought for their rights for more than a decade. The international involvement was a result of this.
- Experience shows that it will be more difficult to achieve peace and democracy in an unstable region if international financial institutions do not take into account the historical proposals of the majority of the population. At the same time, the parties involved in the Guatemalan peace process should bring their internal goals into line with the regional and international context.
- Peace and democracy do not derive from a single factor, as there is a complex system of national and international factors which must be taken into account.
- It is necessary to demand a coordinated definition of the roles of the UN, the International Monetary Fund, the World Bank and the community of donors in the Guatemalan peace process.
- The UN should take measures to convince the community of donors of the need to consider the agrarian issue in its aid projects for Guatemala.
- The community of donors should keep in mind that the agrarian issue cannot be reduced to a programme of land transference.
- It is necessary to establish clearly what financial resources are needed to comply with the agrarian agreement.
- The agrarian issue should be part of a macroeconomic strategy.
- The parties involved in the peace process and the community of donors need to contemplate the importance of the Guatemalan agrarian reform experience of 1944–54 in its social, economic and technological-administrative levels.
- The Guatemalan parties involved in the peace process should build a legal, technical and administrative framework that prevents and resolves conflicts and impediments to the implementation of the peace agreement.
- The Guatemalan parties should formulate adequate specific agrarian legislation.

- It is essential to ensure the participation of peasant organisations in the entire process of discussing and implementing the agrarian agreement because it is a special issue which involves the Mayan people and peasants. This principle could help the resettlement process.

Bibliography

333 Decretos del Congreso de la Republica (1947) *Boletin* No. 7, Guatemala: Tipografia Nacional.

ABECOR Country Report (1994) Distributed by Barclays Bank, UK.

Arevalo Martinez, R. (1971) *Ecce Pericles! Historia de la Tirania de Manuel Estrada Cabrera*, San Jose, Costa Rica: Coleccion EDUCA.

Barry, Tom (1992) *Inside Guatemala*, Albuquerque, New Mexico: The Inter-Hemispheric Education Resource Center.

Berger, Susan (1992) *Political Agrarian Development in Guatemala*, Westview Special Studies on Latin America and the Caribbean. Oxford.

Castellanos Cambranes, Julio (1982) *Origenes de la Crisis del Actual Orden Establecido en Guatemala*, Paper No. 34, Stockholm: Institute of Latin American Studies.

Constitucion Politica de la Republica de Guatemala (1985) Guatemala.

Cronica., Guatemalan magazine.

Civil Society Assembly (1995) *Documents of Consensus*, Guatemala: Representaciones Sache.

Child, Jack (1992) *The Central American Peace Process, 1983–1991*. Boulder and London: Lynne Rienner Publishers.

Costello, Patrick (1995) *Our Land, Our Lives, Guatemala*, London: One World Action.

De Soto, Alvaro, and Graciana Del Castillo (1994) 'Obstacles to Peace Building', *Foreign Policy*, 94, Spring, Washington DC: Carnegie Endowment for International Peace.

El Grafico, daily newspaper, Guatemala.

Estrada Soberanis, H. (1992) *Quinto Centenario de la Conquista y El problema del Subdesarrollo en Guatemala*, San José, Costa Rica: Liga Maya Internacional.

Estrada Soberanis, H. (1992) *Dalla Conquista Spagnola Alle Multinazionali: l'iniziatioa, la Repressione e la Lotta del Movimento Sindicale*, Firenze, Italy: Comitato Regionale Toscana.

Foley, Michael (1995) 'Privatizing the Countryside, the Mexican Peasant Movement and Neoliberal Reform', in Latin American Perspectives, issue 84, vol. 22, no. 1, London: Sage.

Galich, M. (1972) *Del Panico al Ataque*, Guatemala: Editorial Universitaria.

Garcia Laguardia, J. M. (1994) *Politica y Constitución en Guatemala: la Constitución de 1985*, Guatemala: Office for Human Rights.

Garoz, Byron (1996) *CIREFCA y la Atención al Desarraigo en Centroamérica*, Guatemala: Consejo de Instituciones de Desarrollo, October.

Grieb, Kenneth J. (1979) *Guatemalan Caudillo: the Regime of Jorge Ubico,* US: Ohio Express.

The Guardian (20 March 1996) 'Congress Asked to Increase Funds for World Bank', London.

Guerra Vilaboy, Sergio (1985) *Luchas Sociales y Partidos Politicos en Guatemala,* Cuba: Departamento de Actividades Culturales, Universidad de la Habana.

Harrington, Anthony S., Lew Allen Jr., Ann Z. Caracristi and Harold W. Pote (1 July 1996) *Report on the Guatemala Review, June 28, 1996. Intelligence Oversight Board,* Washington: US Government.

Jonas, Susanne (1991) *The Battle for Guatemala: Rebels, Death Squads, and U.S. Power,* Latin American Perspectives Series, No. 5, Oxford: Westview Press.

Informe de la Comisión de Derechos Humanos (1989) Guatemala.

Killick, Tony (1987) 'Reflections on the IMF/World Bank Relationship,' Kjell J. Havenik (ed.), in *The IMF and the World Bank in Africa,* Uppsala: Scandinavian Institute of African Studies.

La Prensa, daily newspaper, Guatemala.

Ley de Reforma Agraria, Decreto 900 del Congreso de la Republica (1945) Guatemala: Tipografia Nacional.

Lieten, G. K. (1996) 'Land Reforms at Centre Stage: the Evidence on West Benga', *Development and Change,* 27/1, January.

Matthews, Jessica (1996) 'Work to Do in the World, but Will Americans Do It?' *International Herald Tribune,* London, 6 February 1996.

Martinez Pelaez, S. (1978) *La Patria del Criollo,* Guatemala: Editorial Universitaria.

Mosley, Paul, Jane Harrigan and John Toye (1995) *Aid and Power: the World Bank & Policy-Based Lending,* London: Routledge.

Noticias de Guatemala, 15 February 1995, Mexico.

Schlesinger, Stephen and Stephen Kinzer (1990) *Bitter Fruit,* London: Anchor Books Doubleday.

Siglo Veintinno, Guatemalan newspaper.

Padilla, L. A., A. Arias, A. Linares and Castañeda (1988) *Guatemala, Polos de Desarrollo, el Caso de la Desestructuración de las Comunidades Indígenas,* Mexico: Gilberto Centro de Estudios Integrados de Desarrollo Comunal.

Prados, John (1986) *Presidents Secret Wars,* New York: William Morrow.

Seguridad, desarrollo y democracia (1989) Managua: Iglesia Guatemalteca en el Exilio.

Skinner-Klee, J. (1954) *Legislación Indigenista de Guatemala,* Mexico: D. F. Ediciones Especiales del Instituto Indigenista Latinoamericano.

Uncertain Return (1989). EUA: Washington Office on Latin America, second printing.

Wilcox Young, Linda (1995) 'Free Trade or Fair Trade?', *Latin American Perspectives,* issue 84, vol. 22, no. 1, London: Sage Publications.

Notes

1. Guatemalan professor and lawyer. He is working in Mayan areas in Guatemala on Mayan Law.
2. With the new migration rules in the United States of America, more of the remittances from Latino-Americans will be cut. Remittances to Latin America are of US$870 millions. *Prensa Libre,* Guatemala, 16 February 1998, p. 4.
3. 'In October 1986 the Special Commission to Aid Repatriates (CEAR) was formed to oversee all government activity related to repatriation. Headed by

Carmen Rosa de Leon, detached from the Ministry of Foreign Affairs, CEAR includes representatives from the Ministries of Defense and Development, as well as the National Reconstruction Committee. Under an agreement with the Mexican Commission to Aid Refugees (COMAR) and the UNHCR, the agency helps refugees in Mexico communicate with Guatemala, facilitates their return, and aids their reintegration in Guatemala.' Washington Office On Latin America, p. l6.

4. More of the lands were occupied by new owners or by government institutions. See Agreements between the Guatemalan government and the Permanent Commissions. Guatemala, 8 October 1992.
5. Delinquency and citizen insecurity raised. The British government warned British tourists of the danger of visiting Guatemala. *Prensa Libre*, Guatemalan newspaper, 10 January 1998, p. 8.
6. *La Situación del Refugio de Guatemaltecos en México y su Proceso de Reinserción en Guatemala*, Comisión Nacional pare la Atención de Repatriados, Refugiados y Desplazados CEAR, Guatemala, September 1996, p. 1.
7. *Prensa Libre*, 11 January 1998, p. 17.
8. *Cronica*, Guatemalan magazine, 12–18 December 1997, 506, p. 34.
9. The last PNUD report on Human Development situated Guatemala in the 117th position before Haiti and Nicaragua. From 1990 to 1997, Guatemala fell down 17 places. *Prensa Libre*, June 1997, p. 103.
10. *La Situación del Refugio de Guatemaltecos*, p. 2.
11. See Byron Garoz, *CIREFCA y la Atención al Desarraigo en Centroamérica*, Guatemala: Consejo de Instituciones de Desarrollo, October 1996, p. 2.
12. The Framework Agreement signed in Mexico on 10 January 1994 by the Guatemalan government, the army and the Guatemalan National Revolutionary Unity, and recognised by the United Nations, gave legal and political support to the proposals of the Civil Society Assembly.
13. Civil Society Assembly, 1995, pp. 69–70.
14. *CIREFCA y la Atención al Desarraigo en Centroamérica*, p. 8.
15. As a result of its work of national consultation and discussion, the Civil Society Assembly has presented a series of proposals in order to create conditions to resolve national problems, which are to be considered as constitutional reforms:
    1. Resettling of population displaced by the armed conflict.
    2. Identity and rights of the indigenous peoples.
    3. Socioeconomic aspects and the agrarian situation.
    4. Strengthening of civilian power and the function of the army in a demo cratic society.
    5. Constitutional reforms and electoral policy.
16. As a result of the counter-insurgency strategy, several Mayan populations had to leave their small towns for the mountains.
17. *CIREFCA y La Atención al Desarraigo en Centroamerica*, p. 3.
18. 'Guatemala is known for its extremely unequal land tenure patterns, which a 1982 U.S. Agency for International Development (AID) study called "more serious than all the other Central American countries and most of the countries in Latin America". Indian highland agriculture is dominated by *minifundios*, plots of land generally insufficient to maintain a family.'

19. Costello (1995) p. 2.
20. Estrada Soberanis (1992) p. 3.
21. 'Exports, although rising by 6 per cent to US$1.4 billion in 1993, have still yet to surpass levels recorded in the 1980s. Sugar and coffee exports rose modestly last year. However, banana export earnings declined sharply. Indeed, the major support to exports was non-traditional exports, which in turn mainly reflected a continued increase in trade with the rest of Central America', *ABECOR Country Report*, July 1994, p. 3. It is also worth noting that the external debt has increased from US$2.5 billion in 1991 to $3 billion in 1995, and the government has faced problems in the process of negotiating with the Paris Club. The debt service is equivalent to more than *Siglo Veintiuno* 40% of exports. See Barry (1992), p. 89, and *ABECOR, Country Report*, July 1994, p. 3.
22. *Siglo Veintiuno*, 5 February 1998, p. 4.
23. Registro de Retornados, CEAR, Guvernamental Commission, 1996.
24. The *Prensa Libre* newspaper has reported an increase in citizen insecurity and some of the articles refer to this problem (*Prensa Libre*, 22–6 March 1996). On 25 March 1996, representatives of the Frente Democratico Nueva Guatemala demanded that the head of the Public Ministry resign because his institution had been unable to ensure that justice was maintained. Central America UPDATE (1996), e-mail.
25. 'The role of the UN in the Guatemalan peace process in 1991 remained helpful and positive, but limited to observing and facilitating the initial talks.' Child (1992), p. 139.
26. 'In recent years, Guatemala has adhered to an economic adjustment programme which has been supported by the multilateral financial institutions' (*ABECOR Country Report*, 1994, p. 3).
27. De Soto and Del Castillo (1994), p. 73.
28. 'Likewise, in the negotiation of the subsequent programme for transferring land to former combatants in October 1992, the UN went off on its own, largely oblivious of the financial pressures the peace agreements were bound to impose on the stabilization program.' De Soto and Del Castillo (1994), p. 73.
29. 'Under the current budget deal, American diplomats are counting pennies, embassies are closing funds; for this year's UN dues will be one-third less than is owed (on top of about $1 billion in unpaid arrears) and funds for peace-keeping and for the IDA will be down by half or more'. Matthews (1996), p. 6.
30. See Foley (1995), p. 62.
31. See Lieten (1996), p. 111.
32. 'The UN then continued to play a central role in ensuring that far-reaching political, social, and institutional reforms agreed to in the negotiations were carried out to prevent recurrence of violence – the post-conflict peace building phase. Meanwhile, here was a second process underway. Sponsored by the IMF and the World Bank, it called for implementing a rigorous economic stabilisation and structural adjustment program.' De Soto and Del Castillo (1994), p. 70.
33. 'At Bretton Woods in 1944 there was a fairly clear idea of the division of labour between the two institutions. John Maynard Keynes then argued

that the Board of the Fund should be composed of cautious bankers and that of the Bank of imaginative expansionists ... Implicit in the division of labour was also a geographic division. The Fund was not expected to be dealing primarily with Less Developed Countries (LDC), and it was not designed as an agency whose policy was intended to tackle the particular type of balance of payments problems which are now associated with LDCs. The Bank was set up to deal with reconstruction after the Second World War and to assist developing countries.' Killick (1987), p. 25.

34. 'By 1989, the IMF had become the lender of first resort, as a consequence of the debt crisis, and was able to force Guatemala to take neoliberal measures just as the World Bank conditioned a $80 million loan for private enterprise on legislation giving new incentives for foreign maquiladora investors. Despite these measures, the IMF and other multilateral agencies judged the Guatemalan government to be still spending too much (and not making its debt payments), and temporarily suspended credit in 1989, while continuing to pressure for stricter policies. In 1990, after the World Bank stopped disbursements on loans to Guatemala, the United States continued supporting the government with large bilateral balance of payments credits.' Jonas (1991), p. 85.
35. These processes are also likely to aggravate the agrarian problem. In Mexico, for example, 'Most analysts predict that Mexican grain production will be undercut by cheaper imports from the United States and that the dislocation of small maize producers is likely to be severe ... Labor productivity in almost all crops is substantially lower in Mexico than in the United States. This is not surprising in most cases, given the low levels of technology used by the majority of Mexican producers.' Wilcox Young (1995), p. 51.
36. 'President Bill Clinton yesterday courted the wrath of Republicans by asking Congress to boost funding to the World Bank and the regional development banks to $1.4 billion – a 24 per cent increase over the deadlocked 1996 budget, writes Mark Tran in Washington. Congress cut the President's request for multilateral development banks by 50% in 1996' (*The Guardian,* 20 March 1996, p. 16).

7

Refugee Women: a Gendered and Political Analysis of the Refugee Experience

Agnès Callamard[1]

Introduction

The focus on refugee women as mandating specific policies and as a distinct subject of inquiry may be traced back to the mid-1970s. This was a time of a growing awareness of women's rights, and of the importance of women's role in the development process, in general and in particular with regard to refugee women. The following 20 years were marked by the proclamation of the UN decade for women, the 1985 Nairobi conference and the 1995 Beijing Platform of Actions which highlighted the situation of refugee women as an area of special concern and gave a new impetus to international and local efforts. Yet, the incorporation of women within the field of refugee policies and refugee studies has been slow, marginal and contradicted by broader structural constraints although marked by important steps towards ending the marginalisation of the issue, including the creation of the position of the UNHCR refugee women's coordinator and the Beijing Platform for Action. The UNHCR, in its never-ending quest for durable solutions, has embarked on worldwide repatriation policies which largely undermine, when they do not contradict outright, the organisation's protection mandate and, in particular, the protection of refugee women. The discrepancy between the public relation statement 'women and children represent 80 per cent of the world refugee population' repeated ad nauseam and the 'voluntary' return (at the barrel of a gun) of a number of these very refugee women and children painfully demonstrates the limits of the rights and protection framework put forward in Beijing, and the obstacles faced in its translation into practice.

In the field of action research in the 1990s two approaches emerged in terms of conceptualising and acting upon the situation of refugee women: development and human rights. Since then, the human rights approach has taken precedence over the former, an evolution sanctioned during the Fourth UN World Conference on Women.

However, the interconnection between development and human rights for refugee women has seldom been fully realised. This state of affairs may be traced back to an incomplete gendered understanding of the refugee experience resulting from the creation of 'the refugee' as a 'generic and essentialised figure' (Maalki, 1992), a political and legal artefact meant to exclude certain aspects pertaining to one's identity or to one's experience of persecution (Tuitt, 1996; Hathaway, 1988, 1991; Goodwin-Gill, 1983). This artefact or generic figure is intended to be ungendered and desexualised, although 'the persecution standard adopted within ... the definition under the Geneva Convention ensures, however, that the few identified within these definitions are adult and male' (Tuitt, 1996, p. 33). This chapter seeks to highlight the gendered and sexual nature of the refugee experiences through a review of existing evidence on the discrimination faced by refugee women in terms of access to international assistance, income and physical protection. It especially argues that discrimination and violence against refugee women are politically determined and politically sanctioned, under the actions or influence of international, national and local actors, and therefore that the situation of many refugee women in camps amounts to persecution under the accepted definition. Moreover, if the militarisation and criminalisation of refugee camps constitute major obstacles as far as the protection of refugee women is concerned, answers to this militarisation, including forced repatriation to unsafe areas, are no less threatening, and constitute a major setback to an already strikingly imperfect protection.

Refugee women, power and social change in camps

Two factors had prompted the international community to notice the existence and functions of refugee women. The first was the emergence, following the publication of Esther Boserup's (1970) seminal work, *Women's Role in Economic Development*, of a new field of research and policy which was labelled Women in Development. The second was a widespread disenchantment with both development and refugee assistance together with the shift of emphasis from national to community development and the provision of basic needs and self-sufficiency (as highlighted, for instance, by the 1974 Cocoyoc Declaration). Although, as noted by Deniz Kandiyoti (1990), the effects of gender inequality did not initially receive separate attention above and beyond those of class membership, concerns with greater equity, grass-root participation and self-sufficiency paved the way for policy proposals and reforms related to women, and eventually resulted, among other end-products, in the production of UNHCR *Guidelines on the Protection of Refugee Women* released in 1991. Drafted for UNHCR and other relief agencies staff, the 1991 UNHCR guidelines recognise and highlight the serious shortcomings of existing (gender-biased) relief programmes. As explored elsewhere (Callamard, 1993) these and other policy papers make claims for refugee women on two bases: the needs or vulnerability of refugee women, and their central role and contribution to the welfare of the refugee community. The assumption here is that projects of refugee assistance that focus on women refugees will be more likely to translate into an amelioration of the welfare of the community.

Key factors which are often underestimated are the political and power structures within refugee camps. The entry point towards addressing and confronting the political nature of refugee women's 'vulnerability' within the camp context has been through a focus on the economic strategies within the camp and/or an evaluation of refugee assistance projects. What has been termed refugees' survival strategies include a variety of activities, ranging from farming and wage-labour to hunting, gathering and the trade of food relief (Mazur, 1991; Refugee Studies Programme, 1989; Weaver, 1988), all of which are heavily determined by the local economic structures (Refugee Studies Programme, 1989). Some of these activities may be defined as 'diet supplementation strategies' in that they aimed solely at diversifying and increasing the (insufficient) food ration allocated to the refugees. Others have a broader objective, namely, to enhance the prospects of economic integration within their country of asylum (Daley, 1991; Callamard, 1995).

Not surprisingly, research also shows that the nature, scope and objective of these economic activities differ sharply among men and women refugees and that individual refugees' adjustment to their new circumstances and the process of social changes within the refugee community as a whole entails a transformation of the gender division of labour; see Christensen's (1983) study of three Ethiopian refugee camps in Somalia and Spring's research (1979) among Angolan refugees. The research of the latter especially highlights the importance of marriage as a vehicle of economic wealth and social integration for refugee women settled in Zambian villages. Johnson's research (1981) in Wad el Hilayew camp for Eritrean refugees in Sudan also revealed the transformation of the gender division of labour, at the expense of women:

> Peoples who had brought drought animals with them such as donkeys or camels set themselves up as transporters of water, firewood and fodder in the camp. This activity had previously been regarded as women's work within the family and as a result of its appropriation by men as a commercial venture many women became even more marginalised in refugee society than they had been in Eritrea.
>
> (1981, p. 420)

The survey by Ager, Ager and Long (1995) of some 200 Mozambican refugee households in Malawi demonstrated that while women were more likely to work than men, they were also less likely to generate any income from their work as their labour was principally domestic in nature. Research conducted in Lisongwe refugee camp in Malawi (Callamard, 1996) points to Mozambican women being expelled from the allocation and trade of food.

Analysis of the factors or forces contributing to the rapid changes of the gender division of labour, in many cases at the expense of refugee women, highlights the interrelationships between structure and human agency as well as among various actors. Christensen (1983) attributes both gender differentiation in terms of economic activities and the emergence of women's consciousness to structural factors, including the unequal sex ratio in the adult population (about two-thirds of the households are headed by a woman) and the fact that refugees belonged to nomadic societies. Other writers have brought to light the role of both pre-flight patterns and relief programmes. For instance, Daley (1991) attributes gender differentiation between Burundian refugees' economic activities to the patriarchal tendencies of the Burundi society and male bias of the settlement programme. Ager, Ager and Long (1995) also recognise the pre-existing gender inequalities within Mozambican society, but nevertheless suggest that relief projects and structures for refugee representation had exacerbated existing gender inequality. As for the structures for representation, they were clearly male dominated and generally insensitive to representing the needs of women (1995, p. 283).

Callamard (1996), studying a different camp in Malawi, reaches a conclusion very similar to Ager, Ager and Long (1995), while she shifts the explanatory emphasis from the relief programme per se to the role of international and local actors, as agents of change. Hence:

> The refugee camp had fostered a culture of its own, constructed by both international, Malawian and Mozambican agents which pictured Mozambican women as essentially backward individuals. Refugee men themselves participated in this ideological construction through fostering a set of ideas that came to justify the male domination of economic structures.
>
> (Callamard, 1996, p. 191)

Supporting Schroeder and Watts's conclusion (1991), my own research points to the need to recognise that local agents are not passive subjects of social change imposed by outsiders and 'external' forces, but that they are able to transform supra-local influences and forces into local forms:

> The initial gender bias and gender-blindness of the international mechanisms of assistance and relief have been consolidated locally to displace refugee women from their usual sphere of work and power, and justified locally on the basis of women's biological characteristics, physical weaknesses and social backwardness.
>
> (Callamard, 1996, p. 192)

What these and other studies underscore is that refugee assistance programmes have failed to recognise that the forces and mechanisms of subordination, domination and exclusion of refugee women are located in both the reproductive sphere of the household (Callamard, 1993, 1994; Ager, Ager and Long, 1995; Forbes-Martin, 1988) and the political and power structures of the camp which, in all cases, reinforce and strengthen the patriarchal tendency of the community (Callamard, 1996; Ager, Ager and Long, 1995). Taken together, the evidence provided by the research surveyed above places emphasis on the interaction and togetherness of a number of actors (the refugees themselves and their leaders, national and international actors) and the relief programme itself in fostering gender inequality.

Dependence and empowerment in refugee camps

A thread that runs throughout the literature on refugee experiences, be it through personal accounts and life stories (Mandani, 1973; Moussa,

1991; Bennett, Bexley and Warnock, 1995), or through other forms of research (Hansen, 1981; Hitchcox, 1990; Maalki, 1992; Jok, 1995) is the profound loss of individuality, self-esteem and independence endured by refugees, and fostered by the dynamics of relief assistance. This is a thread that transcends historical and national barriers to characterise the essence of the refugee camp and the life of refugee populations as a whole. In her 1990 ground-breaking work on South-East Asian camps, Linda Hitchcox embraces Goffman's study of mental asylum and Foucault's on prisons to conceptualise the refugee camp as a 'controlling institution' with control working in two ways:

> First of all, all individuals are constrained to behave as if they were dependent and helpless, which assists the perpetuation of an institution largely composed of workers whose role is to respond to people who have problems and are in need ... Complete control and corresponding dependence is achieved when the person can no longer differentiate between the identity of refugee as it is constructed in the camp and the understanding he has of himself as an individual who is Vietnamese.
>
> (1990, p. 174)

Hitchcox's representation echoes Mandani's personal account: '[T]hey had successfully turned the camp into a total institution, like a prison or an insane asylum ... The Kensington camp gradually became a nightmare in totally controlled living' (1973, p. 96), and Maalki's (1990) description of camps for Hutu refugees in Tanzania as a systematised and generalisable 'technology of power' with the refugees subjected to techniques of control, investigation and intervention. These are the techniques which also elicited demeaning attitudes and behaviours among the Dinka displaced population: portraying oneself as poor and needy, resorting to begging, doing odd jobs or lying about one's conditions, and harsh attitudes and violence against women, and ostracism (Jok, 1995):

> The result of these conditions is an increasing loss of self-determination by the people of Southern Sudan through dependency on relief, and a gradual loss of cultural patterns ... *As the whole society becomes affected, women are constantly pushed to the bottom* ... [w]hen disaster strikes this economy, women suffer most.
>
> (1995, p. 32, my emphasis)

This is not meant to deny that refugee women and men do mediate the effects of the camp as a device of power and control. A number of researches have demonstrated that mediation or resisting may encompass the transformation of consciousness of oneself as an individual and as a refugee. Hence, refugees may struggle against the meanings of refugeeness, repatriation and places of return, imposed by the outside world and the camp management (Stepputat, 1994; Mandani, 1973). The process of resisting what Wood (1985) defined as 'authoritarian designation' may result in the emergence and development of nationness (Maalki, 1990) or in a redefinition of 'refugee' with an explicitly politicised meaning used to extract benefits from international and national authorities (Zetter, 1991). Refugee women's experiences before becoming refugees, in flight and during asylum can lead to empowerment through a process of politicisation and self-awareness (Moussa, 1991; Bennett, Bexley and Warnock, 1995; Christensen, 1983):

> [S]ome of the women have realised that they can manage very well on their own in the camp, or that the husbands in the camp are of little practical help ... Camp life therefore has made the males idle and redundant to a large extent.
>
> (Christensen, 1993, p. 15)

At its 'best', mediation may move from an individual's sense of empowerment to a form of collective movement:

> My name is Maria Guadelupe Garcia ... I am a member of the Organisation of Guatemalan Refugee Women, Mama Maquin. Our women's organisation began in 1990 in three different states in Mexico among the various refugee camps. We have learned many things about indigenous rights, the rights of women and the importance of our participation in the decision-making process.
>
> (Hernandez and Garcia, 1996, p. 265)

These examples also tend to show that the extent and nature of mediation is bounded and determined by individuals' positions vis-à-vis the political and social structures of the refugee community, his or her own sense of worth, and the political and economic circumstances. But examples of mediation, at least as reported in the literature, remain few and isolated. And personal testimonies or life stories are often the ones of 'survivors'. In fact, as Moussa (1991) herself contends, refugee women's experiences may also lead to disempowerment as a result of brutality and violence, a process well demonstrated by McLellan (1996) with reference to Cambodian women refugees. The experiences of Afghan refugee women in Pakistan, as a collective, leaves little doubt as to the extent of oppression, persecution and disempowerment that refugee life may result in, given a set of political and ideological conditions (Amnesty International, May 1995; Forbes Martin and Copeland, 1988). The unequal allocation of food relief may be linked to existing shortcomings at international and national level. But ultimately these shortcomings are given a local form through a collusion of interest between refugee leaders and local actors responsible for its distribution (Rizvi, 1990; Callamard, 1995).

The reality and scope of mediation and resistance should neither be denied nor romanticised. To insist on the political nature of refugee women's vulnerability, on the fact that they are victimised rather than victims (Moussa, 1991) is also to acknowledge that, within the context and setting of a 'controlling institution' (Hitchcox, 1990) which offers little in terms of protection, the 'weapons of the weak' may be quite ruthless in their effects against the weakest members of a given community.

Sexual violence and persecution

One of the most common, yet little researched, forms of suffering imposed on refugee women is violence. Empirical evidence on the violence suffered by refugee women is sketchy, at best, save for the research conducted in Kenya, South-East Asia, and an increasing number of life stories and testimonies. But the (incomplete) picture drawn by these works is harrowing, and the certainty that what is known by outsiders is just the tip of an iceberg of violence makes this picture an even greater concern. In a recent ground-breaking, psycho-social exploration of trauma among 40 refugee women, former political activists in their respective countries of origin, Inger Ager (1994) emphasises the role of sexuality in political persecution. Similarly, the painful picture drawn by refugees, relief workers or researchers centres on the role of sexuality in the oppression of refugee women, in particular, and the functioning of refugee structures in general. For sexual violence does not end with the war, the flight and the attacks at sea, but becomes entangled within the making and functioning of the refugee camp.

Sexual violence within the camp must also be understood in relation to the sexual and political power structures within the societies of origin and countries of asylum. A large number of Somali refugee women who experienced rape in Kenyan camps had fled either similar experiences, or fear of them, in war-torn Somalia (African Rights, 1993; Africa Watch Women's Right Project, 1993). Testimonies also showed that sexual violence perpetrated against them within the confines of the camp, or on the outskirts, by 'bandits', was often linked to clan politics and clan membership. At best, the Kenyan police ignored their plight and request for protection; at worst, they were involved themselves in the criminal acts; in both cases, they were active participants in the *politics of rape*. The role of officials from the country of asylum was especially blatant in Djibouti where Ethiopian and Eritrean refugee women have been raped with a frightening frequency and impunity by border guards, policemen or soldiers (Nyakabwa and Lavoie, 1995; Moussa, 1991; Aitchinson, 1984). In many situations, however, rape and sexual violence remain widely unreported. Even in the case of the refugee camps in Goma, Zaire, that had attracted international attention because of the constant climate of insecurity, killings and presence of perpetrators of the 1994 genocide in Rwanda, attempts to look into allegations of rape were unsuccessful and met with resistance (Halvorsten, 1995).

The role of sexuality and sexual violence within refugee camps is further demonstrated by the prevalence of prostitution, sexual favours and domestic violence, all of which are common characteristics of the functioning of the institutions. Anecdotal evidence underlines the prevalence of these forms of violence amongst Mozambican refugee women in Malawi (Lawyers Committee for Human Rights, 1995), Ethiopians in Sudan (Rogge, 1989), Sudanese internally displaced women (Demeke, 1990), refugee women in Thailand (Working with refugee women, 1989). All studies, and indeed the 1991 and 1994 UNHCR guidelines, argue that the institutionalisation of prostitution and sexual favours within a camp emerges and develops as a result of the shortcomings and inadequacies of relief programmes, including the lack of physical protection afforded to women, which exclude women from formal economic and political structures of the camp (Nyakabwa and Lavoie, 1995, p. 28).

With the exception of the few examples cited above, such abuses remain unreported and unnoticed, or, even worse, are considered by some relief staff as regrettable, yet 'essentially inevitable incidents in refugee life', according to a 1993 in-house evaluation of UNHCR's policy on refugee women (cited in Berthiaume, 1995, p. 12).

At a policy level, the approach embraced by the UNHCR and other relief organisations (UNHCR, 1991, 1994; Working with refugee women, 1989) has been to tackle those factors and conditions that foster gender-based vulnerability, such as the physical planning of camps, the design and implementation of food relief, health assistance, etc. Experience indeed shows that women being forced to walk long distances, along dark or isolated paths, to collect food, water and fuel, the lack of adequate lighting at night and lockable sleeping and washing areas are all factors which erode the security of women. In the Ivory Coast, women refugees were attacked when they left the camp because they could not bring themselves to use camp latrines that were next to those for men (Berthiaume, 1995). In the worst-case scenarios presented by Somali camps in Kenya, the UNHCR put into place the Women Victims of Violence project which provides for counselling, medical treatment and relocation of the victims (Berthiaume, 1995; Nyakabwa and Lavoie, 1995). The Canadian Council for Refugees and the UNHCR have also implemented the Women at Risk Refugee Sponsorship project to assist into the resettlement of women refugees at risk identified by the UNHCR. All these attempts appear to have had some limited successes (Berthiaume, 1995; Marshall, 1995) but, as argued below, the links between sexual violence and women's rights remain to be established at both a conceptual and policy level.

As mentioned in the introduction, the invisibility of gender and sexual violence characterises the codification and intervention throughout refugee experiences, including the process of determination of refugee status. A number of legal scholars, along with the UNHCR, has highlighted the gender biases of the refugee definition and/or of its interpretation by immigration officials. Some (Castel, 1992; Indra, 1987; McKinnon, 1993) have called for the inclusion of gender within the attributes of persecution, implying a redrafting of the refugee convention of 1951. Indra (1987) calls for a redefinition of persecution to give credibility to women's 'private sphere' experiences:

> The key criteria for being a refugee are drawn primarily from the realm of public sphere activities dominated by men. With regard to private sphere activities where women's presence is more strongly felt, there is primarily silence – silence compounded by an unconscious calculus that assigns the critical quality 'political' to many public activities but few private ones. Thus state oppression of a religious minority is political, while gender oppression at home is not.
>
> (Indra, 1987, p. 3)

Others scholars and policy makers (UNHCR, 1991; Greatbatch, 1989; Spijkerboer, 1994; Macklin, 1995) have called for a broader interpretation of the definition of persecution as per the refugee convention, especially underlining the gendered nature of both the 'social groups' and 'political opinions' elements of the 1951 definition. Underlying this approach is the view that the problem lies first and foremost in the interpretation by policy makers and legislative bodies of the convention, rather than within the legal norms themselves.

The debate over engendering the refugee definition is not purely an academic one: gender-specific guidelines have been adopted by the Canadian Immigration and Refugee Board, the US, Australia and New Zealand. The 1991 UNHCR guidelines put forward an interpretation of the refugee convention that suggests that sexual violence, persecution or severe discrimination on the basis of gender, and failure of state protection may constitute a basis for granting refugee status to women. The Beijing Platform for Action (paragraph 137) recognises that 80 per cent of the world's refugees and displaced people, including the internally displaced, are women and children, and calls for particular attention to be paid to sexual violence against such women. It especially refers to 'sexual violence or other gender-related persecution' as constituting a well-founded fear of persecution under the UN Refugee Convention and its 1967 Protocol. Further, a number of ground-breaking cases in the US, Canada and Europe have demonstrated the possibilities of providing refugee status to women fleeing persecution characterised by both their gender-specificity (such as domestic violence, female genital mutilation, or failure to conform to certain discriminatory social norms) and the lack of state protection.

Yet, one cannot but be struck by two dichotomies. The first contrasts legal discourse and debate in the West over the issue with the practice: many refugee women's claims, be they gender-specific or not, are never granted. The UK, especially, has a dismal record in the area (*Marie Claire*, Febuary 1997). Most European states do not even feel obliged to provide gender-desegregated data on asylum claims, a state of affairs demonstrating deeply entrenched gender-insensitivity and/or sexism among national immigration bureaucracies. One can only wonder how resettlement policies, under these conditions, successfully target the refugee populations.

The second dichotomy contrasts the vibrancy of the debate at national and international level with its quasi disappearance as far as the millions of refugee women in camps are concerned. The gendered approach to human rights and the refugee definition has yet to cross the gates (real or invisible) of the refugee camp. The protection of refugee women who do reach the refugee determination process in Ottawa, New York or Paris is thought of, debated and argued in court as a women's rights question, whereas protection of refugee women within the compound of the camps is a matter of good physical planning, well-thought-out assistance programmes and the maintenance of security.

As well demonstrated by Spijkerboer (1993), international human rights, humanitarian and refugee law are unanimous in describing rape as persecution. In all the cases surveyed above, the state of asylum and/or the UNHCR have failed to protect the refugee women from such persecution. The responsibility of the state is especially blatant when its agents (be they policemen, border guards or soldiers) engage, *in total impunity*, in acts of violence against refugee women. Such a responsibility is no less acute when perpetrators are private individuals, but the state is unwilling to prosecute them and fails to offer protection and remedies to the victims. Furthermore, a case may also be made against the UNHCR, on the basis of its failure to offer non-discriminatory or equal protection for refugee women and ensure their right to physical safety within the camp.

Do these claims have a ground in persecution? A large number of scholars, including this writer, will argue that sexual violence is a form of power and control over women. When organised or condoned by the authorities, or, indeed, when these authorities turn a blind eye to incidents of rape, such events should be considered as part of the political structures and, as such, persecution on account of political opinion. But even if one were to take Hathaway's approach (1991) that the harm (or threat of harm) a claimant faces must be linked to her socio-political situation and resultant marginalisation, evidence does give ground for claims on the basis of membership of a 'social group'. Four main arguments may be developed to demonstrate the validity of such claims.

First, the harm tends to be gender specific: refugee women and girls, rather than men, are victims of rape in camps, and, as noted above, rape, or the threat of rape, may constitute persecution (Spijkerboer, 1993).

Second, the victims tend to be the members of social groups which may be gender based or otherwise. Existing evidence indicates that many rape victims are, often enough, without the protection of male relatives (UNHCR, 1991), or are targeted because of their age and the specific domestic activities (such as fetching firewood outside the camp) that are traditionally attributed to this age group (Nowrojee, 1996) or because they belong to a particular clan.

Third, as demonstrated above, the situation of refugee women in camp is characterised by severe gender discrimination, in violation of the general principle of non-discrimination which governs the allocation of all legal rights, including those set by the Refugee Convention. As a matter of fact, the United Nations' Charter, the 1948 Universal Declaration of Human Rights, the International Covenant on Economic, Social and Cultural Rights and the International Covenant on Civil and Political Rights are expressly stated to be of universal application, and include prohibitions of discrimination on the basis of sex.

Fourth, the huge majority of refugee women has not been able to access effective protection, save for the few who have managed to get resettled through such programmes as the Women at Risk Sponsorship. To this writer's knowledge, the authorities of the state of asylum (be it Kenya, Djibouti or Malawi) have consistently failed to prosecute perpetrators of rape, including policemen, soldiers, refugee men or 'outsiders'. Furthermore, the UNHCR itself appears reluctant to bring up complaints of refugee women before the relevant authorities, as the case of Somali women in Kenya underlines (Lawyers Committee for Human Rights, 1995, p. 173; Nowrojee, 1996). It can be contended that, although the writers of the 1991 and 1994 UNHCR Guidelines for refugee women have clearly understood the political nature of refugee women's victimisation, the UNHCR as an institution has been, so far, unable either seriously to challenge the state of asylum (be it Djibouti, Kenya or Sudan) and the donor countries or to tackle the political structures within the camp which condone discrimination against refugee women and abuses of their rights.

Conclusion

There is little doubt that many refugee women's experiences in refugee camps amount to persecution according to the accepted definition. Clearly, the existing conventions and agreements, which regulate the definition of refugees and the ensuing obligations of the international community and the state of asylum are neither sufficient to ensure the protection of refugee women nor, in any case, being enforced by any of the parties to the refugee crisis, be they the donor countries, the country of asylum, some refugees themselves, or the UNHCR. Furthermore, the achievements that have been made on this front, including the aforementioned guidelines and a number of specific gender-specific policies and projects for refugee women have suffered major intertwined setbacks in recent years. Some have taken the form of broader policies or doctrines, such as the artefact of the 'Safe Zone', the Internal Flight 'Alternative' or, more recently, 'voluntary' repatriation following the shelling of refugee camps or the presence of armed forces. Other setbacks, however, not so recent (Zolberg, Suhrke and Aguayo, 1989) have included the militarisation or criminalisation of refugee camps: Goma, as described by outsiders and refugee themselves, appears to bear many more resemblances with Hobbes's description of the state of nature (1985) than with a UNHCR-run camp for displaced persons. But if Hobbes, writing in the seventeenth century, could see in the all-powerful and frightening figure of the Leviathan the solution to the horrors generated by the state of nature, one would expect from the actors involved in the refugee crisis at the end of the twentieth century a different approach to solving problems in refugee camps. Recent experiences with militarised camps and a long-lasting refugee presence have been based upon, or resulted in, a rather reductionist and short-term understanding of 'security'. They have also sharply altered the meaning and scope of refugee protection: refugee women were, in the past, denied protection as women; they are now denied protection as women and as refugees. On the basis of existing internationally accepted standards and principles, mass-expulsion at the barrel of a gun constitutes insecurity. And so are lack of food and sexual violence. In fact, all are also human rights concerns. Notwithstanding the fact that, together with children, women constitute the vast majority of the displaced population, they are also the ones whose rights and protection are most likely to be undermined by a generic, ungendered and ultimately militarised approach to security, refugee protection and assistance.

Bibliography

Africa Watch Women's Right Project (October 1993) *Seeking Refuge, Finding Terror*, 5, 13, New York: Human Rights Watch.

African Rights (September 1993) *The Nightmare Continues*, London: African Rights.

Ager, A., W. Ager and L. Long (1995) 'The Differential Experience of Mozambican Refugee Women and Men', *Journal of Refugee Studies*, 8, 3.

Ager, I. (1994) *The Blue Room*, London: Zed Books.

Aitchinson, R. (1984) 'Reluctant Witnesses: the Sexual Abuse of Refugee Women in Djibouti', *Cultural Survival Quarterly*, 8, 2, 26–7.

Amnesty International (May 1995) *Women in Afghanistan: a Human Rights Catastrophe*, ASA 11/03/95.
Beneria, L. (1979) 'Reproduction, Production and the Sexual Division of Labour', *Cambridge Journal of Economics*, 3, 203–25.
Bennett, O., J. Bexley and K. Warnock (1995), *Arms to Fight, Arms to Protect*, London: Panos Publications.
Berthiaume, C. (1995) 'Do we really care?', *Refugees*, 100, 10–13.
Boserup, E. (1970) *Women's Role in Economic Development*, London: George Allen and Unwin.
Callamard, A. (1993) 'African Refugee Women and Changing International Priorities', *Refuge*, 12, 8, 18–22.
Callamard, A. (1994) 'Refugees and Local Hosts: a Study of the Trading Interactions between Mozambican Refugees and Malawian Villagers in the District of Mwanza', *Journal of Refugee Studies*, 7, 1, 39–62.
Callamard, A. (1995), 'Populations under Fire, Populations under Stress', Ph.D. dissertation, New York: New School for Social Research.
Callamard, A. (1996) 'Flour Is Power', in W. Giles, H. Moussa and P. Van Esterik, (eds), *Development and Diaspora: Gender and the Refugee Experience*, Dundas, ONT: Artemis Enterprise, 176–98.
Castel, J. (1992) 'Rape, Sexual Assault and the Meaning of Persecution', *International Journal of Refugee Law*, 4, 39–56.
Christensen, H. (1983) 'Survival Strategies for and by Camp Refugees in Somalia', *Horn of Africa*, 5, 4, 3–20.
Daley, P. (1991) 'Gender, Displacement and Social Reproduction: Settling Burundi Refugees in Western Tanzania', *Journal of Refugee Studies*, 4, 3, 248–66.
Demeke, T. (1990) 'Refugee Women's Survival Strategies and Prostitution in Eastern Sudan', in *Refugee Participation Network* 7.
Forbes Martin, S., and E. Copeland (1988) *Making Ends Meet? Refugee Women and Income Generation*, Washington, DC: Refugee Policy Group.
Giles, W., H. Moussa and P. Van Esterik (1996) 'Introduction', in Giles et al. (eds), *Development and Diaspora: Gender and the Refugee Experience*, Dundas, ONT: Artemis Enterprise.
Giles, W., H. Moussa and P. Van Esterik (eds) (1996) *Development and Diaspora: Gender and the Refugee Experience*, Dundas, ONT: Artemis Enterprise.
Goodwin-Gill, G. (1983) *The Refugee in International Law*, Oxford: Clarendon Press.
Greatbatch, J. (1989) 'The Gender Difference: Feminist Critiques of Refugee Discourse', *International Journal of Refugee Law*, 1, 4, 518–27.
Halvorsten, K. (1995) *Refugee Camps in Zaire: Security and Humanitarian Issues*, report prepared for the Joint Evaluation of Emergency Assistance to Rwanda, Copenhagen.
Hansen, A. (1981) 'Refugee Dynamics: Angolans in Zambia, 1966 to 1972', *International Migration Review*, 15, 175–95.
Hathaway, J. (1988), 'International Refugee Law: Humanitarian Standard or Protectionist Ploy', in A. Nash (ed.), *Human Rights and the Protection of Refugees under International Law*, Montreal: Canadian Human Rights Foundation.
Hathaway, J. (1991) *The Law of Refugee Status*, Toronto: Butterworths.

Hernandez, G., and N. Garcia (1996) 'Mama Maquin Refugee Women: Participation and Organisation', in Giles et al. (eds) (1996), *Diaspora and Development*, Dundas: Artemis Publications.

Hitchcox, L. (1990) *Vietnamese Refugees in Southeast Asian Camps*, Hampshire: St Anthony's/Macmillan.

Hobbes, T. (1985) *Leviathan*, London: Penguin Books (first published in 1651).

Indra, D. (1987) 'Gender: a Key Dimension of the Refugee Experience', *Refuge*, 6, 3–4.

Johnson, T. (1981) 'Eritrean Refugees in Sudan', *Disasters*, 3, 4.

Jok Madut Jok (1995) 'Dinka Women and the Future of Dinka Society', *Refugee Participation Network*, 20, 31–2.

Kandiyoti, D. (1990) 'Women and Rural Development Policies', *Development and Change*, 21, 5–22.

Lawyers Committee for Human Rights (1995) *African Exodus: Refugee Crisis, Human Rights and the 1969 OAU Convention*, New York, July 1995.

Maalki, L. (1990) 'Context and Consciousness: Local Conditions for the Production of Historical and National Thought among Hutu Refugees in Tanzania', in Richard Fox (ed.), *Nationalist Ideologies and the Production of National Cultures*, Washington, DC: American Anthropological Association, 33–62.

Maalki, L. (1992) 'National Geographic: the Rooting of Peoples and the Territorialisation of National Identity among Scholars and Refugees', *Cultural Anthropology*, 7, 1, 24–44.

MacKinnon, C. (1993) 'Theory Is Not a Luxury', in D. Dallmeyer (ed.), *Reconceiving Reality: Women and International Law*, Washington, DC: The American Society of International Law, 83–92.

Macklin, A. (1995) 'Refugee Women and the Imperative of Categories', *Human Rights Quarterly*, 17, 214–77.

McLellan, J. (1996) 'Silent Screams and Hidden Pain', in Giles et al. (eds) (1996), *Development and Diaspora*, Dundas: Artemis Publications, 238–57.

Mandani, M. (1973) *From Citizen to Refugee*, London: Frances Pinter.

Marshall, R. (1995) 'Refugees, Feminine Plural', *Refugees*, 100, 3–9.

Mazur, R. (1991) 'Self-reliance and Future Orientation among Refugees in Southern Africa: Alternative Conceptions and Interests', paper presented at the 1991 Carter Lecture Series Conference, University of Florida, Gainesville.

Moussa, H. (1991) 'Women Refugees: Empowerment and Vulnerability', *Refuge*, 10, 4, April 1991, 12–14.

Moussa, Helene (1993) *Storm and Sanctuary: the Journey of Ethiopian and Eritrean Women Refugees*, Toronto: Artemis Enterprises.

NGO Working Group on Refugee Women (1989) *Working with Refugee Women: a Practical Guide*, Geneva.

Nowrojee, B. (1996) 'Sexual Violence against Refugee and Displaced Women', in C. Mulei, L. Dirasse and M. Garling (eds), *Legal Status of Refugee and Internally Displaced Women in Africa*, Nairobi: UNIFEM/AFWIC, 273–94.

Nyakabwa, K., and C. Lavoie (1995) 'Sexual Violence against Women Refugees in the Horn of Africa', *African Women*, 10, 26–31.

'Persecuted for being a woman' (1997) *Marie Claire*, February, 52–6.

Refugee Studies Programme (1989), *Food Provisioning amongst Mozambican Refugees in Malawi: a Study of Aid, Livelihood and Development*, report prepared for World Food Programme, Malawi.

Rizvi, G. (1990) 'The Afghan Refugees: Hostages in the Struggle for Power', *Journal for Refugee Studies*, 3, 3, 1990, 244–61.

Rogge, Jones (1989) *Too Many Too Long: Sudan's Twenty Year Refugee Dilemma*, Toronto: Rowman and Allanheld.

Schroeder, R., and M. Watts (1991) 'Struggling over Strategies, Fighting over Food: Adjusting to Food Commercialisation among Mandika Peasants', *Research in Rural Sociology and Development*, 5, 45–72.

Spijkerboer, T. (1994) *Women and Refugee Status*, The Hague: Emancipation Council.

Spring, A. (1979) 'Women and Men as Refugees: Differential Assimilation of Angolan Refugees in Zambia', *Disasters*, 3, 4, 423–8.

Stepputat, F. (1994) 'Deterritorialisation and Community in Refugee Studies: the Case of Maya Diaspora and Return Movement', paper presented at the 4th IRAP Conference, Refugee Studies Programme, Oxford, England.

Tuitt, P. (1996) *False Images: the Law's Construction of the Refugee*, London: Pluto Press.

UNHCR (1991) *Guidelines on the Protection of Refugee Women*, Geneva: UNCHR.

UNHCR (1994) *Prevention of and Response to Sexual Violence against Refugees*, Geneva: UNHCR.

Weaver, J. (1988) 'Searching for Survival: Urban Ethiopian Refugees in Sudan', *Journal of Developing Areas*, 22, 457–76.

Wood, G. (1985) 'The Politics of Development Policy Labelling', in G. Wood (ed.), *Labelling in Development Policy: Essays in Honour of Bernard Schaffer*, London: Sage Publication, 5–32.

Zetter, R. (1991) 'Labelling Refugees', *Journal of Refugee Studies*, 4, 1.

Zolberg, A., A. Suhrke and S. Aguayo (1989) *Escape from Violence*, New York: Oxford University Press.

Note

1. Dr Agnès Callamard is currently the research policy coordinator at the International Secretariat of Amnesty International. The views expressed in this article are her own and should not be attributed to Amnesty International.

   A more complete version of this chapter has been published in Alastair Ager, (ed.), *Refugees: Contemporary Perspectives on the Experience of Forced Migration*, Cassell Series Studies in Contemporary Social Issues, London: Cassell, 1998.

8
Refugees and Internally Displaced Persons: Africa's Liability for the Next Millennium

John O. Oucho

Introduction

At the turn of the twenty-first century Africa is ushering into the millennium the problem of forced migration, which remains a liability in the continent's development. From Algeria to Namibia, Sierra Leone to the Horn of Africa and the Comoro Islands, the number of refugees and internally displaced person (IDPs) has been mounting with no end in sight. In this seemingly endless process, some African states have remained producers (senders) and others recipients of refugees while at the same time toying with the ever expanding waves of IDPs, whose problem affects virtually all states in the region. While the very international nature of refugees has pitched its concern at the international level, including the involvement of the United Nations as well as international non-governmental organisations (NGOs), the national scale of internally displaced persons has localised concerns, with state intervention often partisan. Yet, IDPs and refugees constitute a continuum as most of the former graduate into the latter and as the two conditions interchange from time to time.

This chapter seeks to demonstrate that refugees and internally displaced persons – forced migration – will be Africa's liability well into this millennium unless durable solutions are found to contain the menace. The chapter consists of four sections: the definition of refugees and IDPs generally and in the context of African states; the analysis of the geography of refugees and IDPs; a brief examination of the main determinants and consequences of forced migration; and suggested policies and strategies which African states need to convert the liability to an asset. Selected examples, invoked without prejudice to any state, are provided to illustrate relevant cases and to contextualise the discussion.

Who the refugees and IDPs are: general and African perspectives

The two terms 'refugees' and 'internally displaced persons' have some commonality but are empirically different. It is important from the outset to define them generally and in the context of their usage and interpretation in Africa.

The definition of refugee is based generally on two interrelated documents. First, the 1951 Convention adopted by the United Nations Conference on the Status of Refugees and Stateless Persons held in Geneva in July 1951, which came into force on 22 April 1954. Second, the Protocol on the Status of Refugees adopted by the UN General Assembly on 16 December 1966, which came into force on 4 October 1967. Citing these two, Gallagher (1989, p. 580) defines a refugee as:

> [Any person who] owing to well-founded fear of being persecuted for reasons of race, religion, nationality, membership of particular social group or political opinion, is outside the country of his nationality and is unable to or, owing to such fear, is unwilling to avail himself of that country; or who, not having a nationality and being outside the country of his former habitual residence ... is unable or, owing to such fear, is unwilling to return to it.

This definition, coming in the wake of World War II, took cognisance of populations displaced by the ravages of the war, especially in the main war arenas such as European regions. It places emphasis on flight founded on fears attributed to some discriminatory treatment of victims as a result of specific attributes. It should be remembered, however, that at that time, Africa was still under colonial domination with a few African states embroiled in wars of independence.

Following the formation of the Organisation of African Unity (OAU) in 1963, it became imperative to review the UN-sponsored Refugee Convention and Protocol against the realities of Africa coming out of colonial rule and conscious of situations which had produced and were likely to continue producing refugees. Consequently, the OAU Convention Governing Specific Aspects of Refugee Problems in Africa was adopted by the Assembly of Heads of State and Government at its

Sixth Ordinary Session held in Addis Ababa on 16 September 1969. The OAU Convention of 1969 recognised as a refugee

> one who owing to external aggression, occupation, foreign domination or events seriously disturbing public order in either part or the whole country of origin or nationality, is compelled to leave his place of habitual residence in order to seek refuge in another place outside his country of origin or nationality.

Article II of the OAU Convention on asylum regulates the question of asylum and, in Article V, unequivocally stipulates that repatriation of refugees or asylum seekers must be a voluntary act. This definition broadened the scope of refugees and recognised the fact that refugees may be those fleeing their home or adopted countries as the case may be.

Nearly two decades later, the Cartagena Declaration on Refugees, adopted in November 1984, sought to promote the adoption of national laws and regulations that facilitate the application of the 1951 Convention and the 1967 Protocol. In Africa, the way refugees are handled depends on the relations between the sending and the receiving countries, on gains or losses the receiving countries expect to incur as a result of hosting refugees or on the impact of refugee inflows in the receiving countries. The point to underscore is that the term 'refugee' is restricted to those fleeing across recognised international borders, which in Africa are arbitrary, porous, unpoliced and unpoliceable.

IDPs, in contrast, are those forced to move but within the national territory. The United Nations High Commissioner for Refugees (UNHCR) defines IDPs in terms of those who have moved within their own country for entirely involuntary reasons (e.g. environmental and industrial disasters) or as a result of population distribution programmes employed by governments to counter security threats and to implement large-scale development projects (UNHCR, 1995, p. 41). This explains why the concept of 'environmental refugees' (El-Hinnawi, 1989) has been applied in cases of Ethiopians, Eritreans, Djiboutians and Somalis moving within their countries as a result of floods, drought or famine. Cohen (1996, p. 21) cites the United Nations (E/CN.4/1992/23,14 February 1992, para. 17) working definition, which considers as IDPs those

> persons who have been forced to flee their homes suddenly or unexpectedly in large numbers, as a result of armed conflict, internal

strife, systematic violations of human rights or natural or man-made disasters, and who are within the territory of their own country.

The stress is on 'homes' as IDPs flee to safer or supposedly safer havens. For Africa where armed conflict, diverse forms of internal strife and flagrant violations of human rights have been rampant, the expanding volume of IDPs has become the order of the day, the rule rather than the exception in many African states.

What then distinguishes refugees from IDPs?

Apart from the geographic scale (refugees crossing international borders and IDPs remaining in the national territories), other considerations distinguish the two. Ayiemba and Oucho (1995, p. 4) argue that 'refugee movement is mostly volatile and unpredictable particularly movements of political and economic causes while [movement] of internally displaced is temporary and oscillatory'. However, it has been observed that internal displacement is also volatile and unpredictable and is triggered by political and economic factors, and that refugee movements, too, are temporary and oscillatory. Cohen (1996, p. 23) makes an important distinction in reference to the treatment of refugees and IDPs; she observes that 'refugees have an international agency and legal structure to turn to for protection and assistance [while] ... internally displaced have nothing comparable'. To avoid the distinction which is by no means obvious in African states, it can be useful to refer to both refugees and IDPs as displaced persons (DPs) because their movements are triggered by certain forces and never voluntary. There are instances where some population has remained within national territory (as IDPs) as part of the same group moves to neighbouring countries (as refugees).

The geography of Africa's displaced persons

Much of the literature on Africa's DPs has illuminated the pattern of refugees better than that of IDPs. This is attributed to handier data on refugees than on IDPs, about whom much of the information is concealed, especially because many African states are not open regarding their intervention in the affairs of IDPs. Recently, however, UNHCR, the US Committee on Refugees, the Human Rights Watch/Africa, the Brookings Institution and other organisations have been publishing useful data on both refugees and IDPs, from which instructive perspectives have been gleaned.

Refugees

The tide of refugees in Africa has kept rising and the geographic spread has expanded over the years. In 1990, Sub-Saharan Africa (SSA), which comprises the overwhelming majority of African states, had about half of the world's refugees. Table 8.1 provides an insight, which may be summarised as follows: there were a total of 5.3 million refugees in SSA, of whom about 3 million were in four countries only – Malawi, Ethiopia, Sudan and Somalia. Some 11 per cent of Djibouti's population, 10 per cent of Malawi's, 9 per cent of Swaziland's, 6 per cent of Somalia's and 5 per cent of Tanzania's population consisted of refugees. That was before the deluge of Somali refugees in Kenya in 1991, a time when Malawi hosted mainly Mozambicans and when refugees in Zambia had returned to Zimbabwe and some were returning to Namibia. But in some countries, those returns were only temporary as the number of refugees soared from the same sources in subsequent years.

Some sub-regions generated more refugees than others. In Middle (Central) Africa, the number of refugees increased from 490,000 in 1988 to 521,900 in 1990. The 1993–94 genocide in the Great Lakes region resulted in the slaughter of over 500,000 ethnic Tutsi by the rival Hutus as survivors fled to neighbouring Zaire (now Democratic Republic of Congo), Burundi and Tanzania. In West Africa, as the Liberian crisis exacerbated, there were 800,00 (730,000 alone being Liberians) refugees or 16 per cent of the SSA refugee stock in 1990 (Ayiemba and Oucho, 1995, p. 9). At that point, the political crisis had not started, and when it did later in the mid-nineties, it lingered on into July 1997 when the country held post-civil war general elections. Nor had the crisis in Sierra Leone begun, persisting until July 1999 when the government and guerrillas reached a peace accord, which may or may not hold.

By 1995, Africa accounted for 6.7 million (or 46 per cent) of the world's total 14.5 million refugees and 3.1 million of the world's 4 million returnees (UNHCR, 1995, p. 247). Table 8.2 provides such detail as readily explains the geographical spread of Africa's refugees in 1995.

The major host countries for (500,000 or more) refugees were Zaire (now Democratic Republic of Congo) receiving from the Great Lakes neighbours, Angola, Sudan and Uganda; Tanzania, receiving from the two Great Lakes region countries, Mozambique, Somalia and Zaire (DRC); Sudan whose refugees came from all the contiguous states; and Guinea which hosted Liberians and Sierra Leoneans. Countries

Table 8.1: Refugee population in major SSA countries, 1990

Asylum country	*Estimated population in million(1994)*	*Population of refugees in 1990*	*Percent of total refugees*	*Percent of refugees over population*
Malawi	9.5	909,000	17.1	9.6
Ethiopia	55.2	783,000	14.7	1.4
Sudan	28.6	660,000	12.4	2.3
Somalia	9.8	600,000	11.3	6.1
Kenya	27.0	384,910	7.2	1.4
Zaire	42.5	344,900	6.5	0.8
Burundi	6.0	267,500	5.0	0.9
Tanzania	29.8	266,500	5.0	4.5
South Africa	41.2	201,000	3.8	0.5
Zimbabwe	11.2	186,000	3.5	1.7
Uganda	19.8	170,500	3.2	0.9
Namibia	1.6	25,000	0.5	1.6
Zambia	9.1	135,950	2.5	1.5
Angola	11.2	91,150	1.7	0.8
Swaziland	0.8	71,700	1.4	9.0
Senegal	8.2	56,000	1.1	0.7
Cote d'Ivore	13.9	55,800	1.0	0.4
Djibouti	0.6	67,400	1.3	11.2
Mauritania	1.1	22,000	0.4	2.0
Rwanda	7.7	21,000	0.4	0.3
Mozambique	15.8	700	0.0	0.0
Lesotho	1.9	1,000	0.0	0.1
Total		5,321,010		

Source: E. H. O. Ayiemba and J. O. Oucho (1995), table 1, p. 10.
By 1995, Africa accounted for 6.7 million (or 46 per cent) of the world's total of 14.5 million refugees and 3.1 million of the world's 4 million returnees (UNHCR, 1995, p. 247). Table 8.2 provides such detail as readily explains the geographical spread of Africa's refugees in 1995.

receiving 200,000–400,000 refugees included Côte d'Ivoire, virtually all refugees coming from Liberia; Ethiopia which hosted refugees from all its neighbours except Eritrea; Burundi, receiving from its two politically unstable neighbours of Rwanda and Zaire (DRC); Kenya which suddenly became an important country hosting a large number of Somalis, some Rwandans and those from all its neighbours except Tanzania; and Algeria, with refugees from not only its neighbours but also Palestinians. The spatial perspective of Africa's refugees suggests that no state, sending and receiving alike, can afford to ignore the problem of refugees, especially from the socio-cultural standpoint, given the extent to which international boundaries have divided one

Table 8.2: Refugee population in Africa by country/territory of asylum and origin, 1995

Country/territory of asylum	*Principal places of origin*	*Number '000*	*Total '000*
Algeria	Mali	28.0	
	Niger	22.4	
	Palestine	4.0	
	Western Sahara	165.0	
			219.1
Angola	Zaire	10.7	
			10.7
Benin	Togo	70.0	
			70.4
Burkina Faso	Mali	49.5	
			50.0
Burundi	Rwanda	278.1	
	Zaire	21.9	
			300.3
Cameroon	Chad	42.9	
			44.0
Central African Republic	Chad	21.5	
	Sudan	25.9	
			47.8
Congo	Angola	12.7	
	Chad	2.1	
			15.5
Côte d'Ivoire	Liberia	359.4	
			360.1
Djibouti	Ethiopia	12.8	
	Somalia	20.4	
			33.4
Egypt	Somalia	6.1	
			7.2
Ethiopia	Djibouti	18.0	
	Kenya	8.2	
	Somalia	269.7	
	Sudan	51.8	
			348.1
Gambia	Senegal	2.0	
			2.2
Ghana	Liberia	15.9	
	Togo	97.9	
			113.7
Guinea	Liberia	398.3	
	Sierra Leone	154.9	
			553.2
Guinea–Bissau	Senegal	23.6	
			23.9

Table 8.2: Refugee population in Africa by country/territory of asylum and origin, 1995 *con't*

Country/territory of asylum	*Principal places of origin*	*Number '000*	*Total '000*
Kenya	Ethiopia	10.5	
	Rwanda	2.0	
	Somalia	206.3	
	Sudan	27.2	
	Uganda	2.9	
			252.4
Liberia	Sierra Leone	120.0	
			130.0
Libyan Arab Jamehiriya			2.0
Malawi	Mozambique	88.9	
			90.2
Mali	Mauritania	15.0	
			15.8
Mauritania	Mali	82.2	
			82.2
Namibia	Angola	1.1	
			1.1
Niger	Chad	2.0	
	Mali	13.0	
			15.1
Nigeria	Chad	1.3	
	Liberia	4.1	
			6.0
Rwanda	Burundi	6.0	
			6.0
Senegal	Guinea–Bissau	5.0	
	Mauritania	67.8	
			73.0
Sierra Leone	Liberia	15.9	
			15.9
South Africa	Mozambique	90.0	
			91.9
Sudan	Chad	141.4	
	Eritrea	419.3	
	Ethiopia	160.6	
	Uganda	3.8	
	Zaire	1.8	
			727.2
Tanzania	Burundi	202.7	
	Mozambique	34.7	
	Rwanda	626.2	
	Somalia	3.0	
	Zaire	15.8	
			883.3

Table 8.2: Refugee population in Africa by country/territory of asylum and origin, 1995 *con't*

Country/territory of asylum	*Principal places of origin*	*Number '000*	*Total '000*
Togo	Giana	12.2	
			12.4
Uganda	Rwanda	97.0	
	Somalia	2.3	
	Sudan	180.0	
	Zaire	4.5	
			286.5
Zaire	Angola	160.9	
	Burundi	180.1	
	Rwanda	1,252.8	
	Sudan	111.9	
	Uganda	18.6	
			1,724.4
Zambia	Angola	103.7	
	Mozambique	19.3	
	Zaire	13.5	
			141.1
Zimbabwe	Mozambique	1.4	
			2.2
Other countries			3.7
Regional total			6,752.2

Note: UNHCR states that the figures do not add up due to rounding and because refugee populations less than 1,000 are not shown.
Source: UNHCR (1995), table 3, pp. 248–9.

and the same ethnic groups. That small countries such as Rwanda and Burundi produced 2.2 million refugees (2 million and 0.2 million respectively) by March 1995 (Minear and Kent, 1998, p. 62), shows the depth of the problem in the two countries which represent the most ghastly genocide in Africa in the twentieth century. For countries such as Rwanda, Burundi, Democratic Republic of Congo, Sudan, Ethiopia, Eritrea, Angola and Sierra Leone, the scenario has been the cycle of refugees – repatriation – refugees, placing these countries in strained relationships with their neighbours.

Internally displaced persons

Virtually all African states have been engulfed in the problem of IDPs at one time or another. Of the 5.4 million IDPs worldwide in 1995, Africa had a share of 2 million (UNHCR, 1995, p. 247) or 37 percent.

Table 8.3: Estimated internally displaced persons in selected African countries 1995–96

Country	*Number of IDPs by Year*	
	1995	*1996*
Sudan	4,000,000	4,000,000
Angola	1,500,000	1,200,000
Liberia	1,000,000	1,000,000
Sierra Leone	1,000,000	800,000
Mozambique	500,000	n.a.
Rwanda	500,000	n.a.
South Africa	500,000	
Burundi	300,000	400,000
Somalia	300,000	250,000
Zaire[1]	225,000	400,000
Kenya	210,000	100,000
Ghana	150,000	20,000
Mali	10,000	
Algeria	n.a.	10,000
Nigeria	n.a.	30,000
Uganda	n.a.	70,000
Djibouti	–	25,000

Note: [1]Democratic Republic of Congo since May 1997 n.a. – not applicable – no data available.
Source: R. Cohen and F. M. Deng (1998), p. 33, table 2–2, drawn from US Committee for Refugees, *World Refugee Survey, 1996 and 1997.*

Indeed, by 31 December 1995 seven African countries ranked among the world nations with exceptionally large numbers of IDPs. These were Sudan (4 million), Angola (1.5 million), Liberia and Sierra Leone (1 million apiece), Mozambique, Rwanda and South Africa (0.5 million apiece) (US Committee for Refugees, 1996, p. 6). Table 8.3 illustrates the geography of IDPs in Africa in the two years 1995–96.

The number of countries remained virtually the same in the two years, with the number of IDPs either stabilising or decreasing (but increasing in DRC and Burundi) in individual countries. Political events in Algeria, Nigeria, Uganda and Djibouti produced IDPs in 1996. At the time of writing this paper, the situation has not improved in most countries and it is not surprising that the Organisation of African Unity (OUA) has recently been involved in in-country conflicts, which have generated an increasing number of IDPs.

The two previous sub-sections have revealed one important fact: that African states have entered this millennium with one of the greatest human liabilities, namely, displaced persons (DPs) within and outside their national territories. Added to the IDPs are other liabilities such as the debt crisis, non-performing economies, corruption in public high places and the murky waters of multi-party democratisation.

Some sub-regional perspectives of IDPs

A recent global survey of IDP (Hampton, 1998) devotes attention to some African states where the problem has wrought considerable havoc. In West Africa, ethnic conflicts in northern Ghana caused deaths and displaced 150,000 people in mid-March 1995 (Beattie, 1998a, p. 42); by March 1998 it was estimated that some 750,000 people were IDPs in Liberia as a result of civil war (Nowrojee, 1998a. p. 42); ethnic clashes between the marginalised Tuaregs and the central government erupted in mid-1990 in Mali displacing 15,000–20,000 IDPs and as many refugees (Vohra, 1998, p. 46–7); the clashes between Negro-Mauritanians and Moorish Mauritanians resulted in the expulsion of 75,000 of the former from Mauritania, and persistent drought produced many IDPs (Beattie, 1998b, p. 48); in Nigeria, conflicts in the oil-producing area of the Niger Delta over resources, ethno-religious conflicts in the north and conflicts linked to democratisation generated 1.3 million IDPs of whom only 27,000 received formal assistance (Ibeanu, 1998, p. 51); the Casamance area in Southern Senegal had 40,000 IDPs by 1993 (Beattie, 1998c; p. 53) and Sierra Leone's crisis (Beattie, 1998d, p. 53–5) caused so many deaths and IDPs that recovery after the peace accord of July 1999 may prove extremely difficult.

The Great Lakes/East Africa region took centre stage in Africa's IDPs in the nineties. The crisis in Burundi resulted in 10 per cent of the population being IDPs in the mid-nineties (Mullen, 1998); in the Democratic Republic of Congo it was estimated that there were about 486,000 IDPs between November 1996 and March 1998 alone (Sangara, 1998, p. 63); and Rwanda's genocide of April–July 1994 resulted in the slaughter of 500,000–1 million Tutsis and some Hutus (Kleine-Ahlbrandt, 1998), occasioning the establishment of the United Nations tribunal in Arush-Tanzania to try the principal perpetrators of genocide.

Kenya was engulfed in serious ethnic conflict as multi-party democracy returned to it in 1991, displacing over 300,000 in the Rift Valley Province in 1991–93 (Human Rights Watch/Africa Watch, 1993) and more than 120,000 IDPs in Coast province by the 1997 general elections (Nowrojee, 1998b, p. 64); the first one was a heartless episode that has attracted more critical analysis in some works (Human Rights Watch/Africa Watch 1993; Human Rights Watch, 1997; Oucho, l996a).

Uganda, a country which never witnessed peace in 1971–86, is still riddled with guerrilla warriors in different parts of the country, in March 1998 reporting about 400,000 IDPs (Mugumya and Mooney, 1998, p. 75).

The Horn of Africa has remained the factory of IDPs who easily graduate into refugees and vice-versa. Apart from persistent drought, the development-induced features that displaced population in 1994 (Hansen and Davidheiser, 1998, p. 79) and the Eritrean-Ethiopian war in 1998–99 generated a large number of IDPs and refugees. The same fate faced Ethiopia, whose protracted war from the seventies to 1991, persistent drought, famine and floods have displaced many people (Redding and Hansen, 1998a). Somalia's ungovernability since 1991 has generated many IDPs whom several NGOs have tried in vain to provide assistance to (Redding and Hansen 1998b). In Sudan the 30–40-year-old civil conflict has crippled any development and ruined human resource development, including health and education of children, thereby producing a lost generation of Southern Sudanese. It is estimated that more than one million people have been killed and 650,000 (80 per cent of the area's population) have fled their homes in southern Sudan (Fain, Redding and Swahn, 1998, p. 85). Indeed, the Horn of Africa will remain a liability for a long time in the new millennium.

From the foregoing, it is evident that refugees and IDPs account for a substantial proportion of Africa's population, which implies that the past and current human wastage has already dented the sub-region's demographic structure and accentuated the imbalance in population development. It will take several decades for African countries to arrest the liability of human wastage and embark on human resource development.

Determinants and consequences of population displacement

This section provides highlights of determinants and consequences of population displacement in Africa. Conscious of authoritative works on the subject by United Nations agencies (UNHCR in particular), NGOs and individual researchers, I have attempted to summarise the main causes and determinants in generic categories that are by no means exhaustive.

Determinants

Although refugees and IDPs are often so distinguished for purposes of focusing on each of them, their movements or indeed generation as displaced persons (DPs), are caused by very similar factors. Generically, these range from political to economic and socio-cultural factors and include environmental forces, government intervention and so on. The World Council of Churches (1996) identified seven factors, which I analyse by citing relevant examples in Africa, but which are by no means the only factors.

1. Unsatisfied protection needs of refugees and IDPs
   There are circumstances when DPs fleeing persecution and warfare are treated as genuine refugees and circumstances where those fleeing environmental devastation or economic collapse ('economic refugees') are denied any protection whatsoever. The former may become refugees as the latter become IDPs, the risks of staying in a country notwithstanding. Southern Sudan provides a good case where those fleeing to countries friendly with Sudan are admitted as refugees and those suspected as posing threats to the supposed receiving countries are denied refugee status. Somalis fleeing to Kenya and Ethiopia have been treated thus.
2. Political reasons
   In several African states, the revolutionary struggles, changes of regimes, adoption of multi-party democratisation at the turn of the nineties and disputes over election results, have left in their trail population displacements. Examples which easily come to mind include several and repeated coups d'etat in most West African countries since the mid-sixties, the race towards or the aftermath of multi-party elections in Nigeria (1993), Kenya (1992 and 1997), South Africa (1992–94), protracted war in Mozambique before the peace accord held and in Angola since the mid-seventies, the war in the DRC a year after the overthrow of Mobutu Sesse Seko in May 1997, and civil wars in Liberia and Sierra Leone. Also, partisan state intervention in national, political, economic, religious and ethnic strife has been a powerful force in displacing populations whose complaints remain unresolved.
3. Economic crises
   Apart from the euphoria of independence, which held in the first decade in many African countries, sustaining impressive economic performance then, poor economic performance has been the fashion of these countries. It is not surprising that the 1980s can be cited as Africa's 'lost decade', as most national governments adopted structural adjustment programmes (SAPs). Globalisation romanticised the 'free market economic model' and eliminated restrictions

on cross-border free movement of capital, goods, resources, technology (but not labour), but its artefacts such as SAP and the attendant economic reforms caused increased unemployment or underemployment, stagnation or decrease in earnings for those employed, disappearing job security, increasing poverty, reductions in access to health care, education, public transportation, housing, elimination of public benefits or 'safety nets' for the unemployed causing marginalisation and exclusion (World Council of Churches, 1996, pp. 25–6). The results of these economic experiments inflicted devastating effects on national economies, incapacitating the economies from catering well to the citizenry. Governments adopted unpopular policies which generated migrants fleeing to other countries and displaced populations from a country's poorer to better endowed areas. Indeed, poor economic performance is certainly the one liability which African countries will carry along well into this new millennium.

4. Environmental factors
   There have been numerous instances of population displacement owing to both natural disasters and human-induced catastrophes. The term 'environmental refugees' – those displaced by environmental catastrophes such as drought or floods (El-Hinnawi, 1985) – has gained importance in Africa as elsewhere. It is estimated that the long droughts of the 1980s affected 30–5 million people in Sub-Saharan Africa (El-Hinnawi, 1989; Tolba, 1992), most of whom were displaced. Other environmental problems (such as soil erosion and land degradation), armed conflicts and recurrent famine combine with demographic variables (notably rapid population growth and the demands it generates) and the competition, including conflict, over land, between nomads and agriculturists. Thus, there is a variety of 'environmental migrants' who consist of both refugees and IDPs.
5. Social tensions: ethnicity, religion and class
   Different social tensions, mainly ethnic, religious and class have gripped many African countries. Ethnic conflicts have been at the centre of internal displacements of population (Oucho, 1997) as well as refugee flows in African countries such as Central African Republic under Jean-Bedel Bokassa, Uganda during Idi Amin's eight years (1971–79) of terror, the Great Lakes region countries of Rwanda and Burundi, Sierra Leone way back in 1967–89, resurging in the nineties, and Togo in 1991–92 (Oucho, 1996c, pp. 174–5). In the race towards multi-party democratic elections of the nineties,

ethnic clashes erupted in Kenya in 1991 and 1997 (Oucho, 1996a) and reached their peak in the Inkatha (Zulu)–ANC (Xhosa) clashes just before the April 1994 elections. One model based on Guyana, which comprises two sets of factors, 'predisposing factors' (multi-ethnic society, lack of cooperation, overarching values and internal communal beliefs of separate actions) and 'triggering/igniting factors' (colonial manipulation, introduction of mass democratic politics, rivalry over resource allocation and rivalry over imported political institutions adopted at independence), is instructive for analysing the role of ethnic conflict in population displacements on the African continent. In countries such as Algeria, Nigeria, Mauritania, Chad and Sudan, ethnic animosities combine with religious differences to trigger violence, which results in refugees and IDPs. Finally, in many African countries class struggle has become a persistent feature of the independence era as the rulers and the ruled, the haves and have-nots, exploiters and the exploited often disagree violently, resulting in displacement of the losers in the struggle.

6. The population factor

   Population size, growth and structure and dynamics (in particular migration) have important effects on forced population movements. There have been as many violent conflicts in densely populated as in sparsely populated areas of the continent. Rapid population growth has precipitated population pressure on land and other resources. In the case of land, population pressure has been partly responsible for conflicts in Rwanda and Burundi; invasion of land held by the pastoralist Maasai by Kikuyu agriculturists in Kenya's Rift Valley (Talbot, 1986), as of the Kalenjin, was a major cause of ethnic conflicts of the early nineties (Oucho, 1996a); Kenya's land settlement programme in the sixties and seventies (Oucho, 1996a) laid foundations for ethnic tensions cum displacements; Tanzania's 'villagisation' programme (Ujamaa) (Maro, 1990; McCall, 1985) displaced formerly settled people of these countries; and 'agricultural extensification' redistributed population from densely settled areas to deforested and marginal areas (Bilsborrow and Okoth-Ogendo, 1992) and to marginal areas redistributed population, pitting immigrants against natives. Where immigration in the colonial period and immigration in both colonial and post-colonial periods took place, as in Kenya's Rift Valley, voluntary migration heralded population displacement as a result of uneasy ethnic relations (Oucho, 1996b). It is regrettable that many African countries marched into the twenty-first century with demographic liability that promises to beset their efforts to reorganise themselves to face the challenges of the new millennium.

7. Denial of human rights and democracy
   The last two closing decades of the twentieth century have witnessed blatant violation of human rights and gross failure of democratisation, which has become a buzzword of the time as 'African socialism' was at independence. Publications of Human Rights Watch, the Brookings Institution, church organisations and other bodies concerned with the welfare of the civil society, are replete with empirical evidence of human rights violations and failed democratisation. These liabilities have caused untold suffering in many African countries, forcing populations to flee as refugees or IDPs. Examples which readily come to mind include South Africa during apartheid; Lesotho in a never-ending political quagmire; Nigeria where advocates of civilian rule and the Ogoni environmentalists in the oil-mining area have experienced untold suffering; Sierra Leone, which until recently was 'no man's land'; Kenya, where anti-democracy advocates sponsored ethnic clashes in 1991–94 and in 1997 to try and justify the failure of multi-party politics in a multi-ethnic society; Rwanda, where the genocide of 1994 rocked the foundations of peaceful coexistence between two traditional rival ethnic groups; and Democratic Republic of Congo, where the anti-Mobutu liberators have had to settle their score with the Kabila regime since August 1998.

Consequences

The consequences of population displacement, like the determinants, are diverse and inexhaustible. Generically, they are political, economic and social, but the classification is by no means exhaustive.

1. Political
   African states which have experienced population displacement generally tend to remain 'one state, many nationalities' (Olorunsola, 1972) rather than states par excellence. To amplify, they are states within which live nationalities or peoples whose first loyalty is to their ethnic groups and the second to the state or country. Somalia remains ungovernable nearly a decade after the overthrow of Said Barre's regime sparked off inter-clan conflicts, leading to hundreds of thousands of refugees and IDPs. Sudan, and more particularly the war-torn southern part, can never expect to be one nation in which

the northerners and southerners would live in harmony after the hostilities come to an end. The agreement reached at the OAU Summit in Algiers in July 1999 to the effect that the pan-African organisation will desist from recognising undemocratic regimes in the future sounds theoretically fascinating but in essence is rather hollow. It is a cowardly statement to contain a situation whose very existence is embedded in the member states' chequered past. As long as some regimes in African countries continue to violate human rights, democratic refugees and IDPs whom they produce will persist in aspiring for self-determination or any other appropriate redress of their hopeless situation. Another political consequence is enfranchisement of refugees in a host country in order to augment votes for the ruling parties in parliamentary and presidential elections, and disenfranchisement of refugees and IDPs in the strongholds of opposition parties which, relying on these disaffected groups, may wrench power from unpopular regimes. The opposite is also possible where opposition parties interfere with refugees from voting in their opponents. Finally, refugees and IDPs may infect their host communities with various forms of civil strife meant to destabilise or overthrow regimes; alternatively, the suffering of the DPs might discourage the host communities from engaging government in any strife for fear of victimisation.

2. Economic

   Refugees and IDPs are often placed in situations where they become destitute in every aspect of life. Generally refugees are entrapped in camps where whatever economic activities they might engage in benefits the host country at their experience. IDPs are plunged in a situation where they cannot practise their normal occupations, cannot farm and do not expect much assistance from the state, which is seldom innocent of their predicament. It is not surprising that countries where refugees and IDPs have persisted have experienced some economic downturn, including a drop in GDP and GNP following the collapse of sectors in which the displaced had made a contribution during normal times. Indeed, where conflicts have persisted, loss of state capacities has constrained development in contemporary Africa (Adekanye, 1998), a continent engulfed in an incessant economic crisis where refugees and IDPs have remained a liability within the crisis itself.

3. Social

   Displaced populations suffer from lack of access to social services, notably education, health, housing and entertainment. Families are separated and gender roles completely crippled; children never attend school, nor do they socialise in the normal way; and those who had previously been relying on their own skills, as employed or self-employed, suddenly live in a world in which that is no longer possible. In some circumstances, natives of the host country or community discriminate against refugees and IDPs, rendering them social misfits. In others the displaced live like sub-humans, being herded around like animals and watched over like criminals.

From liability to asset: the challenge for African states

The new millennium will be a time of considerable reflection for African states as they grapple with transforming the current liability into an asset. For that to be realised, a number of institutions and individuals charged with particular responsibilities will have to face up to monumental challenges. In this section, attention is drawn on the post-strife national reconstruction and reconciliation, underscoring forced migration as a priority research and policy concern and considering the search for durable peace.

National reconstruction and reconciliation

There are examples in different parts of the world of war-torn countries where national reconstruction and reconciliation have been undertaken. These include Cambodia, El Salvador, Namibia and Nicaragua where large numbers of people were uprooted in the 1970s and 1980s and where several positive changes – including peace agreements, election of new governments, varying degrees of support from UNHCR and welcoming back citizens who had fled as refugees – have taken place (UNHCR, 1997, p. 25). Three aspects of these were pertinent in the Mozambican programme. First, reintegration of returnees was effected. This involved rebuilding the war-ravaged society through distributing food, providing seeds, tools and shelter materials, and rehabilitating the destroyed infrastructure; creating a viable operational environment for all these to take place; assessing achievements of the reintegration programme, identifying factors that would facilitate smooth reintegration and the UNCHR's contribution against the experience elsewhere; stabilising the population which was necessary for their participation in the activities of the reintegration programme, linking the programme to longer-term development activities, reconciliation and observance of other elements of the peace agreement; inter-agency coordination by UNCHR; resource mobilisation; assessment and thoughts on the impact, sustainability and cost-effectiveness of the whole programme. Second, the reintegration programme was a carefully planned activity. This involved developing a well-conceived strategy, rationalising the planning process, data collection and strategic thinking, planning for continuity rather than for an ad hoc situation and retrospective consideration of the role of asylum countries which had not been envisaged in the initial planning strategy. Finally, implementation was made of reintegration activities, in which six issues featured: field presence and logistical capacity; decentralisation of authority both from UNHCR headquarters in Geneva to Maputo and from the capital city to the Sub and Field Officers; galvanising human resources and staff support; paying attention to the institutional technical capacity, which the harnessing of was delayed; enlisting the support of implementing partners; and sensitivity to community and gender issues (UNHCR, 1997).

Thus the Mozambican example is instructive for countries such as Rwanda, Burundi, Angola (when peace finally does settle therein), Liberia, Sierra Leone, the Comoro Islands and so on. The only important consideration is to be conscious of each country's difference from another and to ascertain the possible key players in the post-war situation. Also, where UNHCR efforts have been constrained by some conditions, it is necessary to evolve a network of international and local NGOs (partners) in the exercise of national reconstruction and reconciliation. Indeed, whereas the former has been successfully implemented in some African countries, the latter is elusive precisely because the actors seldom get to the roots of national strife which generate refugees and IDPs.

Forced migration: a priority area for research and policy

It is important to realise, however, that the agendas of forced migration change from time to time and from one country to another. This was acknowledged in a report of the fifth International Research and Advisory Panel (IRAP 5) held in Eldoret Kenya in April 1996. The meeting recognised new departures for IRAP, among them the founding of an independent International Association for the Study of Forced Migration (IASFM), the holding of IRAPs outside Oxford, its emphasis on conferences for exchange of views rather than as a mere advisory panel and emphasis on research. Also, in addition to acknowledging the challenges facing the international refugee regime, it both reviewed research in progress and considered new research agendas, identifying five areas, namely, forced migration and environmental change, the reception and representation of refugees in host countries, gender issues in forced migration, unaccompanied minors and repatriation and reconstruction; and in the key-note addresses, it reviewed the state of the art, which covered global concerns, contextualisation of empirical case studies in a broader perspective, the lack of theoretical bases for the study of forced migration, the multi-disciplinary nature of the conference proceedings and the temporal dimension of the research presented (Koser, 1996). Regrettably, refugee issues preoccupied the conference, with IDPs not receiving as much coverage as would reflect the magnitude of the problem in African countries. This poses a challenge for African and Africanist researchers of forced migration to try and undertake country case studies of IDPs which threatened to tear apart African countries in the next millennium unless well-conceived deterrents are instituted.

In many African countries migration was hardly a component of national population policy before the International Conference on Population and Development (ICPD) (1994), in the wake of which efforts have been made to incorporate 'population distribution, migration and urbanisation' in some national policies. But most of the policy pronouncements are not based on hard facts or dependable data, from which they find meaning. It is therefore necessary for researchers, planners and policy makers to work in teams to reassess national policies pertaining to migration in order to determine the content and shortcomings of forced migration concerns which might necessitate further work. The outcome of such an effort would most likely include setting up institutions to deal specifically with refugees and IDPs, to liaise with other national and international organisations and to assert at all times that forced migration is perhaps the most disruptive of all disasters as conventionally conceived by governments.

The search for durable peace

As peace has been an elusive precondition for development in Africa, a thorough search has to be made for durable peace. The search is an unending effort and must continue as long as the displaced persons continue to be a menace in Africa.

In the United Nations systems, several agencies have been concerned with displaced persons. The best known is UNHCR, which is mandated to attend to the problems of refugees all over the world. Yet UNHCR has no powers to force any sovereign country, more particularly government, to take decisions that may be repugnant to national interests. This explains why the work of UNHCR has been at variance with that of most governments in handling refugees. It is imperative, therefore, that both UNHCR and national governments work out strategies and modalities for resolving problems of refugees on a sustainable basis. Thus, African governments should stop viewing UNHCR as a watchdog of governments' handling of refugees; rather, they should view the UN refugee agency as a committed partner with whom to work closely. With respect to IDPs, it is noteworthy that in 1992 the UN Secretary-General appointed his Representative on Internally Displaced Persons. Regrettably, the office has not made a significant impact on the world of IDPs, and far less than NGOs and human rights institutions. The office needs reviewing critically in order to determine whether it should be independent or linked to, or even made an integral part of, UNHCR with a redefined mandate. It should be staffed, at the headquarters and in the field offices, with seasoned practitioners, researchers and managers of conflict, all working as teams. Apart from playing an overarching role with displaced persons in war-torn countries, the revitalised and reinvigorated office should endeavour, among other things, to work with governments and NGOs in the implementation of such action plans pertaining to refugees and IDPs as are documented in the Programme of Action of the International Conference on Population and Development (ICPD/PA) held in Cairo, Egypt, in September 1994. That should go for the other displaced persons-based correlated programmes/plans of action, which recent global conferences have adopted. The conferences include the World Summit on Social Development held in Copenhagen in March, 1995, the Fourth World Conference on Women held in Beijing in September 1995, the United Nations Centre for Human Settlements (Habitat) II Conference held in Istanbul in June 1996 and the World Food Summit held in Rome in November 1996.

In Africa itself, the OAU has become increasingly involved in internal conflicts, which trigger refugees and IDPs. Yet while the OAU has had an explicit position on refugees since 1969, it has hardly acknowledged the problem of IDPs well enough either to incorporate them into the definition and treatment of DPs or to address the problem separately from that of refugees. This implies that even the much-touted OAU's position is outdated and needs revision to take on the challenges of the two forms of DPs and not refugees alone. The pan-African organisation should also reconsider the process of handling displaced persons. Instead of going all out to broker peace between perpetrators and victims of displacement, the OAU should start with definition and delimitation of the problems, move on to undertake research on them and use the research results to prescribe appropriate intervention measures. Unfortunately, the OAU is averse to the first two stages of the suggested process and often hastens to determine intervention measures at the behest of the OAU Councils of Ministers and the OAU Summit of Heads of State and Government, without adequate benchmark information.

African governments and NGOs have the challenge to evolve and sustain partnership in handling the problem of displaced persons. They have an important role in facilitating voluntary repatriation and national reconciliation, implementing strategies for peace keeping and peace building in the course of crises, and in ensuring that durable peace exists. There are useful lessons to learn from a number of past strife-stricken countries now enjoying peace. These include Mozambique, Zimbabwe, Namibia, Uganda, Rwanda, Burundi, Ethiopia, Eritrea and South Africa whose 'Truth and Reconciliation Commission' deserves emulation by other African countries. In West Africa, ECOMOG, the peacekeeping force of the Economic Community of West African States (ECOWAS), made an exemplary contribution to solving the crises in Liberia and Sierra Leone. If crises elsewhere in the world are anything to go by, it would appear that the problems of Africa's displaced concern international institutions less than African countries themselves. To this end, the ECOMOG approach provides lessons that the OAU and regional integration/cooperations in different sub-regions of the continent should study more closely with a view to adapting to sub-region or country-specific issues. African governments and NGOs should also consider what the World Council of Churches (1996, pp. 70–83) sees as 'signs of hope' for peace keeping and peace building in the course of crises, namely, (1) awareness building, (2) peace making and peace building efforts, (3) enabling people and communities to resist the culture of violence, (4) monitoring corruption, (5) countering racism (in Africa, ethnicity), (6) promoting multiculturalism and inter-faith dialogue (cultural and religious tolerance), (7) solidarity and networking with uprooted people and (8) empowering refugees (including IDPs) and migrants to return. Also, there is a need to adopt existing legal instruments or adapt them to national situations, acknowledge the special needs of the IDPs, institutionalise data collection on IDPs by particular organisations and make protection an automatic choice (Cohen, 1996, pp. 21–7). But these are possible only if African governments stop their partisanship in handling the problems of displaced persons.

Finally, all the parties already mentioned – UN agencies, international and national NGOs, the OAU and African governments – should endeavour to adopt multi-faceted strategies or mechanisms for handling conflicts. The actions range from prevention, reduction, negotiation/mediation, regulation/management and resolution of conflict (Oucho, 1996a). This suggests that no single option can be expected to succeed in conflict situations in which there are different key players, villains and victims alike.

Conclusion

This chapter has shown that Africa's DPs comprise refugees who easily attract international attention and IDPs who are relatively neglected even by their own national governments. It portrays the problem of DPs as Africa's liability, which the continent will surely carry over into the foreseeable future. For a problem that has attracted considerable world attention, it is not surprising that there have been several key players operating at global, regional, sub-regional, national and sub-national levels. The time has come, however, for new and more innovative strategies or mechanisms for resolving national and international conflicts, which spark off intractable stocks and flows of refugees and IDPs. It is also time for African researchers, planners and policy makers at all levels to work as teams in deciphering problems relating to refugees and IDPs and in prescribing suitable solutions for durable peace and elimination of the menace of Africa's displaced people.

References

Adekanye, J. B. (1998) 'Conflicts, Loss of State Capacities and Migration in Contemporary Africa', in R. Appleyard (ed.), *Emigration Dynamics in Developing Countries*, vol. 1, *Sub Saharan Africa,* Aldershot: Ashgate, 165–206.

Ayiemba, E. H. O. and J. O. Oucho (1995) *The Refugee Crisis in Sub-Saharan Africa,* African Population Paper, 4, Nairobi: African Population and Environment Institute.

Beattie, I. (1998a) 'Ghana', in Janie Hampton (ed.), *Internally Displaced People: a Global Survey*, London: Earthscan, pp. 41–2.

Beattie, I. (1998b) 'Mauritania', in Hampton (ed.), *Internally Displaced People*, 48–9.

Beattie, I. (1998c) 'Senegal', in Hampton (ed.) *Internally Displaced People*, 52–3.

Beattie, I. (1998d) 'Sierra Leone', in Hampton (ed.), *Internally Displaced People*, 53–5.

Bilsborrow, R. E. and H. W. O. Okoth-Ogendo (1992) 'Population Driven Changes in Land Use in Developing Countries', *AMBIO*, 2, 1, 37–45.

Cohen, R., and F. M. Deng (1998) *Masses in Flight,* Washington, DC: Brookings Institution Press.

Cohen, Roberta (1996) 'Protecting the Internally Displaced', in US Committee for Refugees, *World Refugee Survey* 1996, Washington, DC: Immigration and Refugee Services of America, 20–7.

El-Hinnawi, E. (1985) *Environmental Refugees,* Nairobi: United Nations Environment Programme.

Fain, L., S. Redding and P. Swahn (1998) 'Sudan', in Hampton (ed.), *Internally Displaced People,* 84–7.

Gallagher, D. (1989) 'The Evaluation of the International Refugee System', *International Migration Review* 23, 3, 579–98.

Hampton, Janie (ed.) (1998) *Internally Displaced People: a Global Survey,* London: Earthscan Publications Ltd.

Hansen, A., and M. Davidheiser (1998) 'Eritrea', in Hampton (ed.) *Internally Displaced People,* 78–80.

Human Rights Watch (1997) *Failing the Internally Displaced: the UNDP Displaced Persons Program in Kenya,* New York: Human Rights Watch/Africa.

Human Rights Watch/Africa Watch (1993) *State Sponsored Ethnic Violence in Kenya,* New York: HRW/Africa Watch.

Ibeanu, O. (1998) 'Nigeria', in Hampton (ed.), *Internally Displaced People,* 49–52.

Kleine-Ahlbrandt, S. (1998) 'Rwanda', in Hampton (ed.), *Internally Displaced People,* 68–73.

Koser, K. (1996) 'Changing Agendas in Forced Migration: a Report on the Fifth International Research and Advisory Panel', *Journal of Refugees Studies,* 9, 4, 353–66.

McCall, M. (1985) 'Environmental and Agricultural Impacts of Tanzania's Villagisation Programme', in J. I. Clarke, M. Khogali and L. A. Kosinski (eds), *Population and Development Projects in Africa,* Cambridge: Cambridge University Press, 123–40.

Maro, P. S. (1990) 'Resettlement in Africa: Policies, Achievements and Prospects', in Union for African Population Studies, *Conference on the Role of Migration in African Development Issues and Policies for the '90s,* vol. I, commissioned papers, Dakar: UAPS, pp. 55–81.

Minear, L. and R. C. Kent (1998) 'Rwanda's Internally Displaced: a Conundrum within a Conundrum', in R. Cohen and F. M. Deng (eds), *The Forsaken People: Case Studies of the Internally Displaced,* Washington, DC: Brookings Institution Press, 57–95.

Mugumya, G. and E. Mooney (1998) 'Uganda', in Hampton (ed.), *Internally Displaced People,* 73–5.

Mullen, P. (1998) 'Burundi', in Hampton (ed.), *Internally Displaced People,* 57–62.

Nowrojee, B. (1998a) 'Liberia', in Hampton (ed.), *Internally Displaced People,* 42–5.

Nowrojee, B. (1998b) 'Kenya', in Hampton (ed.), *Internally Displaced People,* 65–8.

Olorunsola, V. A. (ed.) (1972) *The Politics of Cultural Sub-Nationalism in Africa,* Garden City, New York: Anchor Press.

Oucho, J. O. (1997) 'The Ethnic Factor in Internal Displacement of Populations in Sub-Saharan Africa', *African Journal of Political Science,* 2, 2, 104–17.

Oucho, J. O. (1996a) *Undercurrents of Ethnic Conflict in Kenya*, Leiden, The Netherlands: Brill.

Oucho, J. O. (1996b) 'Migration and Ethnic Relations in Colonial and Independent Kenya', paper prepared for the Conference on Migration and Culture Contact: Patterns of Confrontation and Coexistence in a Changing World, Amman, Jordan, 11–14 October.

Oucho, J. O. (1996c) 'Refugees and Displacement in Sub-Saharan Africa: Instability due to Ethnic and Political Conflicts', in A. Adepoju and T. Hammar (eds), *International Migration in and from Africa: Dimensions, Challenges and Prospects*, Dakar, Senegal: Population Human Resources and Development in Africa (PHRDA) and Stockholm: Centre for Research in International Migration and Ethnic Relations (CEIFO), 161–87.

Redding, S. and A. Hansen (1998a) 'Ethiopia', in Hampton (ed.), *Internally Displaced People*, 80–1.

Redding, S. and A. Hansen (1998b) 'Somalia', in Hampton (ed.), *Internally Displaced People*, 81–4.

Sangara, B. A. (1998) 'Congo', in Hampton (ed.), *Internally Displaced People*, 62–5.

Talbot, L. M. (1986) 'Demographic Factors in Resource Depletion and Environmental Degradation in East African Rangelands', *Population and Development Review*, 12, 3, 441–51.

Tolba, M. K. (1992) *Saving Our Planet: Challenges and Hope*, London: Chapman Hall.

United Nations High Commissioner for Refugees (UNHCR) (1995) *The State of the World's Refugees: In Search of Solutions*, New York: Oxford University Press.

United Nations High Commissioner for Refugees (UNHCR) (1997) 'Rebuilding a War-Torn Society: a Review of the UNHCR Reintegration Programme for Mozambican Returnees', *Refugee Survey Quarterly*, 16, 2, 24–71.

US Committee for Refugees (1996) *World Refugee Survey 1996*, Washington, DC: Immigration and Refugee Services of America.

Vohra, Shyla (1998) 'Mali', in Hampton (ed.), *Internally Displaced People*, 45–8.

World Council of Churches (1996) A *Moment to Choose: Risking to be uprooted People: A Resource Book*, Geneva: World Council of Churches, Unit IV, Sharing and Service, Refugee and Migration Service.

9
What Was Refugee Status? Legislating the Changing Practice of Refugee Law

Rosemary Preston

Introduction

The tension between practice and the law it informs is a helix. Established law may set a norm for practice until such a point that the two are so far apart that the norm-setting law is changed. As a slow process, this is usually not before continuously dynamic practice has moved on, widening the gap between it and the new law, which is already lagging behind. However small initial deviations in practice from the norms of law may be, it will be organised political pressures conforming to leading ideas of the moment that direct their increasing momentum and the tenor of eventual legislative change.

For social scientists, the period since the Second World War has been characterised by the welfare policies of the post-war and later post-colonial years in different parts of the world and then by the new right liberalism dominating the global political economy since the late 1970s. The first period saw the emergence of the international system of protection of European refugees and, in its wake, international law to legitimate it globally. Former colonial territories endorsed the spirit of this law, using it as the basis of asylum offered to those forced to flee from neighbouring and other states in their regions. Over the next 20 years, these countries modified the law with their own imprints, seeking to make it more comprehensive and socially supportive than its original European version (Organisation of African Unity, 1969; Organisation of American States, 1985).

From a geopolitical perspective, Allen and Morsink (1994) review how the creation and establishment of international refugee law served the Cold War agenda, such that the strength of the emerging international refugee regime's preference for long-term resettlement in third countries of one or other side meant that repatriation was rarely an option. In the late 1940s and 1950s, hundreds of thousands of people from eastern European nations were given long-term settlement entitlements in the US and western Europe, against the wishes of the USSR. In the 1970s and early 1980s, Cambodians, Laotians and Vietnamese, who had fled South East Asian communist regimes, were welcomed in advanced capitalist countries of Europe, North America and Australasia. Over the same period, the Soviet Union, Eastern Europe, Cuba and other socialist states welcomed large numbers of people fleeing European colonial oppressors and fighting for their independence (Preston, 1994).

The waning enthusiasm of the advanced industrial states to offer resettlement, as the durable solution for exiles held in first asylum territories neighbouring the world's conflict zones, has many interrelated and well-documented explanations (Allen and Morsink, 1994). The global transition away from the philosophies of the welfare and centrally planned state has encouraged those of nationalism in a lean market, unemployment and popular resistance to immigration. As the Cold War ended, there was less political capital to be won by East/West bloc protection of or investment in each other's dissidents. Subsequently, there have been previously unknown incidences of conflict and unprecedented numbers of people seeking refuge within their own countries and forced across international borders. This has exacerbated a generalised fear of political, economic and social instability, as a consequence of what are seen in the popular mind as unduly generous settlement/asylum policies. Pressure by the increasingly rich countries of Western Europe, North America and Australasia encouraging first-country receiving states to offer long-term settlement to those seeking asylum from across their borders has rebounded. Less well-endowed, these states have been tightly squeezed by the neoliberal regime. They see their modest resources being further diminished by such policies, at a time when their labour markets are more seriously reduced than those of richer nations, along with their ability to support destitute refuge-seekers in any number. At the same time, it is these nations which are the principal receivers of asylum seekers from neighbouring territories.

The shift from long-term resettlement in third countries to repatriation to countries of origin has been the most significant consequence of these trends (Quick, Chingono and Preston, 1995; Preston, 1999).

No longer taboo, repatriation is now the expected outcome of exile. preferred by involved governments, international organisations and, we are encouraged to believe, by refugees and asylum seekers alike. Although for some writers, the post-World War II unwillingness to recommend repatriation as the conclusion to exile was on the grounds that it would facilitate, even legitimate, *refoulement* (Reid, 1992), its new acceptability does not presuppose the cessation of conflict or changed political structures in the country of origin from which its exiles will have fled in the first place (Larkin, Cuny and Stein, 1991; Cuny, Stein and Reid, 1992). The shift in global preference has been confirmed by the 1992 declaration by UNHCR that the 1990s would be the decade of repatriation, accompanied by pressures on source states to facilitate return and prevent secondary exodus. Policy (UNHCR, 1993) has included: action to resolve conflict so as to enable return; action to prevent renewed conflict and subsequent exit; action to prevent the development of conditions of new conflict and disintegration. Less publicised has been more or less coercive action, in many parts of the world, pressurising refugees and asylum seekers to repatriate, either as individuals or groups.

For some, the complex array of trends captured above heralds the end of the international humanitarian right to asylum and individual protection from persecution (Hathaway, 1991). Preferred strategies of the new regime include: prevention of departure from first asylum countries to resettlement destinations; prevention of departure from countries in conflict; deterrents to refuge-seeker embarkation for specified destinations; refusals to admit asylum seekers; unwillingness to confer refugee status and restricted residence permits for those admitted; collective rather than individual designation of status as determinants of entitlements. Writing on these issues laments the de facto loss of asylum and refugee status and demands the restoration of hard-won humanitarian practice in accordance with international law. Some suggest a strategy to save what can be protected for human rights out of what they perceive to be the impasse created as increasingly restrictive practice has been aligned with the ever more meanly interpreted letter of the law.

Jim Hathaway is one of the most active exponents of this approach. His vision is of an alternative law of temporary protection for those fleeing across international boundaries, which provides for a safe and dignified return to countries of origin at the end of the protected period, under the direction of a supra-national authority (1991). Hathaway has been promoting this idea for well over a decade, as an ethical and pragmatic way of adapting to neoliberal realities, which does not jeopardise rights to protection and *non-refoulement.* Through the 1990s, his commitment has attracted funding for international seminars attended by some of the world's leading theoreticians on refugee law (Legal Working Group, 1993) and for a collection of projective studies on the social applications of his proposed amendments and reflective investigations on what has been achieved. The projective studies included writing on international administration, fiscal burden sharing, temporary protection, responsibility sharing, repatriation in safety and dignity, repatriation and development assistance.

The remainder of the present paper draws on the study of repatriation in safety and dignity, by Quick, Chingono and Preston (1995) and its synthesis (Preston 1995a), written in response to comments from Hathaway (1995a). It describes the formation of the research team and its approach to the research. It reviews the different components of the reports of the study and concludes by highlighting the contribution made by the research, questioning the stasis of the debate and the conditions under which the social environment may change to favour greater levels of humanitarianism.

Studying return in safety and dignity: starting points

Before embarking on the study, there was a need for the research team to resolve dilemmas within Hathaway's proposal, appraise its own resources and identify the questions to which it would seek to respond.

Seeking to identify politically acceptable strategy within increasingly restrictive practices not only condones the practice but also leaves no defence against the mounting threat to international humanitarian law on which the system is modelled. On the contrary, if international law is changed to accommodate proposals such as these, the hard-won achievements of the 1940s–1960s and their *de jure* entitlements will be further undermined. This is the dilemma. The current de facto mode of state compliance with legislative requirements is close to an extreme of parsimony, with the residual margin of generosity serving to promote a humanitarian image through the media. Any legislative reduction of rights, trusting to the goodwill of nations for their fair application, will from the outset be vulnerable to the same extremes, but within a less humanitarian legislative environment.

Difficulties were encountered in meeting the project's criteria that research teams comprise one person located in a part of the world with a healthy economy and another in a state otherwise situated. Reluctant to allocate the limited financial resources available for the research to long-distance air companies, it seemed appropriate to find under-employed researchers who originated from countries that met these criteria, were fortuitously located within low-cost reach of each other and would benefit from the work, professionally and materially. The dilemma only exacerbated the problems. Two colleagues, once they had read the proposal, did not want to be associated with the study because no matter how critical it became, they would risk, through association, being instrumental in serving the neoliberal project throughout the down-grading of the already fragile instruments of international humanitarian law. The group that did form agreed from the start that its role had first to examine worst case scenarios that might obtain in the event of the proposals informing legislative change. Only if the proposed changes were found not to reduce the entitlements of refugees and asylum seekers would they consider strategic mechanisms to optimise this. They were fully committed to not discussing the application of proposals for legislative change that would undermine the spirit of the existing law.

Considering their own resources, members of the research team saw themselves as social scientists with knowledge and direct experience of many aspects of war-related migration in several countries. Susan Quick, then Secretary of the World Development Movement (UK), had worked with refugees in Sudan and Zaire over a 10-year period and was preparing her PhD on pastoralists in sub-Saharan Africa. Mark Chingono was a ZIPRA[1] fighter based in Mozambique, who repatriated after the Lancaster House agreement for independence in Zimbabwe. At the time of the research, he had completed his PhD reflecting on the development implications of the exile experience. Rosemary Preston had over many years researched labour and war-related migration in different parts of the world, including the coordination of a major study of post-war integration in Namibia (Preston, 1993).

While this collective experience afforded the team a wealth of case study material around which to build an argument relating to the application of the proposals being made by Hathaway, no one in the team had previously researched the policy or process of repatriation. Lack of understanding of law relating to repatriation was a further constraint. As important was the lack of information about the boundaries being set by colleagues preparing companion studies and about the positions they were taking on themes common to us all, specifically in respect of the key construct 'return in safety and dignity'. The team began by referring to recent literature to define the component terms of the construct and others related to it, before proceeding to examine its application as envisaged by RLRU/CRS (1994).

Referring to documentation relating to the International Refugee Law Project (IRLP) (RLRU/CRS 1994),[2] the members of the team set out to:

- define return in safety and dignity
- appraise the feasibility of defining and applying criteria for terminating temporary protection
- discuss the feasibility of creating a supra-national authority competent to apply criteria to terminate interim protection and ensure return in safety with dignity
- assess the case for maintaining formal procedures which will oblige agencies responsible to address the needs of individuals and sub-groups, in addition to the needs of the returning group as a whole.

The team reviewed the then limited literature on repatriation and examined the parameters of international law pertaining to it. It then described current trends in practice and examined these in the light of a series of case studies (N = 17). From richer and poorer countries, the case studies provide the basis for the positions adopted by the authors, as their response to Hathaway's position. This is developed as trends in practice are shown to be considerably at variance with the spirit of current refugee law, relating to repatriation. It is from these that Hathaway's demand for the reformulation of law derives and, simultaneously, it is against these that his proposals must be measured. Unlike Hathaway, the authors assume that political, rather than humanitarian, interests will dominate every stage of any reformulation process. From this position, they go on to project the implications of the application of reforms, such as those outlined by IRLP.

Completed research

By the 1990s, there was a burgeoning interest in the process of repatriation and its implications for post-conflict reconstruction. Until then, most writing on repatriation refers to return organised under various forms of agreement between sending and receiving states and UNHCR. Studies of unassisted return and integration are rare, although most people return from exile at their own initiative, without assistance, regardless of any legal constraints upon their action (Cuny, Stein and

Reid, 1992). Beyond the scope of the present study, they are exemplified by Allen's work among the Acholi, moving from Southern Sudan into Northern Uganda (Allen, 1996a) and by references to trial visits as people reconnoitre their prospects on indefinite return to places as far apart as Chile and Mozambique (Wilson, 1994; Preston, 1991a). For Allen and Morsink (1994), the focus of pre-1990s research on organised repatriation has been on the legal parameters of return and on the operational aspects of specific moves, with analyses of the politics of different moves largely serving to promote the cause of particular interested parties.

Cole's account of voluntary repatriations, from 1918 to 1985, is an inventory of experience decade by decade, in different parts of the world (Coles, 1985). It draws upon secondary sources to describe those aspects of the process of voluntary return for which documentation was available. From his report it is possible to trace trends in the principles guiding repatriation, allowing some understanding of how the history of different exile experiences affects the process. If Coles's study provided the most comprehensive assessment of the implications for law in respect of voluntary repatriation, Reid's unpublished thesis was the first substantial political analysis of selected moves (Reid 1992). Based on six case studies constructed from secondary data, Reid related the repatriation process to change in the wider political environment and the extent to which the local political climate at the moment of return was conducive to a more or less hospitable reception on arrival. Neither Reid nor Coles have the data to comment on individual or group experiences of the processes of return or post-arrival integration. More recently, two UNRISD[3] collections on return from exile or internal displacement in different regions of Africa do provide useful insights into the ways in which political, economic and cultural contexts of return may foster integration and stability in countries of origin (Allen and Morsink, 1994; Allen, 1996a) and the collection by Black and Khoser (1999) adopts a similar, critical approach.

Among these writers, Coles and Reid come closest to assessing the implications of practice for the relevance of law. Both perceive commonalities in the modification of law in the cases they present and emphasise the infrequency of indubitably voluntary return. Coles discusses the legal implications of policy to promote voluntary repatriation as the outcome of exile, basing his arguments on the right of refugees to re-enter their country of nationality, associated with rights generated from belonging to that territory. Reid would be reluctant for there to be any legislative weakening of the requirement of voluntariness as a criterion of any move. All of these writers (Coles, 1985; Reid, 1992; Allen and Morsink, 1994; Allen, 1996a; Khoser and Black, 1999) stress the need for systematic basic and policy level research at all levels of analysis on the processes of return and post-return integration. A prerequisite would be for this to be articulated to the practice of current law before any reformulation is proposed, let alone implemented.

Criteria of return in safety and dignity

Quick, Chingono and Preston (1995) review a range of international legal and other instruments concerned with repatriation and the related concept of voluntariness. Drawing from international refugee and more general human rights law, and suggesting in line with Hathaway (1991) that the proposed reformulation may be seen as a move towards the integration of the two, they are guided by the international principle that:

> For UNHCR, charged with protecting refugees and finding durable solutions for their problems, the standard criteria for return are 'voluntary repatriation in safety and dignity', preferably in an organised fashion with the co-operation of the governments of both the host country and country of origin.
>
> (UNHCR, 1992, p. 104)

In this tripartite arrangement, the principle of *non-refoulement* is an essential corollary to the principle of voluntary repatriation.

The instruments of international refugee law in which these principles are enshrined include: the Statute of the Office of the United Nations High Commissioner for Refugees, Article 1 (adopted 14 December 1950); the 1951 Convention relating to the Status of Refugees, Article 33 Prohibition of expulsion or return (refoulement); the Convention against Torture and Other Cruel, Inhuman or Degrading Treatment or Punishment, 10 December 1984, extending the principle of non-refoulement and non-extradition to any State, Article 3; the Organisation of African Unity (OAU), Convention Governing the Specific Aspects of Refugee Problems in Africa, Article V. Voluntary Repatriation; the American Convention on Human Rights Pact of San José, Costa Rica, Article 22.

At all stages of asylum and repatriation, refugee rights must be guaranteed in accordance with the provisions not only of refugee law but also of wider Human Rights Law. These include: the Covenant on

Civil and Political Rights, which provides for protection from torture, slavery, servitude and inhumane imprisonment, the right to liberty and security of person, and the right to freedom of movement; the Covenant on Economic, Social and Cultural Rights, which assures the right to work, the right to safe working conditions, the right to an adequate standard of living and the right to medical treatment, and that plans for refugee repatriation consider whether these conditions can be met upon return; the Covenant on the Elimination of All Forms of Discrimination against Women contains nothing specific to refugee women, although Article 14 on the needs of rural women applies; the Convention of the Rights of the Child which makes specific provisions that refugee children shall be protected; the Convention against Torture and Other Cruel, Inhuman or Degrading Treatment or Punishment, which includes specific provision against *refoulement.*

In addition, various regional conventions seek to protect refugees: the African Charter on Human and Peoples' Rights; the American Convention on Human Rights; the Pact of San José, Costa Rica; the Cartagena Declaration on Refugees; the Convention Determining the State Responsible for Examining Applications for Asylum, lodged in one of the Member States of the European Communities.

Citing Reid (1992), Quick, Chingono and Preston (1995) acknowledge the authority given to Tripartite Commissions (with members drawn from the governments of host and sending states and the relevant UN organisation) as the mechanism authority through which voluntary repatriation might normally be planned and achieved. With reference to change in the global political economy and citing Reid (1992) and Ogata (UNHCR, 1992), they provide documentary explanations for the emergence of voluntary repatriation as the preferred durable solution of people recognised as refugees or who find themselves in refugee-like situations.[4] With examples from western Europe (McDowell, 1995a), they discuss the growing practice of conferring diverse forms of temporary residential status on people admitted to states in which they request asylum. Finally, they refer to the idea of temporary protection, alluding to the UK (*The Guardian,* 1995) and Papua New Guinea (Preston, 1992). With reference to Chimni (1993), they describe trends to prevent the departure, preventative protection, of such people from the country to which they belong and deny them entry to and recognition in the country in which they would wish to request asylum.

The intentions underlying the restrictive practices described above are attributed to the need to reduce the number of refuge seekers with entitlements conferred in association with the Geneva Convention of 1951 and Protocol of 1967. At best, the language of temporary residence may equalise the treatment of all those applying for residence in states other than their own. In this way a process of differentiation operates, in which applicants are granted entitlements according to the activity they will pursue during residence, without reference to their reasons for leaving the territory to which they belong. Such a procedure does not require the denaturalisation and depoliticisation that is a prerequisite of refugee status. At worst, temporary residential status discriminates against would-be seekers of international asylum in favour of those admitted as students or for specified work. Admitted for increasingly brief periods, the permits of those accorded temporary protection may disallow employment, mobility or registration for any course of study. Prospects of renewal on expiry may be minimal and residence after expiry or other infringements can lead to the ascription of illegal immigrant status, followed by deportation, regardless of events in the country of origin. McDowell's work (1995b, 1995c) on Sri Lankans in Switzerland provides harsh illustrations of such cases. In such contexts, the IRLP desire to ensure at least minimal protection is laudable. Setting its parameters, particularly those relating to the termination of residence or temporary protection, is beset with difficulty.

To understand the IRLP thinking, Quick, Chingono and Preston (1995) trace the evolving language of durable solutions to exile and asylum. They note that: the Geneva Convention (1951) made no reference to the term 'voluntary repatriation'; over the years, two permanent solutions (assimilation and repatriation) became three durable solutions, with assimilation dividing into integration in the first country of asylum and resettlement in a third country; the language of third country resettlement has since disappeared and talk of eventual assimilation within the first country of asylum is now rare; today, of what were three durable solutions, the only serious prospect for most refugees is eventual repatriation.

From here, they attempt to distinguish between the currently used term, repatriation, and return, the replacement being proposed by Hathaway (1995a). To repatriate, transitively or intransitively, implies the restoration of people to the country to which they belong and the resumption of normal relationships between themselves and the government of that country. If, as is sometimes argued, voluntariness is inherent to the repatriation of people who are refugees, voluntary repatriation becomes a tautologous term. Return is a broader concept which, transitively or intransitively, encompasses repatriation.

Thought by some to be politically neutral,[5] it refers to the process of going or rendering back (something or someone) to a place. It does not necessarily have the political or legal connotations of repatriation. The right to return has recently entered refugee terminology:

> Within the International human rights framework, the basic tenet underlying voluntary repatriation is the right to return to one's own country.
>
> (UNHCR, 1992, p. 20)

This indicates a significant conceptual shift combining a right with voluntariness to use it, such that it is but a short step to expressing the solution as follows:

> not in terms of the right to choose freely whether or not to return, the traditional formula, but also in the form of the human right to return in safety and dignity, a right to be asserted and implemented.
>
> (Coles, 1989, p. 162, quoted in Allen and Morsink, 1994, p. 3)

While voluntariness is forfeit in this position, it is prudent to interpret the terms 'safety' and 'dignity' before articulating a protest. Quick, Chingono and Preston (1995) take safety, as the principle of asylum, to refer to physical security and *entitlement* to universal human rights, including protection from forced return. IRLP (Tab 7, 4:12) suggests that dignity is to be measured in terms of the quality of life on return. With reference to Vincent (1986, pp. 14 and 17), Quick, Chingono and Preston take dignity to indicate the right of individuals to achieve human potential free from coercion, in ways that are determined by themselves.

The assessment of safety and dignity

The determination of conditions for terminating temporary protection will vary with the interests of those empowered to decide on the safety and dignity of returns proposed in different situations.[6] The authors envisage an international supervisory authority (ISA), such as that proposed by IRLP, to have a function analogous to UNHCR. Unlike UNHCR, it may be newly convened from different institutions with expertise relevant to specific cases. Either way, they find it difficult to conceive that such an organisation will have the capacity to act independently of the interests of sending or receiving states in any situation of involuntary international migration, or of the states controlling global politics or its own funding. Examples abound of the potential for such an authority to decree as 'safe' a place of return which those to be returned perceive as unsafe. They include the forced return of Ukrainians to the USSR 1945–48 (Boshyk, 1988) and the much more recent Tripartite agreement to return Tamils to Sri Lanka in 1991–94 (McDowell, 1995a). The Swiss Tamil example also illustrates cases in which such an authority will conspire with the host state to declare a return to be safe and, in the face of refugee or asylum-seeker unwillingness to agree that this is so, coerce voluntary return by the reduction of rations and withdrawal of other services (McDowell, 1995a). Then there are instances in which refuge-seekers perceive a safe return to be possible, only to find that it is deemed unsafe by the ISA, governments and members of the international assistance regime. A case in point here would be Tigrayan insistence on return to Ethiopia, in the face of opposition from the government, the government of their country of asylum (Sudan) and the UNHCR (Quick, 1995b). Finally, again illustrated by the Tigrayans (Quick, 1995b), there are cases where both refugees and the government of the country of origin agree on the safety of a planned return, which neither the host government nor the international assistance regime will endorse.

While the ISA model indicated by IRLP is problematic it is not clear that alternatives will be more effective. Referring to Crisp (1984), the creation of legally constituted, local voluntary organisations with a remit to negotiate the conditions of return in safety and dignity in respect of local refuge-seeking groups may not have sufficient authority to act in this capacity, even when full members include representatives of all relevant parties, including the refugee community. An approximation to this in practice would be the 1992 case of Guatemalans and the protracted arrangements for their return from Mexico in negotiation with five organisations, which included refugees' organisations and a tripartite commission (Quick, 1995e).

Quick, Chingono and Preston (1995) argue that whatever the capability of structures determining the conditions of return in safety and dignity, mechanisms would have to be devised to gather information acceptable to prospective returners about the situation in the place of return. Media reports are unreliable and information about conditions prevailing in one part of a country may not represent the situation elsewhere. For similar reasons, information obtained from reconnaissance visits by selected members of the returning group may not be relevant to the community as a whole or to sub-groups and other individuals within it. Even when there is a consensus among those contemplating return, other stakeholders may challenge its appropriateness. This was the experience of the Tigrayans in 1980s when some 200,000 set out to walk home in order to plant crops, against the wishes of UNHCR and other aid organisations (Quick, 1995b). Similarly in the early 1990s, with the partial liberation of Eritrea and declining conditions of refugee life in Sudan, Eritreans were unable to mobilise their own return. There was minimal external assistance in Sudan and none within Eritrea, beyond what little the government of Eritrea could provide. UNHCR's mandate was ambiguous, its contribution minimal. Efforts to attract international finance to assist the reconstruction of Eritrea included provision to integrate more than 80,000 returned exiles, but minimal aid was given (Gameladin Ashami, 1995).

While there are strong indications that the safety of return is greater when people travel and arrive in groups, it is also clear that neither international nor refugee organisations can, without coercion, control the decision to move or not. People will remove themselves from ISA protection, as occurred with the return of Ethiopians from Djibouti, 1980–90 (Quick, 1995a). Some will threaten and commit suicide or starve to death, if in their eyes there is no better option. Examples from Ethiopia (Quick, 1995a), western Europe (Boshyk, 1988) and Papua New Guinea in the mid-1980s (Preston, 1995f) come readily to mind. With sufficient incentive, the need to plant at a particular time, people will move, even before their own organisations have time to make arrangements for logistical support. Again Tigrayan experience in the mid-1980s exemplifies this (Quick, 1995b). With such a range of avoidance strategies available, the debate about responsibility for defining the safety of return risks becoming academic.

It is equally unlikely that any organisation will be able to guarantee the safety of exiles, either during return or after. The political problems surrounding any organised return will be augmented by those incurred, for example, with demobilisation, arms control and the demilitarisation of warring societies, all of which militate against such surety, as does war detritus in the form of land mines and other unexploded devices, on the journey or after arrival. This has become the norm in former war zones in places as far apart as Chile and Mozambique, Cambodia and Afghanistan. An important function for any ISA would be to assist in any of these processes and to facilitate arrangements for the clearing of mines.

Appraising the conditions which would assure a return in dignity would also be complex. Exiles may experience a quality of life significantly at variance with the one they knew before. For some, conditions will have differed little from previously, for others they will be either better or worse. For all, it may be difficult to foresee their lives on return. The situation which caused them to leave may have been resolved, but new factors may have come into play which will render unlikely a dignified return.

The logic of the above definition implies that people who experience a relative drop in their quality of life cannot be said to be returning in dignity. For a return to be dignified, people should expect to be able to continue their lives to the same standard as they had before departure or in exile, whichever is the higher. Strategies to facilitate a dignified life after return should be envisaged before the move. They may include arrangements to assist reception and resettlement after arrival and diverse forms of aid to post-conflict reconstruction. Among these may be the provision of inputs to production, opportunities for employment, training and rehabilitation, in ways which foster the integration of returning and stayer groups.

As defined by Quick, Chingono and Preston (1995), the safety of return may be determined by members of any interested group and may exclude those concerned. Any objective assessment of safety will be subject to external factors over which the assessors (who may include those who are to return) have no control. Dignity is dependent on people's own assessment of the situation and their own choice of whether to move or not. It is not necessarily affected by external factors, although they may affect the decision reached. A return in dignity will be based, among other things, on the returners' own assessment of the safety of the move, regardless of whether this conforms to the requirements of an objective assessment. In this way, return in dignity, encompassing returner appraisals of safety, is the more important of the two criteria. It is likely to be the optimal means of achieving physical and psychological rehabilitation and a major factor in long-term stability and security. It is the one ethical criterion for terminating protection.

Quick, Chingono and Preston (1995) doubt the possibility of defining either generally applicable conditions of safety or dignity or locally applicable conditions unless defined with the full involvement and agreement of those whose return is being negotiated. It questions the capacity of any organisation to intervene disinterestedly or autonomously at supra-national levels. These factors, combined with the difficulty of effecting non-coercive control of population movement and with histories of refuge from war (which may last for decades), make untenable the case for specifying preset, generally applicable periods of temporary protection. As the ultimate solution, those terrified at the thought of mandatory return will forfeit their lives to avoid it.

The scope for individual and group-based assessment of fitness to return

Taking the position that refugee communities are not homogeneous, but differentiated in multiple and complex ways, Quick, Chingono and Preston (1995) dismiss the acceptability of arrangements being made for all members of a prospective returnee group without taking into account the particular interests of sub-groups and individuals within it. It will be essential to continue to appraise the prospects of a safe and dignified return for specified sub-groups and individuals who would be vulnerable to abuse if the provisions of their return were undifferentiated from those of the overall group. Quick, Chingono and Preston (1995) argue this position, sometimes in considerable detail, by exemplifying ways in which the appraisal of safe and dignified return will differ in respect of women, children, old people, the mentally sick and physically handicapped, former combatants, prisoners, detainees and victims of torture, as well as those being returned to areas with unexploded mines and other ordinance.

Groups requiring special provision may include: boys and young men brutalised, from very early ages, through fighting and militia survival practices, who will need careful assistance, if they are to be accepted by the returning group and within the home society (Preston, 1997); long-term fighters of opposing sides over the period of disarmament, demobilisation and post-peace return, to prevent hostilities between them (Chingono, 1995; Preston, 1995c); the provision of facilities to those returning with war wounds and other disabilities (Zinkin, 1993); prisoners detained without trial and abused by the leaders of movements to which they had given support (Preston, 1995d); women who had fought for the cause as political leaders and in the militias, who, expecting social recognition on return, find themselves first ignored by male colleagues in the fight for office and then unfitted for their previously normal family roles (Preston, 1995e); children who may have lived in exile for many years in social environments quite other than those to which they will be returned (Dix, 1993).

Sub-group appraisal is often problematic. The uniqueness of each person's experience pervades the literature on the various sub-groups, particularly when people belong to more than one sub-group. A child may be disabled, a woman an ex-combatant, an old man a former double agent and so on. Some categorisation of prospective returners by sub-groups may be useful in order to establish broad categories of need and programmes to meet them, but individual experiences and reactions are unique. Broad criteria and programmes to assure safety may be established, but there must also be in place formal mechanisms to address individual concerns.

The same point is made in respect of group assessment based on membership of different social or political groups. Refugee status is awarded on the basis of well-founded fear of persecution in the country of origin for reason of race, religion, nationality, membership of a particular social group or holding of a political opinion. This implies that once persecution of a particular race, religion, nationality, etc. has ceased then it is safe for persons belonging to that group to return. However, just as people belong to more than one group according to gender, age and class, so they also belong to more than one group according to race, religion, nationality, social group and political opinion. Whereas, for example, the majority of people of a certain race may follow the same religion and share the same political opinion, there will always be exceptions. All this means that no blanket assessment of safety of return can ever be made on the basis of a single aspect of a person's identity. Quick (1995a and 1995d) notes that in the return of Ethiopians from Djibouti (1980–90) and further afield, multiple problems occurred because of international agency support of selected categories of people and abandonment of the interests of others.

While individuated assessment is a principle underlying existing law, IRLP suggests that

> if the ISA has determined that circumstances warrant a return in safety and dignity and a refugee has failed to convince the ISA that her return is unviable, then she must return home. If she fails to do so, then the ISA and the host state will share the responsibility to return her.[7]

This counters an earlier UNHCR position on dangers of this approach.

> The designation of specific countries as 'safe' is both controversial and often highly politicised. If the concept is used as part of an asylum determination procedure, it creates a presumption of ineligibility

> which the applicant must refute. As long as the opportunity for a rebuttal exists, this presents no great departure from normal practices. Most screening processes incorporate information on the general conditions of an asylum-seeker's home country as necessary background for assessing the individual's claim. The dangers of the safe country concept arise if it is used to exclude national groups from consideration for asylum. The political and human rights situation in many countries are difficult to assess with precision, can change very rapidly and may vary from one social or ethnic group to another. The combination of an imperfect classification of safe countries and a rigid refusal to consider asylum cases originating from them could expose individuals to refoulement and subsequently to great personal danger.
>
> (UNHCR, 1993, pp. 45–6)

Quick, Chingono and Preston (1995) conclude that, to conform to the fundamental principles of human rights, safety and dignity may only be applied on a group basis: if this does not violate the rights of individuals; if mechanisms are in place to actively protect those rights; and if the onus is on states and international organisations (including and especially the ISA) to ensure that these mechanisms are used.

Wider implications of legislative reform proposals

Quick, Chingono and Preston (1995) go on to argue that any reformulation of law in accordance with the IRLP proposals will require the consideration of multiple secondary issues, before it can be applied.

In relation to refugee status there are questions of whether:

- temporality of status will, on expiry, lead to lack of protection from forced return
- those accorded refugee status before the application of new law will continue to enjoy that status in accordance with earlier law
- in the context of newly defined temporary protection, action would have to be planned to prevent the 'disappearance' of those fearful or otherwise reluctant to return
- the position of those returning independently of internationally negotiated moves would change.

Questions would have to be anticipated about the social impact of the obligation to exercise the right of return. Examples would include ways in which to prevent return, including:

- having a negative impact on the local economies of host countries dependent on refugee labour
- having a negative impact on countries of origin unable to absorb additional labour
- leading to copy-cat action being taken against refugees of the same nationality with temporary rights of residence in other countries
- causing unrest and negative reaction among established, non-refugee, immigrant minority groups.

Finally, secondary legal issues would have to be investigated. Among others, these would include consideration of implications for:

- the conventions and statutes relating to refugee affairs
- general law on the application of law in respect, for example, of the loss of refugee status
- sovereignty of the creation of a supra-national organisation with the authority to intervene in the affairs of individuals and groups within states
- implications for the laws which govern the exercise of rights, entitlements and obligations.

Beyond the scope of this paper, these are major and complex corollaries of the proposals outlined, of which no account is taken.

Conclusions

The ideas debated in this chapter have been a recurrent theme in international refugee law throughout the 1990s. In spite of severe criticisms (Barutciski, 1996, 1998; Goodwin-Gill, 1996) and evidence that conditions for return in safety and dignity are routinely ignored (Bagshaw, 1997; Vedsted-Hansen, 1997), Hathaway continues to press his case (Hathaway and Neve, 1997). The contribution made by Quick, Chingono and Preston (1995) was in a work commissioned by Hathaway and has not been published. The purpose of synthesising the work in its present form is to highlight what it achieved.

In its own terms, the study succeeds in deconstructing the evolution of the language of solutions to exile, the etymology of return and the political implications of its separation from voluntariness. It differentiates the concepts of safety and dignity and the relationship between the two. It asserts the difficulty of meeting their criteria when decisions are taken relating to return, particularly when the conditions for returning in dignity are not determined by the people who are to move. As the criterion for ending temporary protection, it is they who should decide that return in dignity is possible, if the return is not to be under coercion. The study confirms the necessity for protecting individual rights to status definition, over and above those accorded to any group to which an individual may belong. Grounding its arguments in case study experiences, with reference to individual and group experiences, examples were selected from a wide range of countries, to confirm the global application of current practices.

Practice is increasingly at variance with the original spirit of existing law. This means that any case to investigate the continued relevance of refugee law in respect of repatriation must examine the humanitarian implications of the strategies currently employed to legitimate the denial of refugee status and remove the obligation to ensure that repatriation is either voluntary, safe or dignified. Quick, Chingono and Preston (1995) are concerned that effective mechanisms should be developed to ensure the implementability of any reformulation intended to protect refugee or other refuge-seeker interests. As they stand, neither the IRLP proposals nor later writing identifies ways in which this might be achieved. On the contrary, the IRLP proposals appear to suggest measures close to those which in the past have been ineffective, with supra-national organisational authority and burden-sharing as cases in point. Further, with the requirement to exercise the right of return, IRLP is suggesting legislation that will legitimate the increasingly restrictive practices currently being used and jeopardise prospects of protection.

Several factors combine to make preset, universally applicable or locally agreed short periods of temporary protection irrelevant, were it possible to achieve them. Non-coercive restraint of population movement is not possible. Recent history confirms that the conditions provoking exile are often likely to last for decades, with an attendant need over the entire period for those excluded. Finally, the feasibility of devising any mechanism that will ensure a return that is either safe or dignified may be remote in the majority of cases. The explanation for going into exile is often the lack of affinity between ethnic and class groups with citizenship entitlements in the same state. The choice of destination is frequently determined by refuge-seeker beliefs that this is where such affinities exist. The difficulty of resolving such issues has to inhibit external pressure to return on these grounds. Given the heterogeneity of refuge-seeking groups, account must be taken of ways in which the perceptions of dignified return will vary between sub-groups of population, as well as in the light of the ethnic, religious, political and other histories of individuals.

Under such circumstances, explanations are sought in other arenas for trends in practice which curtail the rights and entitlements of refugees and replace them with inferior alternatives. In many parts of the world, economic reform and the restructuring of labour markets have reduced state capacity to maintain internal stability as increasingly large sections of populations are either without the means to subsist or suffer reduced and precarious means to subsist. Any increase in the numbers of people in these categories, as would-be refugees and asylum seekers, exacerbates what are already politically fragile situations. At present, rich post-industrial societies see little prospect for change and, fearful for their own stability, are keen to legitimate their reluctance to accept or retain refugees and others seeking asylum. At one level of interpretation, the IRLP proposals are symptomatic of this desire.

At some to-be-hoped-for time in the future, the situation will change and as the structures of opportunity improve there will once again be a greater willingness, globally, to receive migrant groups under whatever guise. This means that, in such contexts, there has to be caution before introducing changes in the law. Not only will it take years to introduce, by which time the situation may have changed again, it will take yet more years to undo.

At another level, in a liberal world system, a fundamental politicisation permeates all activities. It is associated 'with strategic networks of state and non-state actors that make up global liberal governance and as a political project in its own right, a complex and networked project requiring its own forms of mobilisation, justification and reward' (Duffield, 2000, p. 7).

If liberal governance assumes the criminalisation of war and the increased exclusion of low-income states, the changing function of states and relations between them may make irrelevant their previous endorsement of international laws within newly emerging patterns of global authority. With reference to Duffield, this might be associated with the shift from territorial to global modes of governance and attendant limited capacities to achieve social change through consensual means. Within this kind of thinking, all international law may be subject to review or abeyance, as part of a process of organisational accommodation to the global liberal regime, with attendant implications for the erosion of standards of justice and accountability (Duffield, 1996). If so, it may seem morally inappropriate if strategically expedient, to initiate such change in respect of the fragile legislation concerned to protect the world's most vulnerable people. The problem is that with this twist of the helix, it is the survival of institutions of law and morality themselves that may be at stake.[8]

Bibliography

Allen. T. (1996) 'Making the Madi: the Invention of a Ugandan Tribe', in K. King et al. (eds), *Ethnicity in Africa*, Edinburgh: Centre for African Studies, University of Edinburgh, pp. 91–116.

Allen, T. (ed.)(1996a) *In Search of Cool Ground: War, Flight and Homecoming in Northeast Africa*, London: UNRISD/James Currey/Africa World Press.

Allen, Tim, and Hubert Morsink (1994a) 'Introduction: When Refugees Go Home', in Allen and Morsink, pp. 1–13.

Allen, Tim, and Hubert Morsink (1994) *When Refugees Go Home*, London/Trenton, New Jersey: UNRISD/James Currey/Africa World Press.

Bagshaw, S. (1997) 'Benchmarks or Deutschmarks? Determining the Criteria for the Repatriation of Refugees to Bosnia-Herzegovina', *International Journal of Refugee Law*, 9, 4, pp. 566–92.

Barutciski, M. (1996) 'Reinforcement of Non-Admission Policies and the Subversion of UNHCR: Displacement and International Assistance in Bosnia Herzogovina', *International Journal of Refugee Law*, 8, 1–2, pp. 49–110.

Barutciski, M. (1998) 'Involuntary Repatriation when Refugee Protection Is No Longer Necessary: Moving Forward after the 48th Session of the Executive Committee', *International Journal of Refugee Law*, 10, 1–2, pp. 236–55.

Black, R., and K. Khoser (eds)(1999) *The End of the Refugee Cycle: Refugee Repatriation and Reconstruction*, Oxford: Berghahn.

Boshyk, Y. (1988) 'Repatriation and Resistance: Ukrainian Refugees and Displaced Persons in Occupied Germany and Austria, 1945–1948', in A. C. Bramwell (ed.), *Refugees in the Age of Total War*, London: Unwin Hyman, pp. 198–218.

Chimni, B. S. (1993) 'Legal and Policy Issues relating to UNHCR's Involvement in the Promotion, Facilitation or Encouragement of Voluntary Repatriation,' papers from Round Table Consultation on Voluntary Repatriation, 2–3 June 1993, Divonne-les-Bains, Geneva.

Chingono, M. (1995) 'Post-Lancaster House: Return to Zimbabwe 1980–1983', in Quick, Chingono and Preston, vol. 2, case study 11, pp. 57–68.

Coles, G. (1985) 'Voluntary Repatriation: a Background Study', prepared for the Round Table on Voluntary Repatriation convened by UNHCR and the International Institute of Humanitarian Law, 16–19 July 1985, San Remo.

Coles, G. (1989) *Solutions to the Problem of Refugees and the Protection of Refugees: a Background Paper*, Geneva: International Institute of Humanitarian Law/UNHCR.

Crisp, J. F. (1984) 'Voluntary Repatriation Programmes for African Refugees: a Critical Examination', *Refugee Issues*, 1, 2, p. 23.

Cuny, F. C., B. N. Stein and P. Reed (1992) *Repatriation during Conflict in Africa and Asia*, Dallas: Centre for the Study of Societies in Crisis.

Dix, T. (1993) Interview with R. Preston, Windhoek, NISER.

Duffield, M. (1996) 'The Symphony of the Damned: Racial Discourse, Complex Political Emergencies and Humanitarian Aid', *Disasters*, 20, 3, pp. 173–91.

Duffield, M. (2000) *Globalisation and Conflict: a Reply*, London: CODEP/DFID Experts Consultation on Globalisation and Conflict, June.

Gameladin Ashami, M. (1995) 'Return to Eritrea from Sudan, 1989–1994', in Quick, Chingono and Preston, vol. 2, case study 8, pp. 51–2.

Goodwin-Gill, G. (1996) 'Comments on the Right to Leave, the Right to Return and the Question of the Right to Remain', in V. Goulland-Debbas (ed.), *The Problem of Refugees in the Light of Contemporary International Law Issues*, Nijoff Law Specials, vol. 12, pp. 93–118.

Goodwin-Gill, G. (1999) 'Refugee Identity and the Fading Prospect of Protection: From Rights to Realities', in F. Nicholson and P. Twomey (eds), *Refugee Rights and Realities*, Cambridge: Cambridge University Press, pp. 220–53.

The Guardian (1995) 'Preventative detention in the UK', 18 January.

Hathaway, J. (1991) 'Reconceiving Refugee Law as Human Rights Protection', *Journal of Refugee Studies*, 4, 2, pp. 112–31.

Hathaway, J. (1995a) 'Commentary on Quick, Chingono and Preston', Toronto: York University, RLRU/CRS, letter to Rosemary Preston, Susan Quick and Mark Chingono, 13 March.

Hathaway, J. (1995b) 'New Directions to Avoid Hard Problems: the Distortion of the Palliative Role of Refugee Protection', *Journal of Refugee Studies*, 8, 3, pp. 288–304.

Hathaway, J., and R. A. Neve (1997) 'Making International Refugee Law Relevant Again: a Proposal for Collectivised and Solution-Oriented Protection', *Harvard Human Rights Journal*, 10, Spring, pp. 115–211.

Khoser, K., and R. Black (1999) 'The End of the Refugee Cycle?', in R. Black and K. Khoser, pp. 2–17.

Larkin, M. A. (1991) 'Preface', in M. A. Larkin, F. C. Cuny and B. N. Stein, *Repatriation under Conflict in Central America*, Washington, DC; Dallas: Hemisphere Migration Project, Center for Immigration Policy and Refugee Assistance, Georgetown University, Intertect Institute, 1991, pp. vii–xii.

Legal Working Group (1993) Reconceiving refugee law as human rights protection: responses from the expert analysts, Toronto, June (cited in RLRU, 1994).

McDowell, C. (1995a) 'Swiss Asylum Policy Reform and Humanitarianism', in Quick, Chingono and Preston, vol. 2, case study 2, pp. 2–26.

McDowell, C. (1995b) 'Day to Day Insecurities for Refugees in Switzerland, 1991–1994', in Quick, Chingono and Preston, vol. 2, case study 3, pp. 27–9.

McDowell, C. (1995c) 'Criminalisation and Deportation from Switzerland, 1991–1994', in Quick, Chingono and Preston, vol. 2, case study 4, p. 30.

Organisation of American States (1985) Declaración de Cartagena, reproduced in *Annual Report on Inter-American Commission on Human Rights, 1984–1985*, OEA/Ser.L/11.6.doc. 10, rev. 1, pp. 90–193.

Organization of African Unity (OAU) (1969) *Convention Governing the Specific Aspects of Refugee Problems in Africa*, UNTS 15691, 10 September (entered into force, 20 June 1974) [Article V. Voluntary Repatriation].

Preston, R. (1991a) 'Education for Young Mozambicans: Report of an Inter-Agency Mission to Mozambique, Malawi and Zimbabwe', in UNHCR,

Mozambique, Malawi and Zimbabwe: Inter-Agency Mission on Education for Young Mozambicans, UNDP/UNHCR, PTSS Report 91/18, pp. 1–91 [MLO].
Preston, R. (1991b) 'The Provision of Education to Refugees in Places of Temporary Asylum: Some Implications for Development', *Comparative Education*, 27, 1, pp. 61–81.
Preston, R. (1992) 'Refugees in Papua New Guinea: Government Response and Assistance, 1984–1988', *International Migration Review*, 26, 2, pp. 843–76.
Preston, R. (1994) 'States, Statelessness and Education: Post-Return Integration of Namibians Trained Abroad International', *Journal of Educational Development*, 14, 3, pp. 299–319.
Preston, R. (1995a) *Dialogue with Reference to a Study of the Social Application of Refugee Law concerning Repatriation in Safety and Dignity*, Warwick: University of Warwick, International Centre for Education in Development.
Preston, R. (1995b) 'After Bashyk: Ukranian Repatriation after World War II', in Quick, Chingono and Preston, vol. 2, case study 1, p. 1.
Preston, R. (1995c) 'UN Administration of Return and Fighter Flare-ups in Namibia (1990)', in Quick, Chingono and Preston, vol. 2, case study 12, pp. 69–72.
Preston, R. (1995d) 'Ex-Detainees in Namibia, 1990–1993', in Quick, Chingono and Preston, vol. 2, case studies 12 and 14, pp. 75–7.
Preston, R. (1995e) 'Namibian Women: On Exile and After (1992)', in Quick, Chingono and Preston, vol. 2, case study 15, pp. 78–84.
Preston, R. (1995f) 'Papua New Guinea in the Mid-1980s', in Quick, Chingono and Preston, vol 2, case study 17, p. 88.
Preston, R (1997) 'Demobilising and Integrating Fighters after War: the Namibian Experience', *Journal of Southern African Studies*, 23, 3, pp. 453–72.
Preston, R. (1999) 'Researching Repatriation and Reconstruction: Who Is Researching What and Why?', in R. Black and K. Khoser, pp. 8–36.
Preston, R. (ed.) (1993) *The Integration of Returned Exiles, Former Combatants and Other War-Affected Namibians*, Windhoek: Namibia Institute for Social and Economic Research.
Quick, S. (1995a) 'Repatriation of Ethiopian Refugees from Djibouti', in Quick, Chingono and Preston, vol 2, case study 6, pp. 31–46.
Quick, S. (1995b) 'Return of Tigrayan Refugees from Sudan', in Quick, Chingono and Preston, vol 2, case study 7, pp. 47–50.
Quick, S. (1995c) 'Amare's Story: an Ethiopian in Canada', in Quick, Chingono and Preston, vol 2, case study 9, pp. 53–4.
Quick, S. (1995d) 'Minority Rights Groups: a Sudanese Woman Living in Britain', in Quick, Chingono and Preston, vol 2, case study 10, pp. 55–8.
Quick, S. (1995e) 'The Repatriation of Guatemalan Refugees from Mexico', in Quick, Chingono and Preston, vol 2, case study 16, pp. 85–8.
Quick, S., M. Chingono and R. Preston (1995) *Social Applications of Refugee Law: Repatriation in Safety and Dignity* (vol. 1) and *Case Studies* (vol. 2), Warwick: University of Warwick, International Centre for Education in Development.
RLRU (Refugee Law Research Unit)/CRS (Centre for Refugee Studies)(1994) *Toward the Reformulation of International Refugee Law: Study in Action of Repatriation in Safety and Dignity. Confidential Background Materials*, Ontario: York University.

Reid, A. K. (1992) 'Political Studies in the Voluntary Repatriation of Refugees', unpublished DPhil thesis, Deakin University, Australia.
UNHCR (1951) Convention relating to the Status of Refugees, Geneva [Article 33. Prohibition of expulsion or return (*refoulement*)].
UNHCR (1992) Draft Protection Guidelines on Voluntary Repatriation, Geneva.
UNHCR (1993) *The State of the World's Refugees: the Challenge of Protection*, London: Penguin Books.
Vedsted-Hansen, J. (1997) 'Analysis of the Requirements for Repatriation', *International Journal of Refugee Law*, 9, 4, pp. 559–65.
Vincent, R. J. (1986) *Human Rights and International Relations*, Cambridge: Cambridge University Press.
Wilson, K., and J. Nuñes (1994) 'Repatriation to Mozambique', in Allen and Morsink, pp. 167–236.
Zinkin, P. (1993) 'Integrating the Disabled', in Preston (ed.)(1993), 7/1–7/28.

Notes

1. Zimbabwe People's Revolutionary Army.
2. It should be noted that the study refers not to any existing proposals for the reformulation of refugee law, but to proposals suggested in the published and unpublished material contained in this IRLP document.
3. United Nations Research Institute for Social Development.
4. Technically, voluntary repatriation refers only to Convention refugees, as long as they retain their refugee status. There are also instances of involuntary international migration where repatriations are arranged in accordance with the Geneva Convention and Protocol, although those affected have not been accorded refugee status.
5. Discussion with A. Shacknove 12 December 1994.
6. Hathaway (1995b) points out that, at present, it is with the state of asylum to decide the safety of the place of return and whether or not to require return to take place. Refugee refusal to comply may have consequences such as those identified in the case studies and examined below.
7. Presumably for reasons of affirmation, Hathaway uses the third person singular feminine pronoun throughout the IRLP documentation and other writing. Its attendant association with the idea that women may be the prime breakers of immigration law in the present and other cases suggests an alternative vocabulary may be more appropriate.
8. This paper was written the Spring of 2000, based on research undertaken five years earlier. Reading the proofs in the summer of 2002, it seems dated. In the intervening time, most of the worst case scenarios identified in the paper have become normal practice. Legal entry is ever more difficult in most parts of the world. Airlines and other transport are heavily fined for carrying undocumented asylum seekers. There are daily stories of desperate alternatives and civil unrest when those admitted trigger resident panic levels to rise above containment levels. As a deterrent, asylum management is punitive. In richer nations, prison-like detention is becoming widespread with no respect for national and cultural differences. Pending status determination, conditions are often so harsh as to provoke riots, and moves

ahead will make them more restrictive. The trend is towards special provision of educational and health services, no longer within national systems, and dwindling options for earning a living. These and other measures are reproducing practices that have long since been the only options available to camp populations in less advantaged countries, their scope and quality miserable (Preston, 1991). For many they seem to imply long-term futures interminably dislocated from home and destination communities. In Britain, as elsewhere, the term refugee now describes those whose fixed-term residential entitlement has been determined. They are compulsorily dispersed across the country.

10
Human Rights Organisations and the Formation of Refugees Regimes

Morten Kjaerum

Introduction

The present chapter deals with developments in the NGO community in the 1990s and their impact on the protection of refugees; it focuses primarily on human rights organisations which have seen much development in recent years. The chapter's main conclusion is that increased collaboration between humanitarian organisations, intergovernmental institutions and national human rights organisations could bring new perspectives into the protection regimes and in particular create a bottom-up approach at the global level.

This chapter is based on the author's work at the Danish Refugee Council in the 1980s, and at the Danish Centre for Human Rights in the 1990s, as well as on the, unfortunately scarce, literature on the issue. Clearly, this is an area which requires much greater attention than it has so far received. In the first place, one needs to identify the relevant NGOs for our subject matter:

1. *Human Rights NGOs* who define themselves as international NGOs. The latter designation usually indicates that such organisations bring together either individuals or organisations from various countries. Generally their interest extends beyond the national level, even if their constituent membership or associations are mainly involved in work at local level.[1] This category includes organisations such as ICJ (International Commission of Jurists), Amnesty International and the International Federation of Human Rights.
2. *Humanitarian organisations* working both at national level and in crisis areas throughout the world. Traditionally, these organisations

define themselves as neutral, and are involved in assisting vulnerable groups in securing their basic needs: food, shelter, medicine and the like. During protracted conflicts, humanitarian organisations often become involved in establishing income-generating programmes, as well as education and skills training programmes. Each organisation establishes its home base in a particular community, but is at the same time involved in networking or in international umbrella(s). Oxfam, the Danish Refugee Council, CARE and church-related groups, among others, belong to this category.

3. The third group of NGOs consists of *human rights organisations* working in the country of their domicile. This type of NGO became increasingly important in the 1990s. Having started out as small, relatively marginal organisations, human rights NGOs working in their own country have come to play a significant role at both domestic and international levels. Among these organisations are: Lawyers for Human Rights in South Africa, the Botswana Human Rights Centre, the Civil Liberties Organisation in Nigeria and the Estonia Legal Advice Office. In this category could be included National Human Rights Institutions as are defined in the Paris Principles:[2]

    - established by parliament – in the constitution or by law
    - vested with competence to promote and protect human rights
    - ensured real independence through, *inter alia*, a pluralist representation of the social forces of civil society

In this chapter the focus will be on how new institutions in the third category are working, and how they, in collaboration with the two other types of organisations outlined above and with intergovernmental institutions, can contribute to strengthening the protection of refugees. It is important to keep in mind, however, that the author's analysis is based mainly on his experiences in Europe and Africa; thus some of the conclusions may not as readily apply to Asia and Latin America.

The development of national human rights organisations

Indigenous human rights organisations do not have a very long history. In Europe and Africa they began to emerge in the mid-1980s, in Latin America somewhat earlier. There are a variety of reasons why these organisations did not develop at an earlier stage despite the need for their services in local communities.

In Western Europe, many problems have exclusively been seen as humanitarian or social issues, while these may have been characterised as human rights issues in third world countries or in the communist part of the world. One example of this is the marginalisation of refugees and ethnic minorities from the labour market in many countries in Europe. Such exclusion, however, is generally not evidence of discrimination, but rather perceived as a social problem. Furthermore, human rights organisations based in the West, such as Amnesty International, Human Rights Watch, ICJ and others, have had their main focus on countries in other parts of the world. Consequently, only a few human rights organisations addressing domestic human rights problems had developed before the mid-1980s.

In Eastern European countries, and in several African countries, oppressive regimes did not allow domestic human rights organisations to work. The Amnesty International principle of not criticising the country of your domicile was in many situations a prerequisite for survival; at the same time, it also created a model which worked against the establishment of indigenous human rights organisations. Evidently, it takes a certain degree of availability to be able to direct one's human rights awareness to issues in other countries than one's own. In fact, when one is confronted with gross and systematic violations in one's own country, it is difficult to mobilise popular support for an organisation to work on violations in a neighbouring country. Such was the situation in many African countries until recently. Consequently, large Western organisations dominated the human rights scenario in Africa, although many of them possessed very little consciousness of African culture, tradition and realities. As a result, the indigenous African NGOs did not have a realistic perspective from which to embark on human rights protection.[3]

Fortunately, the situation has changed dramatically in the last decade. In the wake of the democratisation process in the communist bloc and in several African countries, the space necessary for human rights organisations to operate has become more readily available. Human rights rhetoric became a common language in international fora in the early 1990s, and the 'trickle down' effect consequently made it more acceptable for governments to be addressed in human rights language by domestic organisations. Many governments moved from seeing human rights as a direct attack on their sovereignty to regarding them as constructive norms for guiding the democratisation process.

Furthermore, the UN conferences in the first half of the 1990s established a unique opportunity for domestic NGOs to meet and network. The 1993 UN World Conference on Human Rights in Vienna gave birth to many new networks of human rights organisations, both formal and informal. These networks and contacts have since played a significant role in supporting the emerging human rights environment and elaborating the new agenda. In the latter part of the 1990s, the UN Human Rights Commission increasingly became a platform where national human rights organisations could meet.

These developments were further strengthened by the new human rights agenda of the 1990s – an agenda in which implementation is in focus. How do human rights standards move from paper to the everyday realities of local communities? How are the broad general norms in the international covenants translated into reality in countries throughout the world? The World Conference on Human Rights in Vienna was a milestone for this new human rights agenda. The conference was not about setting new standards, but rather about promoting the implementation of the standards already in existence. To this end, the World Conference adopted a Programme of Action[4] which was the first of its kind in the human rights field. In the programme of action, the participating states express the important and constructive role played by national institutions for the promotion and protection of human rights, in particular in their advisory capacity to the competent authorities, their role in remedying human rights violations, in dissemination of human rights information, and education in human rights.[5] Furthermore, governments recognised the important role of non-governmental organisations in the promotion of all human rights and in humanitarian activities at national, regional and international levels.[6] Finally, states were urged to strengthen national structures, institutions and organs of society which play a role in promoting and safeguarding human rights.[7]

In many countries, the new development marked by this document has improved the dialogue between human rights organisations and governmental bodies. This has resulted in, among other things, the search for ways to give legitimacy to the judiciary, redirect police work, and to relate to minority groups. This global human rights awareness has also begun to be felt in Western Europe, albeit more slowly than elsewhere. National human rights institutions are emerging in various European countries, and humanitarian and social NGOs are increasingly adopting a human rights approach to parts of their work. National Human Rights Institutions as defined in the Paris Principles have been established in countries such as France, Denmark and Ireland. In Germany, the possibility of setting up such a structure is being seriously considered by the parliament and in Great Britain similar considerations are being made, at the time of writing.

In the European Human Rights Commission and Court there is a clear indication of this development; that is, the sharp increase in the number of cases referred to the two organs. In fact, the number of cases received at the Commission has risen from 596 in 1985 to 3,481 in 1995.[8] This cannot be explained by an increased number of human rights violations in the region, but rather by an increased awareness of the human rights dimensions of some phenomena in our societies. A sharp increase in the number of cases concerning refugees and asylum seekers is to be noted.

The role and function of human rights organisations

With regard to the responsibilities of national human rights organisations in the implementation of domestic as well as international human rights norms, three main functions exist: (1) monitoring the compliance of state policy with international human rights instruments; (2) advising; (3) informing and educating.

1. Monitoring

   A key function of national human rights organisations is to monitor state policy in relation to its compliance with international human rights instruments. Human rights institutions will normally follow the legislative process closely in order to come forward with their views should a proposed piece of legislation fail to comply with human rights norms. This work can be done from the institution's offices without attracting much public attention.

   A second important element is the actual implementation of the legislation. In order to monitor its implementation, the institution needs a well-established network within its society. Without such a network it is difficult to identify areas where practice should be changed in order to conform to, for example, the European Human Rights Convention or the African Charter on Human and People's Rights. These networks or community contacts often take the form of strong links with the national NGO community – which is another reason why it is useful to engage civil society organisations in the governing structures of a national human rights institution.

Finally, a third, very direct way of gaining access to information about human rights violations in a country is to have a legal advisory function or a mandate to hear and consider complaints concerning individual cases. In all cases, and regardless of the method of operation chosen, the institution needs to be visible in society in order to be able to carry out its monitoring function.

2. Advising
The advisory function follows naturally from the monitoring function described above. National human rights organisations need to keep abreast of what is transpiring in a society in order to be able to offer serious advice. Since it is the government, parliament, ministries and other state structures who are entrusted with the protection of the human rights of the people within their jurisdiction, it is primarily interaction with these governmental structures that will catalyse the development of the advisory function of a human rights organisation.

In reality, it frequently occurs that over a period of months or even years, the human rights institution raises various issues. The resulting opinions, recommendations, proposals or reports are often neglected, ignored or offered only lip-service. Fortunately, however, experience demonstrates that if an institution is conducting professional work of high quality, governmental bodies will eventually recognise the utility of entering into a consultative process with that human rights institution. At that point, it is perceived to be beneficial to seek the institution's advice before passing new legislation. Similarly, it is considered wiser to alter practices conflicting with the international obligations of that particular country before such practices are being brought to the attention of the international treaty bodies, the media, and the public.

3. Informing and educating
Human rights organisations, together with the NGO community, government bodies and the media, undertake an important task of informing society on all levels about human rights instruments and their relevance in domestic terms. The only way to turn the European Human Rights Convention and other regional or international mechanisms into a dynamic part of democratic development is to make them known to all sectors of society. Unfortunately, in many quarters of different societies, there is still a sense that international conventions are threatening instruments which undermine the independence and sovereignty of the state.[9] This perception can only be challenged through impartial information and education.

Human rights and humanitarian law education should, according to the Vienna Plan of Action, be included *as subjects in the curricula of all learning institutions in formal and non-formal settings.*[10] Human rights institutions should be assisting governments in achieving this aim. One of the most important tasks when focusing on the implementation of international human rights norms is the training of lawyers, judges, police and civil servants in key positions. By targeting these professional groups, a culture of human rights can be developed and strengthened in democratic institutions.

Human rights organisations and refugee protection

Humanitarian organisations have been reluctant to be involved in advocacy work because they feared that their neutrality could be compromised. Using human rights language could previously be perceived as promoting particular political interest, while today it is more broadly recognised that the respect for human rights norms is a prerequisite for protecting the dignity of the individual and securing a democratic society. Humanitarian organisations have thus obtained one more instrument to analyse and comprehend refugee problems within the relevant political context, whereby they can limit the risk of being used as players in the political game of someone else.[11] However, as a consequence of the fear of being compromised, humanitarian organisations have not yet created sufficient human rights expertise. Thus, it has to a large extent been the role of UNHCR to take the lead on these issues.

Human rights organisations working in the area of refugee protection are a relatively new development and therefore many organisations, still young and fragile, are striving to obtain recognition both in civil society and with their respective governments. As mentioned above, it is not on the agenda of many organisations on a continent like Africa to relate to human rights problems in a neighbouring country, and it is almost equally difficult to relate to an individual from a neighbouring country who asks for protection. These are some of the reasons why they still have not been playing an important role in refugee protection. Even in South Africa where civil society organisations for many years have been strong, human rights organisations were not eager to lobby for the inclusion in the constitution of a right to asylum; however, in recent years organisations have begun to address the issue of the protection of refugees and displaced persons more frequently.

In Europe, refugee protection has for historical reasons not been on the agenda of the national human rights organisations. It has been the task of humanitarian organisations, while human rights organisations were dealing mainly with issues in other parts of the world. One exception is Amnesty International which since the mid-1980s has taken up refugee protection issues at the domestic level despite the general policy of not raising issues in one's own country. In recent years, other human rights organisations have begun to address the issue of the protection of refugees and displaced persons more frequently. For example, at the first European meeting of National Human Rights Institutions in 1994, the main topic on the agenda was the role of these institutions in combating racism and xenophobia.[12]

What is emerging in several parts of the world is thus a stronger human rights oriented NGO community at the domestic level, which is concerned with the protection of refugees. These institutions, along with local humanitarian organisations, may deal with individual cases or issues regarding specific refugee groups. Such collaboration should also reinforce the protection work of UNHCR, especially in this period of time, when many governments are seriously working on the implementation of human rights.

A specific case from Denmark may illustrate the potential in this collaboration. For several years, humanitarian organisations had addressed the issue of primary education for children in asylum camps. The Minister of Interior had been approached in so-called 'soft' humanitarian language. Those requests had been turned down, using the argument that it would not be cost-efficient to provide primary education for children who might be expelled from Denmark, should their cases be rejected. In 1994, the Danish Centre for Human Rights wrote to the minister and made her aware that the Danish practice was not in accordance with the right to free primary school education for all children as it is established in Article 13 of the Covenant on Economic, Social and Cultural Rights and in Article 28 of the Convention on the Rights of the Child. To stress the point, a report was simultaneously sent to the UN Committee on the Rights of the Child. Shortly thereafter, a commission was established to look into the matter and, approximately one year later, conditions for children awaiting the decision of their cases had significantly improved. The above illustrates how a case can be moved by applying human rights standards and by using international control mechanisms.

At the regional and international levels, national human rights organisations may in the coming years begin to play a more constructive role by addressing the regional and international human rights mechanisms such as the OAU, the EU, UN mechanisms and others. The following two examples illustrate this point.

The first example relates to the African human rights organisations which meet twice a year during the sessions of the African Commission on Human and People's Rights. These organisations were instrumental in getting the refugee issue into the five-year work programme of the Commission – the Mauritius Plan of Action.[13] The fact that the refugee issue has now become an integral part of the Commission's programme may stimulate the Commission to elaborate new policies in this field. This, in turn, may create new ways of thinking in the NGOs, which, finally, should be directed towards both governments and the OAU. Clearly, there is potential for a new dynamic in this cycle for developing African strategies for refugee protection, which is urgently needed when taking into consideration crises such as in the Great Lakes region.

The second example relates to Europe. In Europe, a new network has been established, namely, the EURO-Med Human Rights Network. It comprises human rights organisations from all the EU member states, and from 12 countries in the Middle East and the Maghreb. The Network relates to the Barcelona agreement which the governments of the 27 countries entered into in November 1995. In the work programme for this EURO-Med network, refugee protection is very high on the agenda. The intention is that the refugee problem becomes an integral part of lobbying the EU countries regarding the human rights situation in the Middle East and Maghreb. Hopefully, innovative strategies can be developed through this network which includes organisations both from sending and receiving countries – including Algeria. The Network is closely collaborating with the European Council on Refugees and Exiles (ECRE) which is a well-established network in Europe based to a large extent on humanitarian organisations.

Another target for NGOs should be the UN treaty bodies and the Human Rights Commission. After years of neglect, the machinery established by the UN to promote and protect human rights has begun to address the human rights of refugees and asylum seekers. Besides the Committee on the Rights of the Child which was mentioned above could be mentioned the Working Group on Arbitrary Detention established by the UN Commission on Human Rights. In its 1997 resolution on arbitrary detention the Commission requested

> the Working Group to devote all necessary attention to the reports concerning the situation of immigrants and asylum seekers who are allegedly being held in prolonged administrative custody without the possibility of administrative or judicial remedy, and to include observations on this question in its report to the next session of the CHR.[14]

This reveals an increased awareness in this and other UN bodies about the concerns of refugees and asylum seekers. Among other initiatives NGOs could submit to the Working Group on Arbitrary Detention individual cases of detained asylum seekers where continued detention appears to pose a risk to the person's health or physical integrity, and many more such issues. There is vast potential for developing new dimensions of protection by using these mechanisms.[15]

Conclusion

In the protection of refugees there is less room for movement or experimentation than in other areas of aid or development. To try to create ideal 'islands' where one sets oneself outside international legal conventions is hazardous, and can easily have lethal consequences to those involved. A profound, exact knowledge about human rights, refugee law and other legal matters is fundamental for successful refugee work.[16]

In this way there is a potential to involve important new groups, who are firmly based in human rights thinking, in strengthening refugee protection regimes. They will need support and encouragement from organisations which have had long experience in refugee work. Consequently, in many societies it will create stronger links between local civil society and the policies on refugees implemented in the particular area. Furthermore, with the present international human rights agenda stressing the implementation of human rights at the domestic level these organisations may be instrumental in conveying to the decision makers at all levels that human rights are for everyone.

Finally, it should be stressed that involving human rights organisations in the refugee protection work should not lead to the creation of a rigid rights regime, where the underlying humanitarian values are forgotten. That would in the long run undermine the very purpose of creating a stronger awareness of the linkage between human rights and refugee protection.

Bibliography

Ambrose, Brendalyn P. (1995) *Democratization and the Protection of Human Rights in Africa: Problems and Prospects*, London: Praeger.

Bahey El Din Hassan (ed.) (1997) *Challenges Facing the Arab Human Rights Movement*, Cairo.

Council of Europe, *Survey of Activities and Statistics*, 1995.

Rodley, Nigel (1997) 'Human Rights NGOs: Rights and Obligations', in *SIM* Special no. 19, Utrecht, p. 45.

Nordby, Trygue (1993) 'Beyond Idealism and Charity', in Morten Kjaerum (ed.), *NGOs and Refugees*, Copenhagen: Danish Centre for Human Rights, 1993.

Notes

1. Nigel Rodley, 'Human Rights NGOs: Rights and Obligations', in *SIM* Special no. 19, Utrecht 1997, p. 45.
2. Paris Principles, Commission on Human Rights resolution 1992/54 of 3 March 1992, GA Resolution 48/134 of 20 December 1993.
3. Brendalyn P. Ambrose, *Democratisation and the Protection of Human Rights in Africa*, London 1995, 99.
4. Vienna Declaration and Programme of Action, A/Conf. 157/23, 12 July 1993.
5. Vienna Declaration and Programme of Action I:36.
6. Vienna Declaration and Programme of Action I:38.
7. Vienna Declaration and Programme of Action II:83.
8. Council of Europe, *Survey of Activities and Statistics*, 1995.
9. See Bahey El Din Hassan (ed), *Challenges Facing the Arab Human Rights Movement*, Cairo 1997.
10. Vienna Programme and Plan of Action II:79.
11. Trygve Nordby, 'Beyond Idealism and Charity', in Morten Kjaerum (ed.), *NGOs and Refugees*, Copenhagen: Danish Centre for Human Rights, 1993.
12. *Report from the First Meeting of National Human Rights Institutions*, Council of Europe and the French Commission on Human Rights, Strasbourg, 1995.
13. African Commission on Human and People's Rights, The Mauritius Plan of Action 1996–2001.
14. Resolution 1997/50.
15. International Service for Human Rights and Amnesty International issued a manual to develop this further: *The UN and Refugees' Human Rights: a Manual on How UN Human Rights Mechanisms Can Protect the Rights of Refugees*, Geneva, 1997.
16. Nordby, 'Beyond Idealism and Charity'.

Index